HARD

LANDINGS

HARD

LANDINGS

LOOKING *into the* FUTURE
for a CHILD *with* AUTISM

Cammie McGovern

AVERY
An imprint of Penguin Random House LLC
New York

AVERY

An imprint of Penguin Random House LLC
penguinrandomhouse.com

Most Avery books are available at special quantity discounts for bulk purchase
for sales promotions, premiums, fund-raising, and educational needs. Special
books or book excerpts also can be created to fit specific needs. For details, write
SpecialMarkets@penguinrandomhouse.com.

Library of Congress Cataloging-in-Publication Data has been applied for.

Hardcover ISBN 9780525539056
Ebook ISBN 9780525539063

Printed in the United States of America
1st Printing

Book design by Silverglass Studio

FOR ETHAN, of course

Also for Mike, Charlie, and Henry

Contents

H ere's what it's like in the early days after your three-year-old child is diagnosed with autism: you never sleep. You spend endless late nights in front of a computer investigating therapies that are only supported by anecdotal evidence, doctors tell you, but there's nothing else to go on. No double-blind studies. No experts who can say, authoritatively, "Do this. It's been proven effective." The only recommendation that's truly agreed on is that early intervention is essential. The younger your child is when you start—and the more hours you put in—the better the projected outcome. This means you spend years alone at home with your atypical toddler, then preschooler, then grade-schooler, teaching him the basics of being a child. How to talk, how to play, how to learn, all with the nebulous goal that at some point in the future he'll reenter the world with some ability to participate in it.

In the midst of it, you try to remember what normal feels like. You imagine what the world will look like when you return. Eventually it happens. You venture forth again. The goals shift from completing a task at home to one in the community, because if your child has autism, the goals must eventually involve other people. He'll ask two questions of his peers. He'll order food at a restaurant. He'll participate in Beginner Band at school. It's hard to describe how vulnerable you feel when you watch your child try and fail at such simple undertakings. At first, you can't bear it. *Let's skip that goal,* you think. *Let's try an easier one where he doesn't look so different.* In other words: *let's put off this business of rejoining the world and go back home to the privacy we've lived in for too long already.*

Consciously or unconsciously, I made that choice for years. Or else I made half-hearted efforts. I called one summer day camp and one children's chorus to see if they'd be willing to accommodate Ethan. When the answer was no—they didn't have trained staff; they worried about overtaxing counselors—I thanked them and hung up. Fair enough, I thought, internalizing the broader message: my child is extra work and I probably shouldn't ask.

Here's the thing, though: you have to ask. You can't stay home all the time and you can't make up reasons why everything he wants to do isn't possible for him. You see it more clearly with every passing year. He's not a child anymore. He's a teenager and then, he's not even a teenager anymore, he's a young adult. He wants to participate in the world. He wants a job. He wants to walk into town by himself. He wants the same friendships and relationships he sees on TV. Your child wants a life.

And it's terrifying.

CHAPTER ONE

Joseph Heller coined the term "catch-22" to describe a military conundrum: a terrified fighter pilot seeking a discharge from armed services on grounds of insanity is declared sane enough to recognize the danger he faces and therefore must keep fighting. The phrase has come to symbolize the absurd vicissitudes of institutional logic and is extraordinarily apt for the generation of young adults with intellectual and developmental disabilities (IDD) coming of age in America today. For Heller, the number twenty-two was arbitrary. For these young adults, it isn't. Twenty-two is the age when they'll leave their school system and lose access to every educational and vocational support they've had since they were three years old. In many states, their twenty-second birthday will mark the last day they have anywhere to go. For nineteen years, they've been part of a system designed primarily around the philosophy of inclusion. They've participated in classes and school choruses; they've gone on field trips; they've learned how to comport themselves in a community that—they will soon discover—has no place for them. The catch is this: they've trained for a life they can't have. They've learned skills for jobs that don't exist or they'll never get. They've practiced independent living but they'll never live alone. Parents describe this moment as "falling off a cliff" without even realizing the worst part—their kids aren't really falling because they aren't going anywhere. They're sitting in their parents' house, waiting indefinitely.

....

Every parent of an autistic child can tell you something about making lists. In the early days after Ethan's diagnosis at the age of three, I made them compulsively: words he understands, words he uses regularly (only a handful at that point), songs he can sing at least part of. I also had lists of goals, composed in bursts of optimism, for what he'd be doing soon: six months from now he will count to twenty, follow two-step directions, tell a stranger his name. At the time, I believed these lists kept us focused, with our eyes on the prize that I made our number one "parent goal" on Ethan's first preschool IEP (individualized education plan): "To enter kindergarten without an autism diagnosis." That was my thinking during our early years in the autism trenches, before we'd learned how complicated and knotty the battles could get.

Ethan was diagnosed just after his third birthday by a gruff doctor with a thick accent we had a hard time understanding. At the start of our appointment, we'd tried to put his developmental delays in the context of a larger picture of medical issues: He'd always been a colicky infant, so prone to sinus and ear infections he seemed to wean straight from the breast onto amoxicillin. He'd had food allergies, terrible eczema, and for the last year and a half, diarrhea so severe we'd never bothered to start potty training.

"Yes, this is autism," said the doctor, who seemed to be missing a few social skills himself. "The first thing you must do is lower your expectations. Don't assume he'll get a job. Hope that he can do a few things independently—get dressed, feed himself, things like that."

I was outraged, of course. Ethan was three years old, and this doctor was already outlining his limited future? My fury dissipated after I did some research and discovered that over half the children diagnosed with autism had experienced chronic ear infections and gastrointestinal issues. The more I read, the more this diagnosis seemed less like a tragic pronouncement on Ethan's future than a thrilling explanation for the constellation of GI problems he'd had all his life. Here at last was a connection, and with it a ray of hope: there were diets to try, therapies to get started on, children like him who were improving physically and catching up on missed developmental milestones.

I read every story I could find of an autistic toddler who'd recovered completely: the nonverbal four-year-old who went from lining up cars to reading *Harry Potter*; the teenager who'd left his diagnosis behind and now had a girlfriend and a software-design company. In these stories, parents described the extraordinary effort required and made it clear—this wasn't an undertaking for the faint of heart. These children will resist being drawn out of their shells; they'll turn over tables or try to hurt themselves. They were right, I learned, and my heart broke as I watched Ethan resist—sometimes sobbing for hours—much of what we were trying to do.

In the beginning, I often returned to those stories of cured children. I needed them because suddenly I had a full-time job I'd never applied for or wanted. I baked every night with the grains that would not aggravate his immune system. I lined up playdates, joined support groups, made flash cards and posted them around the house to surround him with language in manageable doses. I played on the floor till my knees ached teaching Ethan the rudiments of pretend play: "Should we make this banana a phone or a car?" (Early on I'd learned to ask a question with choices buried in it, so an answer was right there for him to grab.) I narrated his world as he encountered it and I stopped thinking entirely about how I looked because what did that matter when there was a child to be saved and this was what it took?

My notes from those early years after Ethan's diagnosis speak volumes to my relentless optimism. In one list I detail goals for the next six months: "Identify four parts of the body. Identify four items of clothing. Name a friend." On that same day, I apparently felt some need to make another list: "What he can do: Name all the instruments in the orchestra. Identify Mozart. Identify eight out of ten of the greatest guitarists of the twentieth century." Reading this now, I easily see how I was grasping at straws, trying to imagine our own future story: He will beat this! Someday when he is a professor of music, we'll look back and shake our fists: *Autism! Ha!*

You need great hope to keep your energy up when every day is a battle to lure your child into joining the world. Most days, I felt like I wasn't myself: I hovered closer than other mothers on the playground and talked like a nervous preschool teacher on her first day: "Here we go up, up, up the slide!" If strangers at the playground didn't notice Ethan's differences, they certainly noticed me, singing in the sandbox, clapping my hands to get his attention. One glimpse at a photograph from that time is enough to recall my omnipresent unease. I look as if I'm wearing a mask of my own face. There's an irony to the arguments I had with my husband and my well-meaning mother who would gently suggest that I relax for a while and leave Ethan alone. I wanted to scream, *I can't relax! I've got to teach this child how to play!*

Now I look back at my determination for Ethan to achieve a full recovery and see all the ways I did us a disservice. I allowed a perpetual cloud to shadow the small breakthroughs Ethan did have: *Yes, he was talking in sentences now,* I would tell myself; *yes, he tantrums less at transitions but* (there was always a but . . .) *why does he still repeat so much? Why does he still jump and flap his hands? Why did he still* look *so autistic?*

The answer, I eventually learned, is simple. This is the way autism works. There are roadblocks in the brain, mysterious and intractable, and for some children no amount of work or determination will change them. Eventually I began to see those stories of cures as addictive and dangerous. Statistically, "recovered children" are a minuscule fraction in the exploding autism population, but their tales fuel a cottage industry of therapies peddled to desperate parents who will do anything to rescue the child they believe autism has taken from them. Not only are these unlikely to work, they set up a struggle that, after a while, begins to break your heart. If you prioritize "full recovery," you must decrease and eventually extinguish all the autistic giveaway behaviors: the jumping, the hand-flapping, the repetitious echolalia. "Quiet body, quiet hands," you whisper in public. "No rocking. No repeating," you say so often you feel like a broken record yourself.

At some point it hits you. You look at your child and realize you're not fighting the autism anymore, you're waging a war against the fundamental person your child *is*. If you hate his bouncing and his squeaks and his flappy hands, that's the same as hating the things that make him happy because these are his purest expressions of joy. Most of the parents of autistic children I've known have gone through this process. They've exhausted themselves for years and then, they've laid down the battle armor and called a truce. *This is my child,* their heart tells them. *My funny, quirky child. I'm not going to fight this anymore.*

Ethan was about eight when this shift happened for us. By the time he was ten, I was so convinced of my earlier folly, I was proselytizing the need for more honest and better clarity around the issue of autism recovery. "I've never met a child who has recovered from autism," I wrote in the *New York Times* in May 2006. "I'm sure it happens but less often than we are led to believe. I wish more parents were told this more clearly from the start. Children won't recover, but they *will* get better. And better is a lot."

At the time I wrote that, "better" for us meant a week going by without needing to pick up Ethan from school following a meltdown or a bathroom accident. Better meant he had four accidents a week, not twelve. Better meant going out to a restaurant and making it through an entire meal. When you've been living for years on high alert, feeling as if your nervous system is plugged into a wall socket, "better" is a twenty-four-hour break from that.

In the years since then, much has been written about accepting our neurodiverse children but far less is out there when it comes to the second great battle most parents will face: helping their older child with autism (or any other developmental disability) find a job, housing, independence and *a life*. "I don't want to think about that," I used to say when someone asked about "life-after-school" plans for Ethan. "We're focusing on other goals right now." Say (or even think) this often enough and a shroud of silence falls around the topic. As your child ages, the unknown grows more ominous. Suddenly you *really* don't want to pull back the curtain and look at what might be your very worst fear: your child who has come so far from the difficult, unreachable toddler he

once was—who is now social and part of a school community he loves—
might have nowhere to go and nothing to do.

....

Just before Ethan turned twenty-one, I published a piece in the *New
York Times* about our final IEP meeting and the difficulty we were having envisioning a full and happy future for him. After four years of vocational placements that had all ended in varying degrees of failure, we
were planning his last year of school-based services before he transitioned into adult services, which aren't guaranteed in most states but
are in Massachusetts for those with IDD. The article prompted an outpouring of responses in large part, I suspect, because we'd arrived, at
least for the moment, at an unexpectedly peaceful place. Ethan had
surprised us by becoming a better worker at his supported farmhand/
landscaping job than we ever expected. Even more surprising, after
years of believing we were solely responsible for planning his future,
he'd written his own vision statement (with the help of his vocational
coordinator). In it, he said, "After I graduate from high school, I plan to
work at Prospect Meadow Farm until I retire and live at home with my
family. I'd like to keep taking music classes at Berkshire Hills. For fun,
I want to go to our cabin in Vermont, mow lawns, and collect business
cards." In other words, he was saying: *I want my life to keep looking
the way it does now.* By writing this out, he showed us, very clearly,
that this was *his* life and he would have a say in it. It was a glorious
moment—one I never would have envisioned in the darkest days of
Ethan's early childhood, when we struggled so mightily to teach him
language and play.

A stream of responses from readers became a flood after Dan Rather
reposted it on his Facebook page, saying he "saw not only the struggles
of a family, but also an echo of our times. Will we reach out to each other
with empathy and understanding? Will we embrace the possible? Will
we put in the work and open our eyes to welcome the goodness and
worth of others?"

Judging by the notes I received, Rather was right: the piece resonated beyond the community of parents of children with special needs. I heard from hundreds of folks with children who had no diagnosis but were still struggling to find a "future vision" for themselves. They appreciated the reminder that if we give our children the space and time to find their own way, they usually will. I did notice one recurring theme, though, in the letters from parents of children with special needs: the story zeroed in on a truth they'd all experienced but hadn't known how to talk about. Over and over, I read about an adult child who had managed school well but hadn't found "her place quite yet" or "a job that will keep him." "He's twenty-seven now and still looking for work, but we haven't given up yet!" one father told me. Or this, from a mother in her seventies: "My daughter is almost forty-five and she's still doing what she's always done: one afternoon a week at our animal shelter. She'd like to do more but we're not sure who to ask. Ethan's story has fueled me to keep trying."

These stories haunted me. I knew, all too well, that Ethan's story was only beginning and the issue of a child with IDD transitioning to adulthood is more complicated than one article can convey. Now that Ethan has stood on the cliff we've dreaded all his life, I've finally looked closer at what lies ahead and it's not a happy picture. Our system of vocational supports and social services for adults with developmental disabilities is, in many states, shockingly behind the times. The history of institutionalization and segregated education of people with IDD is more recent than I realized and both outmoded systems cast woefully long shadows. By comparison to thirty years ago, when many of us attended school without ever seeing a child with IDD, times have changed, though maybe not as much as one might hope.

When Ethan entered high school, for instance, no student with a significant disability had ever participated in the school musical. I pressed the matter because Ethan had brought home a flyer saying, "Everyone who auditions gets in!" I judiciously pointed to the law that guarantees all students equal access to these activities and the school complied. Accommodations were made. At the performance, Ethan couldn't be seen from the audience because he was dancing on the sidelines behind the curtain, mostly off stage, but the next year when I gently asked if we might be able to *see* him this year, we could. He was front and center, singing and dancing and grinning from ear to ear. By the following year, four other students from his intensive-needs classroom had joined him on stage and the beloved theater teacher told me that including these students had become his favorite part of directing the yearly musical.

Most parents I know have at least a few stories like this: small battles won that feel like part of a larger war. Recently, I drove past the high school cross country team and recognized a younger boy with autism from Ethan's classroom running with the pack, a sainted aide huffing alongside him. I was alone in the car and, still, laughed and clapped my hands. Another first! A student from that classroom on a JV sports team!

For Ethan and his peers, victories like this are significant. They mean high fives in the hallway and a dozen interactions he would never have otherwise. They give students with social challenges something to *say* to their peers. "Good luck tonight!" "You're going to be great!" Ethan loves these short, jolly exchanges. He never lingers long on them but that's not the point. Alone in his bedroom at night, I hear him repeat each one like he's flipping through a photo album of happy memories. But what do these wins mean if every door opened shines a light on the empty space that lies ahead? Ethan has been in the same school system for eighteen years and has come light-years from the difficult, uncommunicative toddler he once was. So have his other classmates with disabilities. Many have become outgoing, social creatures with a love of learning that sometimes, even now, catches my breath. But where does it get them if there's no place to bring these hard-won skills after they leave school?

In 2004, the Individuals with Disabilities Education Act (IDEA) tried to address this issue by mandating transition services to prepare students for living and working independently. Those with a disability significant enough that they won't earn a high school diploma are entitled to receive vocational training, including community-based job internships, until they turn twenty-two. This means the federal government guarantees some funding (usually matched by the state) to help students gain the skills they'll need to work. Families who advocate for job placements early can ensure that their child has four to six years of experience under their belt when they head into the world and seek employment. Unfortunately, the reality of the vocational trials often falls short of ideal because many districts don't have the resources to send students into the community and instead put them to work around the school delivering mail, sorting recycling, cleaning cafeterias (jobs they won't be hired to do after they graduate because a new crop of students will be coming up behind them). Still, most would argue these students are getting a better shot at success than they had fifteen years ago, before transition services started. But if you're looking to track their effectiveness, the most disheartening statistic remains more or less unchanged in twenty years: only 15 percent of young adults with IDD will find paid employment—ever. The rest of this group—85 percent—will remain unemployed, consigned to day programs if they're lucky, or nothing at all, if they live in a state that puts twenty-two-year-olds on a waitlist for services. In Pennsylvania, over sixteen thousand young adults (and their anxious families) remain on waitlists for waiver-funding to give them access to *any* services at all. In more than a dozen states around the country, the average wait for a placement in a day program or sheltered workshop is *seven to ten years*. Meaning those young adults will spend most of their twenties—the prime years of their adulthood—rolling back hard-won gains they made in school. With nowhere to go, one parent often must stop working to keep their child safe and cared for at home. In Ohio, the waitlist is sixty-eight thousand names long. In Texas, it's three hundred and twenty-three thousand. Nationally, it's over half a million.

Families are left with fewer choices and one overriding question: If schools spend six years training this population in usable vocational skills, why do so few of them end up with a job and so many end up with nothing to do? How did this *happen*? Are the schools doing something wrong?

Admittedly, Ethan's early high school years were rocky ones. He arrived along with a newly hired teacher for his special-ed classroom who quit after a month, leaving a room of fourteen students and a dozen aides so rudderless they began screening Disney movies in back-to-back double features. When a new teacher was finally brought on, she cheerfully announced to parents that her main goal for the year would be teaching students to make duct tape wallets that they could sell in the cafeteria at lunchtime. Our jaws went slack. After years of skilled teachers who kept a close eye on academic IEP goals, it was our first wake-up call to the lowered expectations the world would have for our children. None of us had duct-tape crafts anywhere on our IEPs, nor were we looking to stigmatize them further by putting them at a lunch table, hawking their wares. We limped through the remainder of the year. That summer I ran into the mother of an older student who'd left the high school a year before Ethan arrived. I didn't know the mother well, but I knew Julia, her daughter, once one of the shining stars of the special-ed room. Julia had Williams syndrome, a chromosomal disorder, rarer than Down syndrome but with some similarities. Most are cognitively disabled with recognizable facial features and a tendency to be extraordinarily friendly (sometimes problematically so) and adept at all the superficial chatter that so eludes Ethan. ("How were your holidays?" Julia would ask. "Did you see your family? How were *they*?")

"You're lucky Julia's out of the high school," I told her mom and regaled her with stories of Ethan's year: the Disney screenings, the duct tape wallets. "I don't think they *learned anything*." Admittedly, parents of students in the special-ed room sometimes speak in broad strokes to make the urgency of our points clear. *It's total chaos! There's no curriculum!* A year of frustration had littered my talk with exclamation points.

Julia's mom said nothing as I filled in the silence with more complaints. Finally she shook her head. "I wish I'd realized years ago— *none of that matters*." Her eyes were shiny, which was odd. This wasn't a woman who spilled her guts at special-ed parent advisory council meetings or cried in public, as far as I'd seen. "All those academic goals and all that effort to get them into clubs. None of that matters if they can't get a life."

I was shocked. Her daughter was one of the few from Ethan's class-room who had genuine ties to the wider student body. Ethan might high-five a few peers in the hallway, but Julia had *friends*—fabulous Best Buddies who arranged movie outings and sleepovers. "Not any-more," her mom lamented. "Those girls are at college now."

I knew Julia had gone to community college as part of a new initia-tive to support young adults with IDD in secondary education. I asked how that was going. "She hated it," her mother sighed. "The work was too hard and no one was friendly. It wasn't the same as being the star of their old classroom." She told me everything else they'd tried: volunteer-ing at a pet shelter wasn't social enough; working a food pantry made her anxious—too many rules and unpredictable clients. I asked about the vocational placement she'd had while she was still in school, shad-owing a hostess at Applebee's, her favorite restaurant. "They couldn't hire her," her mom explained. "A 'rush' of more than two parties at once overwhelmed her—but they also couldn't allow her to volunteer in her old role as greeter."

By the end, the picture was clear: in the year since she graduated, Julia had spent most of her time in her bedroom watching YouTube videos. "She was so successful at school that we always assumed she'd be fine afterward, but I'm telling you now—make sure Ethan has job training. As much as he can get. In every possible setting."

I was most surprised, for some reason, by the Applebee's part. We'd seen Julia at work once and she'd looked so happy, showing us to our table, grinning over menus and telling us our waitress would be right over. Why couldn't she do that job with a little help? I did a little re-search and learned this: the laws in place to protect against abusive practices of underpaying employees with disabilities limit an employer's options. They must still pay minimum wage, even if an employee works at a slower rate or requires assistance. With few tax incentives for hir-ing people with disabilities, companies have little to gain and quite a bit to lose by taking the risk.

I started the new school year fired up. Ethan was sixteen and we wanted him in job placements. "Let's start with a grocery store," I told

Crystal Cartwright, his vocational coordinator. "Baggers have friendly-but-short interactions with customers, Ethan's favorite kind of exchange. They move around a lot. If they have extra energy, they can trot around a parking lot and collect carts. It's perfect!" She agreed, in theory, and then clarified: Ethan wouldn't start out with any position that involved customer interaction. In all likelihood, he'd never be allowed to collect carts in the parking lot. ("For insurance reasons," she told me, cryptically.) He started by "facing stock," which meant turning all cans in the same direction. Predictably, this was fine with Ethan at first and boring after a month, even though he only did it one or two hours a week. When he started complaining at home, I asked his job coach, an older man who'd mentored vocational placements for kids with IDD for twenty years, if Ethan might learn other tasks around the store. Sweeping, maybe.

"That's tricky," he said. "We can't take tasks away from anyone they're paying."

I pressed a little. "What about bagging?"

"Here's the thing about bagging," he said with a sigh. This was probably the fourth time I'd mentioned bagging. No doubt he thought I was a little fixated and needed to understand the truth. "In all the years I've been doing this, I've learned that grocery bagging is one of the best jobs these guys can get. For all the reasons you're saying: it's social, it's a contained skill that can be learned. But here's what they don't tell you: for every bagger with a disability that you see, there are about 150 people sitting at home who want that job." I felt a chill set in. "This store is nice about letting us train high schoolers, but they haven't hired one of our students in over five years. They're filled up. They can afford to keep five or six workers with disabilities. Any more than that and too much falls on the backs of other employees."

It's surprising how rare it is to hear a teacher or vocational specialist speak this honestly. Grocery stores have long been one of the few major employers to hire people with developmental disabilities. The benefits—consistency, longevity, good PR—offset whatever losses they might experience in slightly lower productivity. But grocery stores present both a problem and an irony. Every parent of a child newly diagnosed with IDD spends sleepless nights early on wrestling with the panic-inducing picture of your child bagging groceries for the rest of their life. *There must be more!* you think. *We're going to aim higher!* Every year you compose bold new career goals to include on their IEP to avoid the sad trap of a grocery-bagging future. She wants to be an animal trainer! He wants to work in the music business! Eventually, you narrow your goals to prove you aren't completely delusional. "He'd love to work with an orchestra teacher, helping out. Setting up music stands maybe?" Even as you write, though, you vaguely understand, *This isn't really a job because no one would pay him to do it.*

As it turns out, when the time finally comes to try out real jobs that employ young adults with disabilities, the options are so limited that bagging groceries rises pretty quickly to the top of the heap. It doesn't involve money or making change. It requires a few skills that are easily mastered. Best of all, it's social, which is what Ethan and so many of his peers crave: short, happy interactions with as many people as possible. The more you look at the choices, the more you realize, bagging groceries doesn't seem remotely depressing. In fact, it seems ideal. Which is around the same time you're told these jobs are almost impossible to get. Most grocery stores are happy to hire a few workers with disabilities, but understandably, they have a limit. Add to that the primary asset these workers bring—longevity—and you see the problem. This is a good job and no one wants to leave it. The truth is, I appreciated that job coach and the warning he delivered so early in our search. More parents should hear a chilling statistic like the one he gave me: *for every disabled bagger, 150 people are sitting at home, waiting for that job.* A truth like this gets you thinking more pragmatically. Forget the obvious jobs or the well-worn paths. Think creatively. Look in other places.

I returned to an idea I'd had when Ethan was young. Once, after a freak Halloween snowstorm, we lost power for a week and had to trudge over to the Amherst College cafeteria every night for some hot food and a chance to see each other's faces over a meal. And every night, Ethan explored the nooks and crannies of the cafeteria and hovered around the soda machine, needlessly showing people how it worked. He was only eleven, but no one seemed to mind and we loved watching him in action. "Maybe he'll move over to the silverware and show people which ones are the forks and which are the spoons," my husband, Mike, mused.

"If only that could be a job." I laughed. "I can picture him working here. Being the mayor of his little domain."

It wasn't a crazy fantasy. In fact, in the rare moments when I flashed on grim fears for his future, this was one of the few scenarios I soothed myself with. We live in a town that prides itself for having five colleges within the same twenty-mile radius. *If nothing else pans out, he can always work in one of the college cafeterias,* I thought. Long before we had Ethan, Mike had told me sweet stories about the friendship he and his Bates College pals struck up with Dave, a man with IDD who worked in their cafeteria. He loved hockey and used to come to their rec-league games, a program that didn't have a huge fan base to start with. He was so loyal that in their junior year, they asked him to be a manager of the team so he could travel to away games with them and help haul equipment back and forth. Eventually they invited him to a few of their parties as a way of thanking him for his work. When Mike told me this story, I imagined Forrest Gump wandering through clouds of pot smoke in search of Jenny. "That sounds a little dicey," I said.

"It wasn't," Mike vowed. "We'd met his mom and we knew him really well by that point. He was a great guy. He never drank and none of us would have let anything happen to him."

Though it had been almost thirty years, when Ethan started on this job-hunting track, I googled Dave's name out of curiosity, to see if he still worked at Bates. To my surprise, he not only did, he wasn't the first long-term employee with IDD to work at the college. That honor went to Leon Levasseur, who died in 2011. His obituary told an amazing tale. After being institutionalized for thirty-two years, he was among the first residents of the shuttered facility to move into the community and, with the help of a local attorney, get a job in the Bates cafeteria in 1986, where he worked for the next twenty-five years. "Leon would talk to anybody," Earle Morse, class of '84, recalled at his memorial. It was a quality that challenged his fellow students to rethink their biases. "In a world of people putting up false fronts, Leon caught us all unawares," Morse said.

I thought about the tunnel vision of most undergrads—focused on classwork, on friends, on their own standing in the world—and how these two men offered these students, conditioned to believe that academic success is the clearest measure of self-worth, an alternate perspective. Maybe sports can be enjoyed without being an athlete, maybe parties can be attended without drinking, maybe friends can have brains that work differently. Leon and Dave had a real impact on these students, even ones they didn't know well.

Most astonishing of all was this final detail in his obituary: when he died, Leon Levasseur left his estate to Bates College; worth over $100,000.

I told this story to Crystal, Ethan's vocational coordinator in charge of setting up job internships. She was suitably impressed but warned me not to get my hopes up too high. "I've been trying to put people at UMass and Amherst College cafeterias for a long time and the schools are pretty resistant. They won't let students train on site. Because of insurance issues, they say they can't allow it."

"Aren't students on a job site covered by the high school's insurance?" I asked.

"Yes, but it gets complicated. They say there might be risks to other people."

When I pressed politely, I learned the hesitation was mostly born of uncertainty. "We've never done this before," a woman in the UMass Human Resources department told me.

"You *haven't*?" I said, genuinely surprised. UMass—the University of Massachusetts, Amherst—is enormous—thirty-one thousand students, fifteen hundred acres. It's also about ten miles away from Belchertown State School, one of Massachusetts's "institutions for the feeble-minded" that finally closed down in 1992. I thought of Leon Levasseur; surely some of those residents must have been relocated to Amherst and looked for work the same way he had?

"No," the woman said. "Not that I know of."

When I called Amherst College, I heard the same thing. "It's an insurance issue," I was told. "We can't allow anyone who isn't in our system to work here."

I explained these are students with developmental disabilities who will never learn these skills until they're on site and being shown what to do and how to do it.

"Unfortunately, my hands are tied."

I knew one UMass cafeteria manager had a son with multiple disabilities and I asked his wife if I might ask him directly. "You can try," she said. "There's not much he can do. They have a lot of red tape and regulations they have to follow."

We weren't asking anyone to give Ethan a job. We also weren't asking them to supply support staff. We were, essentially, asking if Ethan could come over with a job coach and voluntarily help them clean up after a meal.

"I agree with you," the manager's wife said. "But they don't see it that way. They see it as extra work which also carries risks."

In a litigious world, it's the first and easiest excuse. *We've never seen people with IDD doing this job before. There must be a reason. It's dangerous for them, perhaps, or unsafe for the rest of us.* But why haven't those assumptions been challenged? We have (for the most part) grown to accept a student with Down syndrome or autism in our public schools and understand there's no danger or risk, but how rare is it to be served mac and cheese in a college cafeteria by someone with IDD? It's probably only happened to you if you live in Lewiston, Maine, near Bates, or near the University of Iowa or another school that has incorporated hiring people with disabilities into the fabric of their employment philosophy. It's telling that once the barrier is broken with one hire, others follow suit. When people *see* it on a daily basis, the fear falls away as does the nebulous sense of danger.

I kept pushing until eventually UMass relented and gave Ethan a chance to come over after lunch and bus tables with an aide. He was too young to be in the dish room near machines, they said. This was the best they could do. Fine, I said.

What followed was a story that many parents of a child with a developmental disability will probably recognize. After I lobbied hard and fought for his chance to do this, Ethan wasn't much interested in proving that I was right or working hard to earn his way to the spot where I thought he wanted to be. He loved college cafeterias for their food, their soda machines, and their college kids. None were present when he arrived for his shifts to bus dirty dishes and wipe dirty tables. It was boring work and he wasn't particularly conscientious about it. Ethan didn't care if he walked around all day with a zigzag of ketchup down the front of his shirt; why would he care if he left the same behind on the tables he was cleaning?

Fighting to get this opportunity for Ethan launched us into one of the many gray areas that are so tricky to navigate, we've discovered. Here I was delivering sermons on the importance of opening doors for kids like Ethan and here he was, happy to walk over the threshold and shoot himself in the foot. He didn't like cleaning tables. It was hard and they wouldn't let him eat any of the food left over on the plates. Exacerbating the problem was the plan to reward him by letting him have one soda at the end of his shift. Apparently he pitched a fit. "Why?" I said.

"The soda machine was turned off," his aide sheepishly explained.

Of course it was. This is life in the real world, and these are the details that accumulate and shape a big part of the battle. At this point, Ethan didn't care about impressing future employers with his work ethic or good attitude. He also didn't care about getting a paycheck one day. He cared about the soda.

The more important lesson here is one that must be taken into account by the policy makers determining the future funding toward community-based employment for people with developmental disabilities. The assumption that these folks want to work "like everyone else" isn't necessarily true. One of my favorite aspects of *Riding the Bus with My Sister*, Rachel Simon's groundbreaking classic about spending a year riding public busses with her sister, Beth, who has IDD, is how defiantly and insistently Beth refuses to work. She had worked in the past, but she hated it and she quit. As she would say, "Working isn't *fun*. I ride busses." Beth isn't alone. More than half of the adult population with developmental disability—a whopping 56 percent, according to a 2014 survey—have never worked. According to another 2017 survey, only a quarter of adults with ASD (autism spectrum disorder) receiving services have community-based employment as a goal in their service plan. Working is—well, *work*.

How can someone who has never felt ambition be taught to get some? How could we tell Ethan the stories of Leon Levasseur and Dave so he would see the larger purpose to the drudgery of cleaning messy tables? The answer was: we couldn't. We forced him to stay with it for the six weeks we originally negotiated. He never went back.

It was frustrating and infuriating to Mike and me who are both genetically wired to be hard workers. We love drawing up to-do lists and ticking off items. To have Ethan seem so, well, lazy was dispiriting. For Rachel Simon's family, Beth's refusal to work became a breaking point for some members. She *could* work—just as she could live independently and navigate a byzantine small-city bus system—she simply chose not to. She didn't like working; she liked riding busses. By packing her lunches and limiting her expenses, she survived on her limited social security income. The irony is plain—she's high-functioning enough to see through the charade everyone was peddling. She has enough money. She doesn't *have* to work, so why should she?

Toward the end of his career, Wolf Wolfensberger, an early pioneer of the deinstitutionalization movement, began to believe that pushing all people with disability toward community-based employment was a mistake. "No matter what people will say about finding jobs for them, it's lies, lies, lies, and more lies. . . . Very few people will end up with paid jobs." He believed that work was no more of a requirement for a successful, independent life than getting married or having children is. What is required is having a connection to other people. In this way, volunteer positions can be just as significant as paid work, but having a role in the lives of others can also be unofficial. *Riding the Bus with My Sister* is an elegy to that possibility. Beth has a role to play, a job she's given herself and one she wakes up before dawn every morning to get started on. She is there to buy coffee and snacks for her beloved drivers, to chat with other passengers, and, as her sister observes—with initial embarrassment that gradually shifts to admiration—she's also there to *be herself* and, in so doing, to remind everyone who walks by her, to be their truest selves, too.

This participation in the world is what every family is looking for when they fight for job placements that seem out of reach or—even worse—of no interest to their child. We're terrified of them having no place to go beyond the sofa of our home or lost in a loop of YouTube videos alone in their room. How we judge their success—and whether it necessitates a paycheck or not—is up for debate but no one will argue that isolation at home, after nineteen years of schooling, is the definition of failure.

These conversations are taking place in growing numbers around the country. A decade after federal funding mandated transition services for all students with IDD, a huge swath of young adults are transitioning backward, to a level of isolation they haven't felt since their preschool days. By most measures, even for those who do get state funding after they turn twenty-two, outcomes haven't changed much. Unemployment figures remain stubbornly high, meaning the majority of those who get funding will participate in day programs, where the quality varies widely. Some create innovative, enriching programs. Many do not. Some offer a combination of vocational skill building, social opportunities, and health and wellness activities. Others might put on a workout DVD and not worry too much if no one follows along.

For the most part, policy makers are well intentioned in their attempt to correct old wrongs. The emphasis placed on community-based inclusion speaks volumes to the mistakes they're trying to avoid. In arguing against federal funding going to any "congregate settings," they make it clear—they don't want to fall into the traps of the past. Many institutions started as beautiful havens, but bucolic views and lovely gardens didn't mean much to the people trapped inside. In 2014, Medicare and HCBS (Home & Community Based Services), the government entity that funds residential services, issued a strong warning against "intentional communities," even ones with appealing perks like swimming pools, fitness rooms, and life-skills classes. Congregating disabled people would lead to segregation and abuse, they argued.

These warning words severely curtailed the development of residential options in many states, including my own commonwealth of Massachusetts, where most group homes are limited to four residents and cannot be clustered with any other group homes nearby. The guidelines were so strict that the net result is a small number of group homes run fairly smoothly, and an estimated 80 to 90 percent of adults with IDD who live with their parents into middle age. Massachusetts legislators point with well-deserved pride to the absence of any waiting list for day services. If a person qualifies, they will have some place to go when their schooling ends, but if that same person (or family) mentions a residential placement, everyone will look nervously away. It's unstated but understood—residential services are only available for those in the direst situations. For terminally ill caregivers, for people who are a danger to themselves and others, for individuals in residential placement before leaving high school. Everyone else should hunker in place until an emergency arrives.

In the year I spent traveling the country and doing research for this book, I saw this contradiction play out in different ways over and over again. The fear of repeating the tragic, past mistake of institutionalization has put state providers into a paralyzing loop: Shutting down sheltered workshops for exploitative practices, but offering little if anything to replace them. Moving residents out of old institutions only to discover abuse and neglect happens—sometimes with fatal consequences—in group homes, too. What are the right answers? Has any state found the balance of dividing the money fairly among an ever-growing number of people in need?

When Ethan was younger, I never asked these questions. I was so averse to thinking about his adult life that I often avoided the parents of older kids. I said to myself, *I don't have time to worry about what the future might hold. We've got goals to work on now. One thing at a time.* As it turned out, not thinking about the adult Ethan would inevitably become wasted a lot of time. Never looking at his realistic job options meant we vaguely imagined him going the Applebee's route: *he loves this restaurant, maybe if we ask nicely, he can work here someday.* Occasionally these scenarios work out, but I wish I'd heard more often back then: *Don't count on it. Look around. Find out what others who are older with similar abilities and interests are doing. Start making lists and expand from there.* Being realistic begins with understanding what the reality is. For far too long, I was scared to squint into the darkness of Ethan's future. From where I sat, I saw only closed doors: He wouldn't go to college. He wouldn't get married. He probably would never live on his own. What's left?

A lot, as it turns out. Being realistic means leaving behind an idealized notion that you might find an employer who will magically love your child's fixations and pay him to pursue them. It means readying your child from a younger age to widen his outlook, trying options that might be valid ways to spend their days, working through tasks that are hard at first. Changing the dire unemployment statistics will only happen with concerted effort on both sides. Yes, companies and employers need to figure out ways to include this group more; yes, legislators must offer more tax incentives and rewards for the companies who find ways to do this successfully. But we families also need to prepare our child from early on for the real challenges of working hard to live the fullest life possible.

The goal shouldn't be finding perfection or even, in some cases, employment. *Riding the Bus with My Sister* stands as a testimonial to the possibility that a full life can exist outside of employment. The goal is *participating* in the world. The goal is having a community beyond your family—people your child can spend time with comfortably because they know him and he knows them. The goal is finding a way—any way—for your child to contribute positively to others because it will make them feel worthwhile.

The goal is getting your child out of their bedroom and out of the house.

....

As a nation, we are in the midst of some fiery debates about what the next steps should be to ensure the fullest life possible for what is rapidly becoming one of the largest minority populations in the country. There are approximately seven million people with developmental disability in the US. As more infants survive their perilous beginnings and autism diagnoses rise, these numbers will only grow. After schools have spent hundreds of thousands of dollars educating these children, consigning them to waitlists and returning them to the emptiness of their parents' home indefinitely must not remain as the only choice they have. One day this will be viewed as a cruelty along the lines of the old days of institutions.

We can do better. All around, options are springing up, often spearheaded by parents meeting a need for their own child and bringing others into the fold because instinctively they know the real goal of these projects is the creation of community. Traveling the country and visiting these places was as reaffirming as anything I've ever done. I saw tailored work sites, residential communities, and day programs focused on visual and performing arts. Many were launched without any government funding at all. "We had to start that way," I heard over and over. "Otherwise, regulators would have told us what to do."

Some programs are new. Some have existed a decade or more, proving both the essential role they play to their constituents and also their financial viability. Policy makers are, at long last, paying attention. Instead of fighting these rule-bending start-ups, they are seeing the necessity of partnering with anyone who has a good idea and the willingness to work hard to see it through. If this is the civil rights movement of the twenty-first century, as many have called it, I suspect it will be waged in small victories like these, and in reminders to this generation of adults—the first to have been educated in inclusion classrooms—that the peers they knew from their school days have grown up, too. They're also waiting to take their rightful place in the world. Remembering that will help, as will every action taken to make room for them—in homes, in jobs, in social gatherings.

These efforts alone won't solve the problem, of course. My research has included talking to families of the severely disabled who have the highest needs and are far too often left out of the debate. Most egregiously for them seems to be the rigid limitations set on residential options in the name of avoiding anything that might—even superficially—suggest institution. For them, collective care in larger settings—meaning more oversight, and, most importantly, lower staff turnover—might very well be the only humane option. Yet families are denied this option in pursuit of small group homes which have, in many states, proved to be more dangerous.

There is a middle ground to be found, I feel sure. I've seen evidence of it across the country: innovative programs that reflect a partnership combining government funding with local energy and talent to offer homes, jobs, and engagement to a group that was, only a decade earlier, left to founder in isolation, virtually forgotten. But we need more.

The disabled are the largest minority group in the country. They are also the only one that any person might join at any time. The communities we build today—accessible, accommodating, accepting—will be as much for ourselves as they are for our children.

CHAPTER TWO

B orn in 1996, Ethan is part of the first generation of children with IDD to be given a proper education and—equally important—to go to school alongside nondisabled peers. Before 1975, schools had the legal right to refuse any student they believed "uneducable," which meant that in some states only one out of five children with special needs attended school. After the Education for All Handicapped Children Act passed, children with disabilities were given the right to an education, but many school systems complied by relegating them to basement classrooms and separate facilities. It wasn't until 1990, with the passage of the Individuals with Disabilities Education Act (IDEA) that they were guaranteed access to the same local schools their nondisabled peers attended. Along with this guarantee came a raft of provisions that have become the cornerstones of special education: It introduced IEPs that brought parents into the creation of their child's education plan and called for regular evaluations to measure progress. It also guaranteed the "least restrictive environment possible," meaning every effort must be made to include them in the same classrooms as their nondisabled peers. By comparison to the crumbs they had been given in the past, it was radical and groundbreaking.

When I first learned how recently these changes were instituted, it took me a while to wrap my mind around it. Here was the reason I had never met, or even seen, anyone with autism or Down syndrome when I was in school. For years, I thought this was evidence of the exponential increase in autism. When I learned about IDEA, I finally understood: they were there all along, hidden in plain sight, relegated to secluded classrooms. But how did such a transparently separate but equal system hold on for decades after *Brown v. Board of Education*? Having once believed the historical mistreatment of people with IDD was a grisly story best left in the distant past, I've come to believe the opposite is true. Learning this history is essential to understanding where we are today and how the dangerous stories once peddled about people with IDD shape a collective narrative that lives with us still.

Institutionalization began with the best of intentions in the mid-1800s, when Samuel Gridley Howe, a social reformer and headmaster of Massachusetts's Perkins School for the Blind, proposed opening a new school founded on research coming from Europe about the capacity of "feeble-minded" children to learn not only basics of reading and math, but enough job skills to become independent and productive members of society. The idea was revolutionary. "They can be taught to do some kinds of labor, to acquire some kinds of knowledge, to attend to their own persons and take care of themselves," Howe wrote. His idea was to bring these children together in a residential school, where they would learn basic academics and work skills. When they graduated, they would return to their communities to become fully participating members of society. By all measures, Howe's experimental school was resoundingly successful, and over the years served as a model for dozens of others around the country.

Within a decade, though, finding employment for graduates who returned home became harder. A rapid rise in immigration meant fewer jobs, lower wages, and more competition. Many former students of Howe's ended up in poorhouses or jails. To avoid this fate, superintendents began keeping graduates on in their laundries and kitchens to support the growing numbers at these "schools for feebleminded," which had filled up with children who had physical handicaps as well as disabilities like cerebral palsy and epilepsy. As they became more and more crowded, the schools shifted their focus away from education entirely.

After visiting some of these sites, modeled after his own, Howe grew increasingly worried that many had become custodial warehouses of a vulnerable population. In 1866, at a groundbreaking ceremony in New York State, he stunned the crowd by critiquing the building they were all there to celebrate: "Institutions are unnatural, undesirable, and very liable to abuse. We should have as few of them as possible, and those few should be kept as small as possible. The human family is the unit of society." Toward the end of his life, Howe made a plea to the governor of Massachusetts to suspend the construction of such institutions entirely: "Let us try for something (where) the morbid peculiarities of each are not intensified by constant and close association of others of his class." He concluded with a warning delivered in the language of the time: "Even idiots have rights which should be carefully considered!!" Instead, after Howe's death, his former school was moved and expanded. At the opening of the larger site, Governor Butler argued against educating these children at all. "Give them an asylum with good and kind treatment, but not a school. An idiot awakened to his condition is a miserable one."

This dramatic change in attitude was fueled, in part, by the burgeoning field of social science begun in 1859 after the publication of Charles Darwin's *On the Origin of Species*. Though Darwin was opposed to the idea of applying natural selection to humans, others were not. His cousin Francis Galton, eager to get in on familial acclaim, coined the term "eugenics" and proposed taking steps to "breed a better gene pool of humans." The idea caught fire in America, thanks to a Harvard zoology professor named Charles Davenport who launched a public relations campaign for his book *Eugenics: The Science of Human Improvement by Better Breeding*, in which he wrote, "Three or four percent of the population is a fearful drag on our civilization. Society must protect itself. . . . The tide is rising rapidly."

At the time, a massive demographic shift was underway, and eugenics stoked Americans' fears about their changing society—fears that only multiplied when superintendents of these institutions began speaking out about the "abnormally strong and utterly ungovernable sexual drive" of their residents. In 1912, W. E. Fernald, the newly installed superintendent of Howe's school, wrote in the *Journal of Psychoanalytics,* "It is well-known that feebleminded women and girls are very liable to become sources of unspeakable debauchery and licentiousness . . . and if at large, usually become carriers of venereal disease and give birth to children as defective as themselves."

By that point, the eugenicists had a receptive public, in the US and around the world. The idea that "half-wits" might reproduce uncontrollably resulting in more progeny like them took hold. Involuntary sterilization of institutionalized adults began in Indiana in 1907 and spread over the next six years as twelve other states legalized the practice. The development of the IQ test in 1905 by Dr. Alfred Binet and Dr. Théodore Simon added fuel to the fire of the eugenicist's argument that intelligence was inherited and unchangeable. Binet pushed back—"We must protest and react against this brutal pessimism," he said—but his words were ignored by a new branch of social scientists looking for a way to weed out the "genetically inferior." Not only was schooling a waste of resources, they argued, it endangered the population at large by keeping the feebleminded in their midst.

The biggest threat, according to university-associated eugenic scientists like Davenport, were the higher-functioning cases. Those who were only mildly affected—the ones who might "pass," limping through school and into the mainstream—could now, thanks to the IQ test, be identified and separated early on, before they hit their reproductive years and began having defective offspring.

Davenport not only won over a receptive public but received substantial research funding from Andrew Carnegie and John D. Rockefeller. Alexander Graham Bell—in spite of having a deaf wife and child—became the chairman of the board at Davenport's research base, the Eugenics Record Office in Cold Spring Harbor, New York. With such esteemed backers, his influence grew. Magazines like *Ladies' Home Journal* and *Cosmopolitan* ran articles about using sterilization to do away with "diseased or crippled" babies for good. The Museum of Natural History in New York hosted an International Eugenics Congress, which boldly announced its mission to "prevent the spread of and multiplication of worthless members of society."

After being named the director of Davenport's Eugenics Record Office, Harry Laughlin proposed the involuntary sterilization of the "most defective and undesirable Americans, estimated to be at least 10 percent of the population." In other words, roughly fifteen million people. If "carried out thoroughly," Laughlin argued, they could "wipe out defectives within fifteen to thirty years." Surprisingly, some of the greatest proponents of eugenics were progressive social reformers, including Margaret Sanger, champion of the birth control movement, who believed the elimination of the weakest in society was more humane than the alternative—allowing them to die of starvation or disease. Others also saw this as a humanitarian solution to a larger problem. An early meeting of the American Academy of Medicine formally declared: "If we prolong the lives of weaklings, we make it possible for them to transmit their characteristics to future generations." Most significantly, in 1927, Supreme Court Justice Oliver Wendell Holmes—who was hugely popular with progressives for his rulings on economic regulation and free speech—gave eugenics a boost in *Buck v. Bell,* which not only upheld Virginia's sterilization law, but delivered a call for other states to follow suit. "It is better for all the world if, instead of waiting to execute degenerate offspring for a crime, or let them starve for their imbecility, society can prevent those who are manifestly unfit from continuing their kind. . . . Three generations of imbeciles are enough." The court ruled eight to one in favor.

In the decade that followed this victory, involuntary sterilizations quadrupled and Davenport's Eugenics Office grew more ambitious. They argued that it wasn't enough to simply sterilize the feebleminded individual. In order to make real progress, "We have to go up higher into the upper strata and find out which families are reproducing these degenerates. The remedy lies in drying up the source." The parents of any child with IDD, and even their siblings, should be sterilized as well.

Eight years after *Buck v. Bell,* the tide began to shift. In 1935, after it became known that Hitler used Davenport's research to justify his own experiments in purifying the population, the Carnegie Institute pulled its financial support of the Eugenics Record Office. Other funders followed suit. Over the next decade, the propaganda machine created by Davenport and Laughlin died away, but the work it set in motion would continue. A class of powerless citizens had been vilified as a danger to society, and that assumption would live on for decades.

....

Though there's plenty of writing describing how people with IDD were viewed at this time—"little more than animals," "born criminals," "worthless," "a drain on humanity"—it's almost impossible to find any writers or parents who were brave enough to publish stories about their lived experience. There's no counterweight on record. What was it like to be the parent of a child with a developmental disability at that time? With a near-total absence of community support and a mainstream education impossible, did institutionalization feel like a humane response?

I don't know the answer to this, only a story about my grandmother's younger brother, Hank, born in 1907. According to family lore, he developed normally until the age of four, at which point, he suffered brain damage from either spinal meningitis or encephalitis, depending on who you ask. (The fact that there's disagreement suggests that my family—like many at the time, and still—were eager to point a finger at anything but genetics.) By the time Hank was six years old, the extent of his cognitive disability was clear, and his parents refused to send him to school. This was in Augusta, Georgia, now the second largest city in the state, then still a small town where such a choice might not have been so unusual, perhaps. By keeping him out of school they also shielded him from the prying eyes of neighbors. Unfortunately, it also meant keeping his younger brother, Ed, home. When Ed was eight years old—obviously bright, and eager to learn—his parents relented and sent him to school, but after that, keeping Hank out of the spotlight grew increasingly difficult. My grandmother, Margaret, Hank's older sister (who was smart enough to eventually leave home and attend Wellesley College, a rarity at the time for a young woman from the

South), wouldn't bring friends or dates home where her brain-damaged brother "might be sitting next to the fireplace, drooling," according to my aunt. With his father's death in 1923, Hank's mother decided that she "could no longer control him" and sent him to the Georgia State Lunatic, Idiot, and Epileptic Asylum in Milledgeville, Georgia. By that point, Hank was old enough that on the eve of his departure, he found his father's duck hunting gun and tried to kill himself. He didn't succeed but lived with a permanent scar on his forehead from then on.

Not surprisingly, this story didn't get told often in our family, but when it did, the lesson was always this: Hank's parents had made a terrible mistake keeping him at home as long as they did. It would have been better for the family—and less embarrassing certainly—if he'd been institutionalized sooner. There was also this undercurrent: it would have been better for Hank, too. "The cruelty was waiting," my aunt insists. "By then he was used to family life. He didn't want to leave it."

Though it was built in 1842 as an asylum for "lunatics," Georgia State Hospital had a long history of serving patients with IDD, as many of the state asylums did at the time. Like others, it began with the goal of creating a humane residence for mentally ill and intellectually disabled people. By the 1920s, though, when Hank was committed, it was the largest institution in the country, housing thirty-five hundred residents, and struggling to survive under the weight of such numbers. During the Depression, food shortages meant that patients ate primarily soups and porridges; eggs and milk were a rare treat, meat even scarcer. Worst of all was the shortage of doctors, one for every 275 patients. By the late '40s, it was nearly a thousand patients to one physician. After the war, the overworked staff relied on what were believed to be the necessities of custodial care-management: straightjackets, lobotomies, insulin shock, and the newly heralded electroshock therapy, lauded because it left no marks and afterward, the patient wouldn't remember anything. The doctors referred to it as the "Georgia Power Cocktail."

"[The hospital] has witnessed the heights of man's inhumanity and the depths of his degradation," Dr. Peter G. Cranford, the chief clinical psychologist at the time, wrote. In 1950 alone, three patients died attempting to escape. Another managed to commit suicide by hanging himself with a bed sheet. Finally, in 1959, the *Atlanta Constitution* published a series by reporter Jack Nelson detailing the atrocities he'd witnessed: a nurse performing surgery without a doctor's supervision; a quarter or more of the doctors with a history of alcoholism or drug abuse; and this startling tidbit: several physicians had been hired directly off the hospital wards after they had received psychiatric treatment themselves. The inmates were, quite literally, running the asylum. Nelson won a Pulitzer Prize for the story and the state began a series of long-overdue reforms, but by then it was too late for Hank. Our family tree records his death in 1957. No one knows how he died.

The eugenics craze came to Georgia late. In 1937, it was the last of the thirty-two states to enact a program of involuntary sterilization of institutionalized patients, after two hundred leading citizens of Augusta signed a letter delivered to the state legislature strongly supporting the eugenics law. "How much of our money are you willing to contribute to the growth of a yearly increasing crop of half-wits?" the letter demanded. "Within the next hundred years there will not be enough normal people to care for the sub-normal." Was my great-grandmother among those "leading citizens" calling for an end to the perpetuation of half-wits? Her husband was a respected doctor in town, their family a pillar in the community, secrecy surrounding Hank aside. So how did she feel when the sterilization bill passed the Georgia House of Representatives on March 7, 1935, by a landslide vote of 117 to 29 and the editors of the *Augusta Chronicle* rejoiced: "The very intelligent campaign for a sterilization law in Georgia which was conducted by a number of prominent Augusta women did much toward educating the members of the Legislature and the people of Georgia generally as to the great necessity for such a law in this state"?

Hank's is just one of hundreds of thousands of stories lost to history. His life has been reduced in our family's history to the valiant effort his parents made to forestall the terrible fate they ultimately couldn't save him from. I know they visited him. I know my grandmother hated going and after a time, refused to anymore. Her feelings about her brother were always described as "mixed." My father's main memory of the uncle he never met boiled down to: "I know my mother felt sad about the whole thing. She didn't like thinking about him."

But surely she did. Surely having such a brother meant internalizing a fear of her own potentially defective genes at a time when eugenics was taught at every major college and university as part of their standard biology curriculum. Did his specter haunt her thoughts when she became pregnant in 1945, at the age of forty-two with a baby she named Margaret, after herself, who seemed healthy at first, if a little slow developing? Did she panic when my eleven-year-old father came home from a friend's house and commented, innocently enough, that his friend's infant sister could do a lot more than baby Margaret could?

I think about my own complicated dance with denial when Ethan was still less than a year old. I knew something was wrong, but I was terrified of doctors putting a label on him that would limit how others saw him. For my grandmother, the stakes were infinitely higher. If this child was labeled, she would have to give her up.

In all my father's childhood scrapbooks, I've only seen one picture of Margaret. She's the infant sitting in her mother's lap in a family portrait—parents seated, siblings gathered around in front of a fireplace. Everyone looks off in different directions, seemingly lost in their own thoughts. Only my grandmother smiles into the camera, surrounded by her brood, with no idea yet that in less than a year's time, doctors will tell her the terrible truth about Margaret, along with the accepted wisdom of the time, what her own mother must have heard and resisted as long as she possibly could. *To spare your other children, you must relinquish this one.*

"Disability is most often viewed through the lens of whatever social issues and cultural anxieties seem central to society at a given time," historian Katherine Castle writes. It was 1947. The war had ended, ushering in a decade that would prioritize idealized families and general prosperity. Instead of being told to institutionalize their child against the danger they might one day pose to society, the threat was now closer to home. Parents were told they must make this impossible choice for the sake of that child's non-disabled siblings. One superintendent of a Virginia state institution issued a report concluding that the "psychic trauma wrought upon the normal children in the family of an idiot sibling is incalculable." For children under six, the rate of admissions to public institutions doubled between 1945 and 1955.

Margaret was born in 1946. When the extent of her disabilities became clear just after her first birthday—she was developmentally delayed, with limited mobility and issues with her vision—my grandmother made the decision to put her in an institution "before she would have any memory of living at home with her family," my aunt tells me when I ask about this story. She remembers helping her mother care for the baby, and then, because her father couldn't bear it, accompanying her mother to look at different institutions. The private ones were nicer, of course, but "there was no guarantee they would stay that way. They might lose their funding or their director and change completely. The state hospitals seemed like a safer bet." She also remembered this haunting detail that caught my breath when I heard it: before delivering baby Margaret to state care, her mother signed do-not-resuscitate papers, a measure of how little hope she must have had that a worthwhile life was possible for her daughter.

My father never saw his sister again. A year later, she died. Again, no one is sure exactly how. "She was just very sick," my father told me, shaking his head. "Everyone said it was a blessing." He never forgot the effect she had on his mother, who became sad and quiet in the aftermath of her youngest child's placement. Once, when he was playing a Paul Robeson record in his room, he opened the door to find her standing in the hallway outside, weeping. Only then did he realize the song playing was "Sometimes I Feel Like a Motherless Child."

By the time he told me this story, he was well into his eighties and far more emotional than the father I grew up with. He cried easily, sometimes embarrassingly, at TV commercials, passages of literature, music, sadness in other people's stories. Often it was hard to pinpoint what had set him off. He'd be in the middle of a story and start sobbing. My sister and I would widen our eyes across the dinner table—*here he goes again*—and wait for the spell to pass. We gently joked about it because it seemed safe to do so. Our dad's life wasn't sad. He was beloved by his children and friends, happily married for over fifty years. Now I wonder if he was, in his final decade, feeling emotions he might have witnessed or experienced but set aside in his mind.

Toward the end of his life, he got much chattier and more willing to sift through the past. When I asked about his baby sister, he recounted everything he could remember. She was a late-in-life baby and because of that, his mother had worried when she was pregnant. Then she arrived and was seemingly fine. A happy baby who babbled and stood up in her crib. As he talked, the connection seemed to slowly dawn on him: I was asking as the mother of a child who seemed fine at first, and then wasn't. By the time we got to the coffee shop we'd been walking toward, he was weeping. "It must have been so hard for my mother. I look at you and Ethan . . ." He struggled to speak through his tears. Finally he calmed himself enough to say this: "A mother wants to be with her most vulnerable child."

Yes. A mother wants to be with her most vulnerable child, and for my grandmother, this wasn't possible. These fragments of my family story are a glimpse into what must have played out around the country for decades. I suspect few willingly gave their child up. To succeed in such a mass effort, reality itself must be reframed. A population that had always been pitied in the past, as "harmless idiots" or "God's eternal children," had become dangerous, sex addicts, a threat to society. Your family will be irrevocably hurt. Your other children will suffer.

The revelations of Nazi atrocities might have ended the eugenics craze, but it didn't alter the trend to segregate and institutionalize. By demonizing people with IDD for so long—in popular thought, in statutory codes, in educational systems, in the judgment of professionals—their image as being dangerous and uncontrollable persisted long after the eugenics talk died away. Even after a surprising 1930 report from the National Children's Council warned *against* placing children in institutions, saying such situations "pushed them beyond limits that were scientifically sound or socially useful," instead, recommending "appropriate education and suitable employment in the community" the number of children institutionalized tripled over the next three decades.

....

Pearl Buck, the first American woman to win the Nobel Prize for Literature, for *The Good Earth* in 1931, was also the first writer of note to go on record and tell the story of having a child with IDD. Her daughter Carol was born in 1920, but it took three decades for her to work up the courage to tell her devoted readership the secret she'd carefully guarded: "I have been a long time making up my mind to write this story. It is a true one, and that makes it hard to tell." First published in *Ladies' Home Journal,* and later as a book called *The Child Who Never Grew,* Carol's story became one of the earliest and most widely read narratives to counter the negative stereotypes that had permeated the culture. It was also the first to articulate what my grandmother and countless others must have felt: having a child with a disability changes one's thinking. Though Buck was raised by intellectuals, her child taught her "to understand so clearly that all people are equal in their humanity and that all have the same human rights." She is almost at a loss for words trying to explain what so few writers ever had: her daughter's sense of justice and fairness, her love of music, her passion for the outdoors. "What I am trying to say is that there is a whole personality not concerned with the mind. The mind seems to have very little do with the capacity to feel."

Buck's story is also a testimony to the fact that even a mother with plenty of resources and the respect of the professional world was left with few options to care for her daughter. She details the year she spent when Carol was seven, traveling the country, meeting with leading doctors and professionals in search of a solution to the problem of where her child could live most productively and happily. She wants to keep her at home but isn't sure that's right. She talks to other mothers of children who tell her what it was like for them in no uncertain terms: "The neighbors don't want them around. The other children are mean. What shall we do? Where can we go? Our child is still a human being. He is still an American citizen. He has some rights, hasn't he? It's not a crime to have a child like ours. But people behave as if it were."

Ultimately, even a pioneer like Buck couldn't find a way to keep her child out of an institution, but still she is determined that Carol's life will have meaning. "If her musical gifts can never be expressed, her energy never creatively used, then her existence must be of some use to people. In one way, if not the other, her life must count." The only way she can think to do this is, in itself, a radical act; she tells her story, and in so doing, offers her most poignant advice to other parents: "Be proud of your child, accept him as he is and do not heed the words and stares of those who know no better. . . . You will find a joy you cannot now suspect in fulfilling his life for and with him. Lift up your head and go your appointed way." By the end of her book, she makes what was, at the time, her boldest argument of all: people with IDD deserve the same civil rights as everyone else. "I come from a family impatient with stupidity and slowness and I absorbed the family intolerance of minds less quick than our own. . . . It was my child who taught me to understand so clearly that all people are equal in their humanity and all have the same human rights."

Buck never considered herself a disability activist—the cause was too personal, the movement too nascent—but her words galvanized a growing community of parent-activists to tell their own stories. Dale Evans, one half television's hugely popular singing cowboy duo along with her husband, Roy Rogers, took inspiration from Buck and wrote a bestselling memoir, *Angel Unaware,* about their experience parenting a daughter with Down syndrome who died at age two. Later Buck wrote about the galvanizing power of parents' sharing their experiences: "[When you find other parents] you're not alone anymore, waging a battle with a fragile toddling soldier at your side. You're part of something larger, a web of strangers bonded by shared grief and steely determination."

Over the next two decades, support groups began to unite under the umbrella of the National Association for Retarded Children (NARC) and start a systematic push for schooling, more funding, and more support for families to keep their children at home. It was a slow, uphill climb, most often waged locally when parents sued a school district that had deemed their child ineducable, but in 1960, their cause got a huge boost with the election of John F. Kennedy and the revelation—long kept a family secret—of his sister Rosemary's developmental disability. Another sister, Eunice Kennedy Shriver, was the galvanizing force behind going public with their story. Two years after his election, she wrote about Rosemary for the *Saturday Evening Post,* the most popular magazine in the country. Instead of focusing exclusively on the personal, as Buck had, she put the story of her sister and their family into a larger context by describing the plight of "so many people with mental retardation in the country today, living in overcrowded wards of a hundred or more, unloved, unwanted, some of them strapped in chairs like criminals."

If Buck told one truth—that she believed in her daughter's humanity and her right to a decent life—Shriver went further and filled in the story that people didn't want to hear but needed to: too many people were being abused by the government charged to care for them. Six months after her brother formed the first President's Committee on Mental Retardation to oversee his commitment to fund the expansion of research, educational opportunities, and institutional overhaul, he was assassinated. Shriver ensured that the committee continued its work after his death, but the last issue—improving the institutions—proved to be the most intractable. Even after her brother Robert visited Staten Island's Willowbrook State School in 1964 and appeared on the TV news that night to declare it "no better than a snake pit," very little about those horrific conditions changed.

In December of that same year, frustrated by what seemed to be a national acceptance of blatant abuse, Burton Blatt, a professor of special education at Syracuse University, turned to activist tactics. With a photographer who had a hidden camera attached to his belt, Blatt gained access to four institutions and captured images of people restrained, naked, sitting in their own excrement beneath festive holiday decorations.

Blatt titled his work, "Christmas in Purgatory" and sent a copy to every member of Congress. After *Life* magazine ran the pictures, the impact was dramatic. Public pressure increased and the following year, the President's Committee on Mental Retardation assembled a group of experts to write up a frank analysis of "what to do about the institution issue." Legislators were willing to invest in change, but no one could agree on what that change should look like. Expanding the overcrowded wards? A return to the educational model? Simply hiring more staff?

Included in that group of experts charged with addressing these questions was a twenty-five-year-old German émigré named Wolf Wolfensberger, a researcher at the University of Nebraska with experience working in several state-run institutions around the country. The report he coedited, with contributions from leading researchers around the world, came to a clear conclusion: hiring more staff and making reforms wouldn't solve the problem when the system itself was so fundamentally dehumanizing. "If you can view them as animals, you can keep them as animals, physically," he decreed. "Until the attitudes change, all the money in the world is not going to make a good institution."

Their report, "Changing Patterns in Residential Services for the Mentally Retarded," concluded that institutions couldn't be fixed, they had to be closed down. The cornerstone of this argument lay in an essay by Bengt Nirje, a Swedish researcher, called "The Normalization Principle," a concept that caught fire, in part, for its simplicity: people with mental retardation should have lives that mirror all the "normal" rhythms and rituals of life for nondisabled people. For years, Nirje had observed how residents were routinely dehumanized: adults sleeping in cribs, eating dinner at 3:00 in the afternoon, never visited by family members, unaware of holidays or recreational opportunities. Niels Erik Bank-Mikkelsen, a colleague of Nirje's, said, "For children, normalization means living in their natural surroundings, playing, going to kindergartens and schools, etc. We are trying to integrate the retarded into the community in the best possible way."

Instructed to come up with recommendations for improving institutional care, Wolfensberger and his colleagues essentially argued that it couldn't be done. The very foundation was rotten. Then Wolfensberger raised the bar even higher: these people deserve to have *a life,* he argued, like everyone else. The solution was integration through small group homes where they'd be able to participate in activities they hadn't been allowed to do for seventy years, i.e. go to restaurants and movies, choose their own clothing and haircuts, cook for themselves, work in the community. The idea was met with trepidation. Even Blatt, the writer of "Christmas in Purgatory," still believed in the possibility of a "good institution." His example was Seaside Regional Center for the Mentally Retarded in Connecticut, which he called "The Promised Land" because it provided a nightstand beside every bed, a stuffed animal for every child, and curtains on the windows. But among the young professionals starting out in the field, Wolfensberger was hugely influential. Steve Holmes, who began his career as a nineteen-year-old at Fernald State School (once Howe's school), remembers arriving to his first day of work and being assigned to a ward of twenty-eight men, all of whom slept in metal cribs. "People who weren't in wheelchairs basically lay in bed all day in diapers. That was it." When he read Wolfensberger's book, everything changed. "It swept through our field. It became one of those enlightening moments for everybody . . . [mostly because] it made so much *sense.*"

By 1973, Wolfensberger had moved to Toronto and consolidated his ideas in a book called *Normalization* that became a Canadian nonfiction bestseller. Within a year, he was invited by Burton Blatt to join the Syracuse University faculty, where his legend grew. He used three overhead projectors and a stack of hand-colored transparencies during his speeches—high tech at the time—to illustrate the all-important specifics of making normalization a reality. His lecture halls filled to capacity. It was the early '70s, and graduate students in education and social work saw this as a civil rights revolution that they weren't too late to join.

Though the idea behind normalization was simple, the execution was not, and Wolfensberger saw these students as his foot soldiers. He armed them with checklists and protocols for what it should look like:

clothing and haircuts must be age appropriate, activities must be culturally "normative." No more sitting around with coloring books or stringing macaroni necklaces all day for groups of adults. The word spread. *Newsweek* ran the cover headline, "Is Basket Weaving Harmful?" Wolfensberger's response: *Yes, when no one in our culture weaves baskets anymore except for people locked away in institutions.* One of his overriding points was that nothing much would change until society's attitude changed. Having people with intellectual disabilities go to school, movies, and restaurants would alter their lives dramatically, yes, but it would also change how they were *seen:* "Prior to the 1970s many handicapped people had never made a phone call, never cooked for themselves . . . never been on a picnic or vacation. They'd certainly never selected their own clothing or shopped for groceries." When given the opportunity, many learned to do these things with ease. "This was a phenomenal eye-opener for everyone," Wolfensberger remembered in *Valuing Lives,* a documentary released in 2016 about his life's work.

Small changes could make a big difference. To college students who were studying with him and working part-time as community-inclusion aides, he said, "Just be with someone. Walk beside them, not in front of them. Speak with them as an equal. Ask questions. Listen to their answers." In other words: *treat them as people,* which was still a radical enough idea that people went to university to hear someone explain how to do it.

To understand how people with IDD had become so mysterious and misunderstood, Wolfensberger looked at their depiction in art and literature over time, and the damaging roles that had so often been assigned: menacing threat or object of pity. He blamed Pearl Buck for battling one stereotype by creating another—the eternal child. John Steinbeck gave us Lenny, who embodied both extremes at once—a hulking man-child, unaware of the lethal dangers of his own innocence. All had effectively isolated and dehumanized people with IDD. They'd never been viewed as ordinary citizens, capable of playing ordinary roles in our society. Every poster child for a March of Dimes fundraiser undermined the adult jobseeker that child would one day become. This devaluation, he argued, was the real enemy. Fighting it meant finding positive and valued social roles for this group.

As deinstitutionalization became an accepted goal, the challenge shifted to finding acceptable alternatives. Community-based group homes were the first logical step, but in the beginning, those didn't look much like ordinary homes, especially when eighteen to twenty residents lived there. Even as the houses got smaller, Wolfensberger realized that the residents and staff still had an institutional mindset. The residents didn't receive furniture or decorations; they still wore their ill-fitting coveralls. They'd been given a home, but nowhere to go.

Wolfensberger redoubled his efforts at getting to the heart of changing society's attitude. He challenged his students to question their own biases about what people with IDD were capable of. His workshops became juggernauts—intense and unrelenting—with demands that everyone present become a true agent of change. Black-and-white footage shows him in front of packed halls promising the assembled crowd, "You are going to get frustrated with me. You are going to get exasperated when you ask me for the simple, easy solution to a problem and I have to tell you, over and over, there is none."

"He had a style of training like what the Green Berets might do—let's not eat, let's not sleep, let's see what happens," one participant remembered later. His protégées loved it. He developed a system called PASS (Program Analysis of Service Systems) with hundreds of checklists for evaluating how successful day programs and group homes were at supporting independence and integrating their clients into the larger community. The more intensely he worked, the less satisfied he was with what he saw in the field. Service providers touted normalization in their brochures but failed to follow through on the protocols. John Armstrong, one of Wolfensberger's students, recalls, "The idea was that the institution was evil and if you were to deconstruct the institution brick by brick, then you would have removed the evil. But of course as people moved into better settings, we found that the culture of the past followed people."

Eventually Wolfensberger became so disheartened that he shifted his focus to a single core issue: social role valorization (SRV), the idea that having a valued role in a community is the most important single predictor in quality of life for all people. A job, paid or unpaid, a sense of responsibility to others. "You can bring someone into a community, but unless they have a valued role to play, others won't see them as being part of it," he said. A devalued person "will behave in ways that are socially expected of him/her." If we perceive the role as having value, we're more likely to raise our expectations and act positively toward them. "Our respectful treatment results in higher achievement."

Implementing SRV meant longer workshops and an even more exacting template, and Wolfensberger lost a good chunk of his followers. He also became more emphatic about speaking the truth as he saw it. Twenty years after it began, deinstitutionalization had been a failure, as far as he was concerned. Too many people had been "dumped" into community settings without enough support. They didn't have jobs. They hated their day programs and did everything they could to avoid them. Unconnected to neighbors who didn't want them living nearby in the first place, residents became vulnerable to predators who encouraged drug and alcohol use. "An amazing new development is the large number of retarded people who have become alcoholic!" Wolfensberger lamented. "In the bad old days one hardly ever encountered an alcoholic retarded person." Worst of all, there had been an explosion of sexual abuse. "It is altogether ironic that a larger percentage of these people were safer inside institutions than outside."

Bengt Nirje, the pioneer who originated the term "normalization," stayed more positive about the developments that Wolfensberger found disillusioning. Nirje pointed out that for any individual—disabled or not—achieving true independence meant allowing for an element of risk. When presented with a full menu of adult life choices, some people will make bad ones. If they have the right to live as they choose, they also have the right to make poor decisions. Robert Perske coined the phrase "dignity of risk" in 1972 to describe what he believed was an essential aspect in creating new service models: "In the past, we found clever ways to build avoidance of risk into the lives of persons living with disabilities. Now we must work equally hard to help find the proper amount of risk these people have the right to take. We have learned that there can be healthy development in risk-taking and there can be crippling indignity in safety."

For Wolfensberger, the risks were too great and this population was too vulnerable. He thought the push toward independence and the self-advocacy movement was a mistake, leaving too many people without the support that they desperately needed. Here is the balancing act parents, professionals, and advocates still wrestle with: How much protection do our kids need? Does the rigorous pursuit of independence leave them too vulnerable to exploitation, or simply their own bad choices? Wolfensberger believed that the bloated, government-funded system was part of the problem, too. It was too rigid to adapt to individual needs, too bureaucratic to ensure humanizing support. Toward the end of his life, he seemed stumped. Institutions were not the answer, but community-based living hadn't worked for the most severely impaired. Study after study showed that those in community-based group homes still experienced very little social integration, with a majority of them reporting that they had "few or no friends."

What was a better solution? By that point, Wolfensberger had no answers. "People should consider living with a family member or trusted friend and advocate," he suggested in defeat.

Ultimately, he believed the greatest threat to people with IDD was spending their adult lives in idleness. There had been a lot of talk about employment, but it had never panned out into a measurable reality. In 2009 he said, "There is no solution in sight for the problem of adult unemployment for the vast majority of people with any serious handicap. No matter what people will say about finding jobs for them, it's lies, lies, lies, and more lies." He'd been at this too long and had seen too many failed efforts. In his mind it was clear: "Very few people will end up with paid jobs."

Acknowledging and accepting this reality is crucial to ensuring that people with IDD not "waste their lives away in the devalued role of idleness," he argued. To this end, he insisted that the most important thing was to find work, even if those jobs are unpaid. "We could insert handicapped people in any number of places where they could perform valued adult work. Of course this is only possible if they haven't been brainwashed into thinking that unpaid work is undignified and should be rejected. Unfortunately this has been one of the dogmas in recent years. Now you have handicapped people who won't work if they're not paid and their whole lives go down the drain as a result."

This was how bleak Wolfensberger's outlook had become. By the time he delivered the only one of his legendary workshops that was taped in its entirety and is available online, it was 2009. He had seen too many horror stories to believe that a few successes presented an accurate picture of where the population was thirty years after the normalization principle had swept through the field. "You might tell me some people are doing fine, but I'm telling you most are not. You all don't see them. They're in jail, they're homeless. If they're not homeless, they're living in worse conditions than they ever were back in the institutions." The majority of them had been "dumped," he said, becoming the among the most vulnerable, preyed-upon segment of our population.

By this point (understandably, perhaps) Wolfensberger had a hard time filling his legendary workshops, but in *Valuing Lives,* countless students remember his early work and say he did more than any other figure in the second half of the twentieth century to improve the quality of life for people with IDD. Though the term "normalization" isn't used anymore (it sounded too much like an attempt to make disabled people "normal"), the basic idea has morphed into the approach most parents of children with disabilities are familiar with: person-centered planning and self-determination. Steve Eidelman, professor of human services policy at the University of Delaware says, "These ideas lie on a continuum and they depend on the same principles. You put the person at the center, you figure out who they are, what they want and what they need, and you figure out how to support them."

Wolfensberger's army, sent out to change the world's thinking about the least understood minority group among us, is mostly gray haired now. Many are retired after long careers in disability service. They all look back wistfully on their time in "the Wolf Pack." Some had ruptures with Wolfensberger, philosophical and otherwise, as his thinking grew more rigid and their work demanded more flexibility; some distanced themselves even as they admired his unwillingness to back down. "We need people like Wolf," Chas Mosely, now a court monitor in Rhode Island, says. "We needed him then and we need him now to pull the veil away and help steer us back on course."

After watching all ten hours of his workshop online, I had to agree: The later message that people didn't want to hear seems just as important as the earlier one that masses flocked to. Not because of his negativity, which does feel excessive at times, but because of the unexpected honesty of a man who devoted fifty years of his life to a mission and in the end, admitted that he had no clear answers. He no longer ruled out congregate-living situations. In fact, he'd become an ardent supporter of L'Arche, a model community begun in France by Jean Vanier in 1964, as a compassionate "shared-living" experiment where people with and without IDD live side by side. He didn't see employment as the only viable option for a meaningful life, either. More important to him was finding valued roles in the larger community, be it as a volunteer or a member of a high-quality day program. Idleness was the gravest danger; meaningful activity the solution. Connections beyond immediate family. As little reliance on the "collapsing social service structure" as possible. He strongly criticized the overuse of technology to replace caregiving and human interaction, afraid of the same things all of us are: our children at home watching endless YouTube videos on their phones.

Wolfensberger died in 2011 but his ideas remain relevant because the questions he raised remain unresolved. He wasn't afraid to name the failures of the movement he'd set in motion. After deinstitutionalization, vulnerable people were left unmoored and unsupported. Too many lived in unacceptable isolation. Putting such a large percentage of adult service federal money into employment programs was a mistake when so few have ended up with paying jobs. It's chilling to hear him articulate in 2009, what he sees ahead for this population—a loneliness and abandonment that might be even worse than they experienced in institutions. Many will dismiss a vision this bleak, but I have to wonder: What if he's right?

CHAPTER THREE

F or most of Ethan's childhood I never thought much about the fact
that we live less than ten miles from the abandoned site of Belchertown State School, formerly known as Belchertown School for the
Feeble-Minded, the second largest institution for people with IDD in
Massachusetts. In the early days after his diagnosis, I occasionally met
older therapists who'd once worked there which always mystified me.
"You *worked* there?" I'd say, privately thinking, *Isn't all of that ancient
history?* I never asked what it was like because I assumed it would be
rude, like asking an elderly Southerner about the Jim Crow days. Institutions were universally seen as a mistake and best left in the past, like
segregated lunch counters, I thought. They had nothing to do with
Ethan and certainly played no part in his future. It was only as Ethan
approached his first forays into working outside of school that I saw how
the history of institutionalization had shaped the world he'd be allowed
to join. His struggle to get a cafeteria internship at UMass and Amherst College was our first encounter with the invisible walls institutionalization left behind. How was it possible to hear so many nos
to what seemed like such a benign request—can my son volunteer to
clean up?

Learning the history explained a lot. In 1972, eight years after Robert Kennedy's visit, Geraldo Rivera famously smuggled a camera crew
into Willowbrook to record what continued to be the brutal, inhumane

treatment of the six thousand residents there. It aired on ABC with a warning to viewers: *These images are graphic and difficult to watch.* Indeed they were. The exposé is often credited with raising public awareness and bringing the institutional era to a close.

It's interesting how frequently you hear this about Rivera's report when it simply isn't true. Willowbrook remained open for another fifteen years. But it did herald a plethora of similar reports around the country that ran on local news stations about other institutions with equally grim footage: gaunt adults sleeping in cribs, day rooms filled with naked or scantily dressed inmates. In 1972, the same year as Rivera's exposé, Belchertown had its own version, an hour-long Public Affairs presentation from WTIC based in Hartford, Connecticut. Sparked by a class action suit from the families of residents calling conditions at the school "shockingly oppressive, unsanitary, unhealthy, and degrading . . . an affront to human decency," two reporters went to investigate and were— surprisingly—granted permission to film anywhere on site. Even more shocking is the chilling candor from the administrators and staff.

"Is it true that feces particles can be found on the walls?" one reporter asks.

"Very true," Robert Knudson, the plant supervisor, replies. "Many of our residents aren't toilet trained. The problem is when it's been on the wall for more than a day."

When asked if cockroaches really run over the residents confined to beds, Knudson hesitates: "I'll give you a terrible answer to that. I don't know if it's true, but if a resident is confined to a bed all day, maybe a cockroach is a welcome diversion."

Though it takes a few minutes to figure this out, eventually it's clear: the conditions are monstrous, but these administrators aren't monsters. They're playing a longer game, looking to get attention from legislators, hoping to spark a bonfire of public outrage that will get them the money they need. As more supervisors are interviewed, the atmosphere is almost surreal, as if they've all received a directive to whitewash nothing and tell only the truth. "Yes, most patients regress when they get here," Robert Agoglia, staff psychologist, says. "Inmates suffer injuries regularly, many of them self-inflicted. Employees are also regularly injured."

"Doesn't the state of Massachusetts *care*?" the reporter asks.

Agoglia hesitates. "I think if they would come out here and look around, they would have to respond. The other choice is to make people aware so they will force the state to respond." Later, he corrects himself to point out that the governor had visited the year before and called conditions "appalling" and a "monumental disaster."

"Then why has nothing changed?" the reporter asks.

Agoglia shakes his head. "The answer to that runs into the very fabric of our society which has always focused on differences between people. The residents at Belchertown are more similar to you and I than they are different. They have the same needs. When people can see them as human beings—not as sub-human beings—I think it will be a little more difficult for them to tolerate the existence of such conditions."

When asked what's needed to improve the barbaric conditions they've just filmed, Agoglia has a ready-made list: More staff, safer buildings, sanitary conditions, for starters. They'll need teachers again, and an educational curriculum. They'll need therapists of every discipline—OTs, PTs, speech and language, psychologists. He never mentions closing the place down, a concept that was still years away.

Eight years later, when the shutdown started and Belchertown residents began being placed in group homes, these exposés were the only picture their potential new neighbors had and the resistance was fierce. Neighbors rallied in opposition. Some towns tried to enact by-laws against group homes. In *Purgatory: An Historical Analysis of the Belchertown State Schools,* a documentary about the closing of Belchertown State School, Joyce Riley, the psychologist overseeing these community placements, gets a little emotional at the memory. The public didn't know anyone with a developmental disability, she explains. "They associated them with mental illness. They were all very dangerous. They were all crazy . . . they were all lumped together." It dated back to the fears stoked by the eugenics movement, she thinks. "People were scared they were going to get out in the community and start breeding."

Setting up group homes was a long, slow process of meeting with neighbors and explaining, over and over, "These people aren't criminals. They weren't locked up because they did anything wrong. People were still scared. I got a letter from one father saying he was afraid of his daughter getting raped."

Bill Zimmer, the assistant superintendent at Belchertown and part of a team of relocating residents in the late 1980s, remembers it a little differently. "The law was on our side. We had a federal court mandate that this had to be done, so we never backed down, even when some communities were pretty resistant," he tells me. They held public forums and made it clear that the group homes were coming: "We told them we didn't need their permission but we wanted this to go well. We wanted neighbors on board." Did it work? Zimmer hesitates before answering. "Eventually we learned that getting people housed was easy. Making them *part* of the community was not."

Zimmer is self-reflective about having both witnessed and participated in such dramatic change. "We had a hope that churches and synagogues might help us create some community inclusion for these people coming out of the institutions and largely that never happened. Nor did we get much help from community service organizations like the Lions Club or the Rotary clubs. It was disappointing. It seemed like a natural part of their missions." He couldn't think of a single example of an organization that included this group in their community events. "It's always been a struggle. I'd argue that it's continued to be a struggle ever since. Maybe we didn't emphasize it enough because we didn't think we had to. We believed the isolation would end when residents weren't physically isolated anymore."

Ruth Sienkiewicz-Mercer is arguably the most famous former patient from Belchertown State School thanks to her memoir *I Raise My Eyes to Say Yes,* published in 1989. A wheelchair user with cerebral palsy that also left her nonverbal, Ruth was part of a small group of physically disabled but cognitively typical residents who were moved out of Belchertown in 1982 and into Linden Towers in Springfield, Massachusetts, a building designed as an active retirement community for residents, with a daily schedule of group activities. The hope was that the social atmosphere there would help facilitate connections, but it didn't. "I can't tell you how many people pinched my cheeks and called me 'cutie,' 'sweetie,' or 'poor little thing,'" Sienkiewicz-Mercer writes. "We hoped that given time with the chance to get to know us, our neighbors' resentment and lack of understanding would fade away. Unfortunately, it didn't work out that way. We were never accepted there."

Zimmer, who later went on to serve as Franklin Hampshire Area Director of the Department of Developmental Services (DDS), isn't sure what could have been done differently to ensure better community integration. "I wonder if some individuals were over staffed. We promised families a lot when we brought people out of Belchertown. We perpetuated this idea that they couldn't do things alone in the community, that they needed staff with them to go anywhere. It set up a lot of expectations that ultimately limited how much independence they had because no family ever wanted to scale *back* on staff."

I suspect this happened around the country. Focused on the safety and health of the relocated individuals, many of whom had complex medical needs like Sienkiewicz-Mercer, the quality and content of the life they were offered wasn't measured until later. Ruth's memoir ends with her marriage to Norman Mercer, a fellow Belchertown resident, a joyous affair by all accounts, shadowed only by the afterword summarizing the nine years of their life since marrying: "The biggest problems Ruth and Norman currently face are boredom and a tight budget." Having finally achieved their independence, they had nowhere to go and nothing to do. These are demoralizing words to hear about pioneering disability activists—but also an explanation for why we heard so many nos when we first began looking for internships for Ethan. Few of the residents coming out of Belchertown State School got jobs. Community integration didn't happen magically.

Belchertown finally shut its doors only *four years* before Ethan was born, but throughout his childhood, I never saw a single adult with IDD working any job besides bagging groceries. Admittedly, no one wears a badge with their diagnosis, but I had a keen eye for the signs—the repetitive tics, the rocking, the random conversations starters. In other words, I was looking *all the time*. I *wanted* to see versions of what Ethan's life might one day look like—a twitchy, giggly man in a paper McDonald's hat, a broom-pusher whispering to himself in an orange Home Depot apron. I never did. Unable to imagine anything else, I obsessed over grocery-store bagging.

When we first started looking for job internships and heard so many nos, I assumed the people in charge were nervous for Ethan's safety. I told them that Ethan was actually a very cautious person. Like many with autism, he has a fear of breaking rules and will regularly (and annoyingly) remind others of rules they shouldn't violate, either. Finally one man said to me, "We have to think about the safety of our equipment and the other workers."

I was so surprised I didn't respond. Was he afraid that if Ethan got near a dishwasher, he might go berserk and press all the buttons at once? Turn on someone with a butter knife? Now I understand; this is what happens in the absence of role models. If people have never seen something before, they assume *there must be a reason*. Consciously or unconsciously it still flutters in the background: *these people are dangerous*.

For half a century, it was the story we were sold. It's not hard for people to believe it still.

CHAPTER FOUR

The research is pretty clear that preparing for vocational placement and independent living should begin long before these students leave school, but when that training should start and what it should look like remains up for debate. Bryna Siegel, a developmental psychologist specializing in autism and founder of the Autism Center of Northern California, sparked some controversy with her book, *The Politics of Autism,* by declaring that transition services and life skills classes should begin at age ten, about six years earlier than most programs today do.

Like Wolfensberger, she believes millions of dollars in government funds have been badly misspent.

"Present spending on autism research has almost no practical value. We still don't have genetic tests for autism, or reliable genetic markers; we still can't look at the brain of an individual with autism, find something to alter, alter it and see improvements in the symptoms of autism," she argues. Only 25 percent of those research funds were directed toward initiatives that would actually improve the day-to-day lives of those on the spectrum and their families. Her point is well taken: the rise in autism diagnoses has been with us for thirty years and the outcomes haven't changed much. As she points out, the majority of adults with autism will live with their parents into adulthood. Ninety percent of them will be unemployed or underemployed. Siegel's toughest argument is where the focus of educating autistic students *should* go. For the last two decades, she believes schools (and parents) have put far too much emphasis on maintaining academic progress to align with the general curriculum and not enough on independence and life skills. She says the students struggling the most academically should drop reading and math goals and focus on life skills much earlier, around third or fourth grade. Many parents bristle at this idea because they think of life skills as a euphemism for giving up on real learning. Every parent I knew from Ethan's special-ed class had a great fear of this fate; we rolled our eyes and called it "macaroni-stringing," assuming that once "life skills" got going, real learning stopped.

These days, I see it differently. Now that Ethan has turned twenty-two, the old bars that we used to measure his success by—reading levels and math scores—seem laughably unimportant when looking at the shape and scope of his adult life. The real measure of his success and that of his peers is almost exclusively related to their independence skills. Can they take a public bus? Make their own reasonably healthy meals? Take their medications? How much of their life can they access and live independently? The sticking point here is that many of these skills are hard for schools to address. How can schools reasonably teach kids about their own medications? How can they do more than corral a small group onto a public bus to do what these kids often do just fine—follow orders and wait to be told what to do? How do teachers instill these kids with the skill set to *not need them*?

I *have* seen it happen. Ethan was so determined to make the half-mile walk into town by himself that we wrote the goal in his IEP and, the year he turned eighteen, he and an aide began practicing regularly. She walked a few feet behind him at first and then lengthened the distance, while still watching his every move. We used to laugh about the Skittles he marched into town to buy for himself. At one point, though, she got serious. "He can do this," she said, pressing my arm so I understood—she meant it. "He *can*. He crosses the street safely. He stays focused on where he's going. He doesn't get sidetracked or wander off."

Until this conversation, I hadn't thought that Ethan would really do it on his own. It was a theoretical goal, yes. But a reality? We'd never considered it because *we'd never seen any of his peers do it.* I'm ashamed to say one of my thoughts was: *If we let him do it, will people see him and think we're irresponsible?* Ethan was nineteen the year I finally began to understand what developing life skills means: learning what he needs to live the life he wants. And schools can help with that, especially if students and parents are clear on what they want to learn.

The last year we insisted on including Ethan in mainstream academic class with a modified curriculum, he was in eighth grade. We knew it would be a stretch, but we promised to do whatever it took to help him keep up. As luck would have it, his special-ed teacher was designing a science class that would include a mix of students, some with significant special needs, like Ethan, and some with milder learning disabilities. "Great!" we said. "Perfect!" For months we worked diligently, helping Ethan spell the words that he needed to fill in the blanks of his homework. When it came time to do the work on his own, I'd try to assist as little as possible. As he looked for the word to describe the plant's process of converting the sun to energy, I'd give him the start. "Pho—"

"Forest?" Ethan guessed.

It went like that all year. He didn't mind the homework. He liked coloring the parts of the cell using different pens, but when he had to memorize the vocabulary for the "big test," I understood how little this all meant to him. For nucleus, he wrote "Nuclear," which was at least close. For ribosome, he wrote, "Ribs," which wasn't. When asked, "What is a cell?" he wrote, "I don't know." When asked to explain what a nucleus does, he wrote, "I have no idea," in letters big enough to fill in all the space provided.

This wasn't the teacher's fault. In a way, it was ours. "He had these answers the night before!" I lamented to Mike, not yet seeing the bigger picture—he didn't have them for the test because they didn't mean enough to him to hold on to.

To this day, I'm grateful to the teacher who complied with our request to challenge Ethan academically and I'm glad to have learned that having Ethan memorize the parts of the cell wasn't worth the effort it took to not do very well on the test anyway. Maybe we should have seen the bigger picture earlier, but we didn't.

Part of the problem was that Ethan, like many of his peers, is a surprisingly enthusiastic learner. He's the only one of his brothers who still loves museums and asks to visit one in every city we travel to. He likes listening to stories on tape, going the library, and watching documentaries. We never knew when his interest would pique for a topic so we wanted him in real classes, exposed to all of it. Somewhere along the way, he developed an affinity for Martin Luther King that has lasted a lifetime, especially when he discovered that his speeches can be accessed and played on Spotify. Gearing up for MLK Day, Ethan will put one on in the car and mouth all the words. "I say unto you, we are being tested. . . ."

Ethan isn't unique in these passions. He's grown up alongside a boy with Down syndrome who loves genealogy and can discuss it in all its granular, Punnett square details. Perhaps not coincidentally, Martin Luther King resonates for a lot of them, as do stories of the civil rights struggle. The parts of a cell might be too abstract, but the concept of fairness isn't. They can all relate to the idea that separate water fountains and bathrooms wasn't right.

We aren't crazy or deluded in wanting modified curricula of advanced subjects for our kids. Sometimes these topics open up a world they can carry with them for years. But does focusing on academic interests take time away from learning the independence skills that will matter more in the long run? Siegel doesn't mince words: "To my mind, such an accommodated curriculum is a waste of time and of educational resources and accrues no knowledge this child will ever use."

It's harsh and off-putting and entirely misses the notion of learning for learning's sake, but she's also right to some extent, and it's important for parents of younger children with IDD to hear what the parents of older children often think: *I wish we'd worried less about academics.* At the same time, Ethan benefitted from laboring through homework the way all students benefit from it. It provided him with the same rhythm as his brothers at the other end of the dining room table—get your homework done, then you get free time. "Charlie and I are doing our homework," Ethan would announce in the evening as I made dinner. *"Then* we can watch TV."

Never having any homework at all, or homework along the lines that Siegel suggests—making burritos to learn reading, measuring, and following step-by-step directions—would have widened the already growing divide between him and his peers. The real answer, of course, lies between the extremes. Parents shouldn't be expected to teach their children *all* the living skills that elude so many of them. By the same token, how can schools be expected to take them all on? Doesn't it make sense to have schools provide Ethan with exposure to interesting subject matter and some academic skills and trust that parents will take on burrito-making on their own?

Even this line of thinking presumes a lot. As every parent will tell you, it is much easier to do a task yourself than to walk your often-resistant child through it, step by step. Can Ethan do laundry? Yes. Does he do laundry? No. Over eighteen years of contributing to IEPs and writing hundreds of goals with even more benchmarks to record your child's progress, it's remarkably easy to lose track of the bigger picture. The real endgame is helping them build a life of their own. Math should be taught as it relates to cooking and money skills, reading and writing as it is needed for interacting with friends and family online and accessing information they're interested in. Siegel believes that forcing children to learn difficult or impossible material will risk making them avoid school altogether. Her other proposals support this line of thinking: bring in functional academics starting in middle school, bring back the vocational education classes that disappeared from most high schools long ago.

I suspect she would not be a fan of a new Massachusetts law that provides all students with developmental disability access to a year of college experience if they want it. A sticking point in making high schools responsible for educating these kids until the age of twenty-two is obvious: everyone can see that they're older than their peers. Call them what you want—"super seniors" was our school's moniker, or "postgrads," or "our transition bunch"—the effect is the same. The world is moving on and they aren't. They're past their due date.

Massachusetts was one of the first states to offer the option to take at least one of these transition years at a local college. In Ethan's case, UMass was literally up the road. Working with their disability department, they sent a teacher over from the high school with a small group of students. In the morning, they'd have a life-skills class on campus, in the afternoon, they could audit a class or explore other resources. As is always the case, the success of such a program hinges on many factors, and for whatever reason UMass has a long history of not loving ideas like this. Two years earlier, Ethan was only begrudgingly allowed to clean up in the cafeteria for a six-week job internship that he had no interest in repeating. Now "exploring resources" meant he had an open invitation—at long last—to eat there.

And eat he did. Like any first-year college student unleashed on the daily buffet of a college cafeteria, he made the most of his time and by all accounts, stopped only after he'd cleaned three plates of food.

Did he do anything else in his time at UMass? Not that he remembers. The program was unsupported by the administration and disorganized by all accounts. (A few years later, it had become so unproductive that parents of a younger student brought in lawyers to help navigate the many issues that, I hear, have since improved.) As it was, students and aides spent most of the day wandering campus aimlessly, thinking of destinations, killing time. They visited the gym and the music classroom but with no reason to be there, they didn't last long. It turns out strolling the halls and grassy paths of a university does not a college student make.

Happily, there are far more successful examples of similar programs, ones that have established relationships with interested professors who have found ways to include these students meaningfully in classes they can keep up with, or at least get something out of. The best of these programs run mentorships that assign each student with IDD a peer who commits to spending two or more hours a week together, going to lunch, gym, classes, etc. This is a better model than having a student move everywhere with an aide at their side. Aides are essential for giving students access to the wider world, but they don't last forever and shouldn't be relied on as if they will.

Siegel asks a bigger question, though: For these students, is a college experience worth it if it postpones learning job skills and entering the real world? "Some children will not learn to read and write, even with eighteen years of IEPs aimed at that," she writes. "Herein lies the problem: How do we, as a society, have an honest dialogue that can lead to ways that realistically support the best future for which we can educate our children with autism? The truth in special education is a very vulnerable commodity."

She also poses a crucial question that all parents must wrestle with sooner or later: *What should we realistically expect schools to achieve?* Our job as parents is to be advocates, to raise expectations, to show that we're serious about their education. So when do you set aside the battle armor and say, "Okay, that's enough, let's work on life skills now"? The question of expectations makes me think about the scene when Ethan was first diagnosed. He had just turned three and was, in our optimistic viewpoint, a hugely social creature with a significant language delay. With the neurologist, we emphasized this over and over—he loved people, loved toddling between the knees of strangers at an airport, touching them and grinning from ear to ear. Was this the behavior of an autistic child?

"Yes," the doctor said curtly. He specialized in epilepsy, but yes, he insisted, he saw this a lot. "This is autism." When we asked for any resources or books he recommended, he thought for a moment. "*Rain Man* is a good movie," he finally said, then added, perhaps in response to our stunned expressions, "The main thing is, you'll need to lower your expectations. Forget about college. Hope that someday he can write a check, manage his money, things like that."

For years we told the story about that stupid doctor and his *Rain Man* recommendation. A gut-wrenching prognosis feels especially cruel, delivered in the same hour that parents are absorbing the psychic body blow of a diagnosis. It bonded us with other parents who had their own stories of dismissive doctors underestimating what a toddler might someday accomplish. *Those doctors were all wrong! Let's show them all what our children can do!* At a time when you have little in the way of energy, it's remarkable how galvanizing a few cruel words can be.

Now I look at Siegel's work and I see an explanation, at last, for why doctors diagnose a young child with a developmental disability and, in the same breath, deliver the grimmest possible picture of what parents should expect. Someone has to. Perhaps they've been told, in medical school or elsewhere along the line, that this is their responsibility. If, as Siegel argues, overly high expectations have wasted resources and even caused harm, who is responsible for delivering a more realistic picture of what parents should fight for and expect?

I hope the message most parents get these days is closer to what I say whenever I meet someone with a newly diagnosed child: there's a huge range of outcomes. Work hard early on, access as many resources as possible, find other parents, listen to your child and follow their lead. Even if they can't talk, you'll learn what they're telling you. Most importantly (I always save this for the end because it *is* the most important), it will get easier. Whatever happens—regardless of how much language they get or how much they "improve"—your life will get easier than it is now and there will be a lot of joy along the way.

I don't know who should be responsible for steering parents onto a path of realistic expectations. I appreciated our pediatrician's response. After he got the neurologist's report, he called us right away and invited me in to talk. I confess now that I didn't want to go. Partly, I was scared of getting emotional, and partly, I was embarrassed by the way I'd mitigated Ethan's deficits in all his well-check-ups, putting a cheerful spin on his delays, part of an elaborate performance of trying to seem fine. But I'll never forget the first thing our pediatrician said to me when we got to his office that day: "Pretty soon you'll know more about this disorder than I do. It's possible you already do."

It had been a week since Ethan's diagnosis. A week spent almost entirely on the internet, finding links to Ethan's constellation of mysterious ailments, his food allergies, his chronic ear infections. Our doctor was acknowledging a deeper truth: reading obsessively was the right thing to do. Information is reassuring, knowledge a balm.

"It's possible I already do." I laughed, tearing up at the same time.

He then did something that's rare for doctors. He listened as I ran through all the research I'd done on links between autism and overuse of antibiotics. Ethan was a baby beset by almost chronic ear infections. Sweet amoxicillin produced one of his few early phrases: "pink medicine." I wasn't blaming the pediatrician. I suppose I just wanted him to know what was out there, what parents were saying. I also wanted him to roll his eyes at the other doctor, which he did.

"*Rain Man?* Really? It doesn't sound like you were asking for movie recommendations."

When you're in the frantic early days after your child's diagnosis, it's easy to forget the humanity of the professionals you're sitting across from. I was hyperconscious of being judged and overly judgmental myself. How often did my mother-friends and I make fun of "stupid doctors"? With distance, though, it's easy for me to see that doctors are right to offer some warnings early on. Having unrealistic expectations puts parents and their child in a long, frustrating battle that can eat up years and run through life savings without producing much in the way of satisfying results.

Pearl Buck wished that doctors had spoken more honestly when her child was three and not yet talking. For her, "the truth is so much dearer than any comforting falsehood, so much kinder in its clean-cutting edge than fencing and evasion." In my experience, hearing such negative words from a doctor alongside his diagnosis was off-putting but also energizing. Those early years demand a level of commitment that can only be fueled by a furious faith that your child will get better. After a certain point, most of the parents I knew stopped buying into the recovery talk. We weren't looking for miracles, we were looking for *better*— we wanted our children to have the language they needed to make life more manageable. We wanted to understand their frustrations and mitigate those. We wanted simple things: to go out to dinner, to travel, to stay with family without meltdowns and scenes. Were we all secretly harboring dreams of more? Did I sit in IEP meetings and insist on including unrealistic goals and benchmarks? I'm sure I did. Should the teachers who knew Ethan and understood the bigger picture, have spoken up and said, "No, these goals aren't realistic"? All I can say now is that I'm not sure it would have worked. To parents, it feels like the fight is our job. Who will insist that our child can learn if we don't?

For many years, it felt wrong to relax in an IEP meeting, even with teachers who loved Ethan and wanted to tell us funny stories about things he'd done. *We can't let our guard down,* I remember thinking. *If we relax, so will they and he'll never get anywhere.* It's hard for any parent to change this mindset and harder still for a professional to persuade them to do it. For me it happened slowly, watching other parents I admired let go of certain battles without the world caving in. "Yeah, we pretty much gave up on teaching her to read. It's so hard for her and there are so many apps that can read for them now," I remember one mother telling me with a shrug. "Now we don't have a battle every night with those stupid flash cards." This is how it happens—slowly, over time. Picking new goals for the relief of letting others go. Redefining your future this way is devastating at first and then, slowly, it becomes liberating. For years you work on money and making change with baggies of play coins and then when that doesn't work, you try real coins. Eventually, it dawns on you: he's never going to get this. It will never make sense to him that two big nickels equals a dime. You get mad at him and then at whoever invented our money system. *Why is a dime so small and why does a nickel look so much like a quarter? What were they thinking?* It's frustrating until it's not. "He's not good at making change" becomes "He can't do it." It's liberating. It's acceptance.

I can't say exactly when it happened for us. I can only say this: For years we resisted having Ethan's IQ tested, thinking it might give teachers permission to stop trying. We finally relented when he was in middle school and when we got the number I'd spent ten years afraid of, and it was even lower than I'd ever imagined—42!—I didn't feel devastated. Quite the opposite. I felt a surprising mix of pride and relief. If this was really his IQ, maybe Ethan, with his fourth-grade reading level, was something of an overachiever. By that point, we'd let go of college. We'd also let go of other, more specific dreams that had once seemed possible—playing a musical instrument being the main one. Each time, there was sadness, yes, but not as much as I expected. *This is him,* I thought. Every parent wants to know who their child truly is. It was a relief.

In a 2008 speech given at the Perkins School to parents of newly diagnosed children, writer Jane Bernstein, mother of Rachel, a thirty-year-old with IDD, and author of two wonderful books about her experience, called this the most important thing parents of young children should remember: "Make your child as independent as possible. It's the only thing that really matters. Write it in big, banner letters and hang it up where you'll see it every day." It won't be easy, she acknowledges. Stepping back as her daughter got dressed by herself was agony at times. "I mean, she has motor problems. Watching her struggle to get a turtleneck on . . . whew! It's exhausting, and she is rather an oppositional human being, and so it's loud and exhausting, but I have to say, I'm so glad that I let those fights happen, and I let her be as independent as possible, because the more independent your child is, the more freedom and dignity your child will have. . . ."

To me, the last phrase is everything: *the more independent your child is, the more freedom and dignity your child will have.* These would have been the best words to hear from a doctor diagnosing Ethan at age three. Acknowledgment that it won't be easy, that your goal will not be getting your child to look and act like other children (or to parrot the same knowledge), but to one day be able to enter the world on their own terms, the fullest and truest versions of themselves.

I n the spring after Ethan's first few job trials—when we learned that he hated "facing stock" and would probably never get the grocery-store bagging job that I coveted for him—I worried enough about what lay ahead to take a tour of Riverside Industries, our local sheltered workshop, that employed the largest group of adults with IDD in the area. Though it had a good reputation, I had a preconceived vision of what such a place would look like: disabled adults sitting at tables, bent over busywork they were being underpaid to do. The whole idea sounded antiquated and depressing. Someone once told me that they'd seen workers filling baggies with utensils and napkins for airline meals, and I stopped them from saying any more.

In truth, I wasn't there to see the workshop; I was trying to learn more about an off-site program that sent "enclaves"—small crews of three or four workers with one job coach—to do landscaping jobs at the local colleges. This sounded like a possible answer to Ethan's internship struggles. The few he'd had by that point hadn't gone well. Alone with a job coach at a site, he and his cohort were often left unsupervised and unsure what to do. Sometimes they were given pointless tasks like sweeping a floor that had just been swept, or picking up sticks on a lawn that had just been mowed. I hoped that on a crew, doing real work, surrounded by others who were working hard, too, Ethan might get a better sense of what it meant to do a job and feel good about it.

As it turned out, I was right. The enclaves *were* successful and popular—and the waiting list might be years, Kyle Scheller, the director of admissions at Riverside, told me. "We'd want to get to know Ethan first and see what his skills are." I read between the lines: to get work off-site, he'd have to put in his time in the depressing workshop.

Or that's what I assumed before I took the tour, and nothing was what I expected. Yes, it was in an old riverfront factory building that once housed paper mills, but instead of feeling like a throwback to a sweatshop past, it had oak floors and vaulted ceilings and felt like a big, sunny museum gallery. Floor-to-ceiling windows opened up a glorious view of the river that brought in a dancing pattern of dappled sunlight. There were about fifty people on the workshop floor, all of them engaged in a wide variety of tasks. In one corner, a group of eight made tiny springs out of wires; in another area, a group of ten packaged Deepak Chopra CDs. Everyone seemed remarkably focused, though they didn't mind stopping for a moment to answer questions. I admired one woman's work. "Wow. How do you get that spring so small?"

"It takes a lot of practice," she said. "I'm very good at it now."

At another table, two men were finishing up a job from Hasbro, the game company, headquartered nearby, putting little gray battleships and pegs in separate baggies. One man filled bags, another operated a machine to seal them. "Battleships!" I said. "That's so cool."

They smiled but didn't stop. "They're on a deadline," a staff member behind them said. "We've got a pretty big order."

"Very big," the man operating the machine agreed.

I watched, mesmerized. They worked seamlessly: fill, seal, fill, seal. When they got to the end of their order, they high-fived, hugged, and bent over to catch their breath.

"Okay, *now* we can talk," one said, grinning at me.

I was thoroughly won over, and then shocked when Scheller told me, after the tour, that the workshop would probably be shutting down in the next two years. Riverside would still be here, she assured me, but the workshop would not. When I asked why, she said, "This is where we're headed. The state doesn't want to fund segregated workplaces indefinitely."

Though Riverside had other offerings—an art studio, a café, and a new garden center—the workshop was clearly the heart of the place, filled with the most people, all of whom seemed focused, happy, and proud of their work. While it was hard for me to imagine Ethan having the attention span or the fine motor skills to do these jobs, it wasn't hard to imagine him at Riverside, finding friends and community. And even if it wasn't ideal work for Ethan, it was obviously a great fit for the people I'd just met.

At home, I did more research. Riverside had a forty-year history of running a highly successful sheltered workshop, with an involved parent group and a dedicated staff, many of whom had been employed there for thirty years or more. Was it really going to close down in the name of preventing abuse and exploitation that no one was accusing it of? As it turned out, yes. Two years after my visit, Massachusetts did indeed order the closing of all sheltered workshops, and Riverside transitioned into a vocational training center providing Community-Based Day Services (CBDS).

Sheltered workshops came into being in the 1930s, initially as a way to help returning war veterans and people with disabilities learn vocational skills in a setting where they would be paid "commensurate with their work." Because this meant everyone was earning less than the newly instituted minimum wage, they were considered training grounds and no one was meant to stay in one forever. Eighty years later, the reality was a far cry from that original intention. The vast majority of workers with disabilities who went to sheltered workshops—almost 97 percent—never left. The lower-skilled folks couldn't manage it, the higher-skilled folks couldn't be spared if the workshop was to maintain its work quota.

The push to close sheltered workshops began in 1999 with a Supreme Court ruling called the Olmstead Act, which declared that segregated services for people with disabilities are a form of discrimination.

It gained momentum in 2014, with a court case in Rhode Island brought by the families of disabled adults who said that the sheltered workshop system had both exploited their employees—some earned an average of fourteen cents an hour—and limited their opportunity to work anywhere else. A key part of their argument was that students still in high school were being shuttled into sheltered work programs without an opportunity to try competitive employment. That same year, more examples of egregious exploitation were exposed. CNN investigated Goodwill Industries and found that CEOs were making $750,000 while many workers were earning an average of twenty-two to forty-one cents an hour. In March, the *New York Times* ran a feature about a jury that awarded $240 million in damages to a group of thirty-two men with IDD who had been subjected to twenty years of severe abuse while working at a turkey processing plant in Atalissa, Iowa. The plaintiffs, known as the "Boys in the Bunkhouse," had once been residents in Texas institutions. Promised that they would earn money and be taken care of for the rest of their lives, they went to work for Henry's Turkey Service which, since the 1960s, had trained over a thousand men from state institutions in agricultural and food processing work and sent them in work crews around the South and the Midwest. This group was the farthest from home and had the least contact with their families back in Texas. After complaints from family members, social services finally investigated and discovered the men were eating roach-infested food, working ten-to-twelve-hour days and, after twenty years of service, had never been paid more than their starting salary: sixty-five dollars a month. The idea that such abuse could take place in plain sight, in a small Iowa town, became a clarion call to action. In response to the Rhode Island ruling, the *New York Times* published an editorial from their board equating sheltered workshops with modern-day slavery. "The need to end the economic servitude and social exile of people with disabilities has long been clear. The [Rhode Island] agreement is a promising but overdue starting point."

A few months later, Massachusetts announced a two-year plan to phase out sheltered workshops, to be replaced by employment programs that promised to put workers with disabilities in community-based jobs earning minimum wage or better. Dale Dileo, once a director of an award-winning sheltered workshop in New Hampshire, believes this is the only way to go. "Sheltered workshops are fundamentally flawed in how they approach employment," he tells me. They start everyone in the same basic skills program. From there, they'll move into a vocational program where they might learn job skills like recycling and paper shredding. Then, they might enter a sheltered workshop where they'll get paid—if work is available—but the pay is minimal and unpredictable. After that, they might get onto an enclave and then, if they're lucky, get a job in the community. "One study from the University of Oregon found that it took the average person *fifty-six years* to move through this system. Everyone is spending their whole life *getting ready* to have a life!"

The same thing happens with independent living skills, Dileo explains. "We have these checklists that parents have to go through. In order to live independently, a person needs to have these 30–40 skills. No one has them all! We could spend twenty years teaching coin identification to someone who's never going to really understand money concepts or we could spend a few days teaching them how to use an ATM card. Parents figure this out early on with shoe-tying. You could spend six years on shoe-tying or you could buy some loafers. Most parents do the latter. They prioritize necessities. But then they let providers tell them their child isn't ready and needs to master this checklist of skills."

He's right about this. Those skill assessments sent a wave of shame through my heart every time they were brought out. When Ethan started his transition program, we filled out voluminous questionnaires that asked similar questions, slightly rephrased, as if they knew you might be fudging when you said, early on, *yes, he dresses appropriately for the weather* or *yes, he can zip a heavy parka independently.* By the end, you feel like you've been focusing on the wrong things for far too long. *Why didn't we stick with shoe-tying back in elementary school?* you think. *He could once make change for a dollar—why did we let that skill slip away?* Every parent begins again with every new age their child reaches. *We didn't know this would matter. We thought taking part in the high school musical was more important.* It's impossible to know what to prioritize until it's too late.

Dileo offers some reassurance for parents who fear the worst mistakes made might have been their own. "If we wait for someone with a disability to master everything needed to live, work and play in a community, there is almost no chance he or she will get there. This person will spend a lifetime getting ready to have a life." Parents should remember the crucial lesson they learned early on. *You don't have to master shoe-tying to wear shoes.*

I meet Dileo at an APSE (Association of People Supporting Employment First) conference in Orlando, Florida. Though it began thirty years ago, Employment First is a model that has turned into a movement in the last decade or so. Their basic premise argues that when a student leaves school, instead of working through a system of vocational training workshops, they should first try competitive employment. "It's a reverse of the old formula," Dileo explains. "Instead of training forever in the hope of a placement, we should place, then train. These are hands-on learners. No one will know what they can do until they're given a chance to try."

One of the core principles of Employment First is that everyone, regardless of their disability, is capable of working. For some, this will depend on finding the right job match and putting enough supports in place, but they are serious and ambitious in their goal to get all people with disabilities earning minimum wage or higher, interacting regularly with nondisabled employees, and having advancement opportunities. Since its inception, Employment First advocates have moved to the forefront of disability service, especially in the wake of growing unease about sheltered workshops. The conference I attend has over a thousand people there, mostly professionals—job coaches, transition specialists and special-ed teachers—and Dileo, a thirty-year veteran in Employment First, is a keynote speaker.

As Dileo speaks, I realize that Ethan has already been the beneficiary of their work. It explains his school's unexpected responsiveness when I asked for help with job placements after running into Julia's mother. That was in 2014, the same year that Massachusetts adopted the Employment First model. Because it was still such a new concept, they didn't have many employers on board yet—hence the nervous hesitation when I called to ask about interning in the cafeteria—but eventually it happened. Ethan was placed at the grocery store, where he worked once a week for two hours and finished up by announcing he didn't want to do *that* anymore. Next, he tried a nursing home—one of his first choices because he loves older people and their equipment, especially the wheelchairs and the oxygen tanks. Though the job description wasn't specific, I got the sense that he was meant to help out at social times—pass out Bingo cards, do exercise classes, things like that. I thought it might be a good fit. After his first day, though, Crystal, his vocational coordinator, called to say that Ethan's self-talk—usually a mash-up of movie lines—was disturbing the residents. My heart sank. If you don't know him, it would be disconcerting to see a young man standing alone in a hallway running lines from *Elf*, like "Son of a Nutcracker! Not now, arctic puppet!" But I also knew Ethan wanted to be there. After dinner that evening, we told him the rule: "If you quote movies or talk to yourself, you won't be able to go back."

At his next shift, his aide said he spent about half of his time there quoting movies. He tried to offer suggestions. "Maybe don't let him watch *Elf* the night before a shift?"

Ethan went back once more, talked to himself 80 percent of the time, and we gave up.

After that, Ethan interned at an organic farm where we had a CSA membership. Again, I was hopeful. He'd always loved farm equipment and used to talk about driving a tractor one day. After his first few visits, he told us he liked it except for the smell. And this ominous observation: "I don't really do anything except say hi to the animals."

Perhaps the most discouraging episode came after he got his long-awaited chance to work in a college dish room. On the first day, he was taught the most important rule of hygiene: any time he touched his nose or mouth, he'd have to wash his hands. Suddenly he couldn't keep his hands away from his face. "He spent most of the day at the sink washing up," his aide reported. "We'll try again tomorrow."

The next shift, the same. And the shift after that. It was infuriating. Each time Crystal called to say another job trial hadn't been "quite the right fit," I felt like another door was closing on a shorter and increasingly darkening hallway. *How many chances will he get?* I thought after his third placement ended in less than a month.

"It doesn't mean he'll never work," Crystal assured me. "It means he won't work *here*."

To any parents approaching transition, I would say this: I wish I'd understood from the start that failure is a built-in part of the process. We can't know how our kids will do until they try, which means experimenting with jobs that are a reach and might not work out. I also wish I'd recognized, much earlier, that there is comfort in learning, clearly and unequivocally, what Ethan isn't interested in and what he can't do. Clarifying the picture means less second-guessing down the line. Having once imagined Ethan working on a college campus, we learned that except for the food and the soda machines, Ethan didn't love being on campuses. They were large and overwhelming, so full of distractions that he was never able to focus on one thing or decide what he wanted to do.

Also not the right fit: a hair salon where his job was to carry towels to a laundromat next door, wash them, and fold them. He loved it at first. The machines were thrilling, as was the pocket full of quarters he was given to get them going. He loved the women who ran the salon and made such a fuss over him that he once brought me in on a Saturday to meet all his "work friends." I was so grateful, I hugged them all and thanked them profusely for letting him wash and fold their towels. (They seemed confused, especially when I got a little emotional and said, "You have no idea how hard this has been.") So why, after a month and a half at the salon job, did Ethan come home one evening and announce that he'd quit?

"What?" I asked, stunned. "You can't quit. You love that job."

He shrugged. "I didn't love it *that* much."

This was our first introduction to a simple, but profound concept called self-determination. Ethan was eighteen years old by then, an adult in the eyes of the law. If he quit a job, neither I nor any job coach could make him go back.

Believe me, I tried. "He didn't mean it!" I told Crystal. "Call them back and tell them he was in a bad mood! He has to work!"

"I can't," she explained. "He's in charge of these decisions now. We can't force him to do anything."

It's a nearly impossible mindset adjustment for a parent to make after a lifetime of not-so-gently nudging your child into situations and activities that he resists and then loves. He won't get on the merry-go-round, or the pony; he is scared of a fairy-tale theater show because he's seen a wolf in costume standing backstage. You coax him through it because your certainty is bigger than his fears. "You'll love this," you whisper, because giving in to a meltdown means barricading this activity forever. In the past, you've almost always been right. Afterward, thrilled, he shakes the wolf's paw and asks for his autograph. But this time is different. This time he really does get to decide for himself. His friends at school had their own struggles with jobs and many were telling each other the secret: they could just walk away! "It's okay to quit," Ethan told me. "I'm allowed to because I'm an adult. That's what William says."

....

Employment First advocates argue that closing sheltered workshops is a necessary step in the goal of getting more people with disabilities into competitive jobs. They point to the stubborn unemployment figures and argue that allowing segregated work sites is part of the problem. They hold job developers back from doing the hard work of finding and supporting people in community-based jobs. "The people at Employment First are going with the idea that if they don't drive this principle very hard—and close down the alternatives—they won't be able to overcome the inertia of the status quo," Bill Zimmer, who retired as the Franklin/Hampshire Area Director for the Department of Developmental Services in 2014, believes.

It's a reasonable argument, but not an easy one to make to the estimated three hundred thousand individuals around the country who are still employed in sheltered workshops and their families, who are fighting these threatened closures. In Arizona, the debate about closing sheltered workshops began in 2014, the same year as the Rhode Island ruling, and came to a head when parents gathered in Tucson in 2017 for a talkback session with service coordinators to explain their opposition. They were clear: community-based work was fine for those individuals who can manage it, but none of their children could. They knew this. They'd tried it. One father described his daughter's attempts to keep up with a job that was over her head. She couldn't multitask or follow three-step directions. Other employees had to pick up the slack. "It created a caustic environment. They all got paid the same, only one person was doing less. It was unsustainable." Another father recalled his daughter's experience in a restaurant job: "After two months, she thought she was finally getting the hang of the job. Then one night she came home, and someone had written 'Retard' in magic marker on the back of her jacket." She'd been put in an untenable situation, he argued. "Never again." He shook his head. "That's all. Never again." Without the workshops, the Tucson parents argued, their children would have no option other than staying home. One mother argued, "If you want these children to be more of a burden on the system, abolishing sheltered workshops will accomplish that. They'll have more health issues from staying home and eating all day, and more police interventions when they wander outside." Another parent shook her head. "People are going to die because of this."

When Pennsylvania threatened to close its sheltered workshops, Jane Bernstein joined the fight after visiting the day program that would have been her daughter's only other option. "I was chilled by what I saw, reminded that the shuttering of work sites will bring as much human misery as it is meant to correct." In the end, Pennsylvania and Arizona did not close their sheltered workshops. With budget constraints and lengthy waitlists, they couldn't offer parents a reasonable alternative.

In 2013, Massachusetts planned ahead for this process—and potential family opposition—by releasing a plan called "Blueprint for Success" allocating $26.7 million to support moving the sheltered workshop population into community employment. Over the next three years, the funding fell short of provider requests, but nevertheless the mandate was honored and, in 2016, all workshops were closed. Since then, providers have juggled tough budget realities. As anticipated, the cost of transporting and supporting a client in a community-based job is substantially higher than running a standard day program. DDS reimburses provider agencies about fifty dollars an hour for supported employment services and eleven to fifteen dollars an hour for a standard day program. Most adult service providers offer a choice: for each hour of supported employment the participant works, they must give up four hours of day programming. For families, it looks like this: if your kid wants to work for three hours at CVS on Monday, they don't go anywhere on Tuesday and Wednesday. Some families are willing to make that sacrifice. Most aren't. The real problem is that even for those families willing to forego other services in pursuit of a community-based job, there aren't nearly enough of those jobs for everyone leaving sheltered workshops. For each person who finds a job, ten are now in a day program with no paycheck.

At the APSE Conference, Dileo is the only person I hear address these discouraging statistics directly. According to a 2016 report from the Institute for Community Inclusion, the percentage of individuals in integrated employment has actually gone down slightly in the last ten years. In 2008, 20.3 percent worked in integrated jobs; in 2016, 18.8 percent did. "Employment First has been around for thirty years now," Dileo asks the crowd. "So why aren't we doing better, folks?"

For Dileo, the answer goes back to the historical segregation of this group. Prejudice dies hard, and society is still catching on to the idea that people with disabilities are reliable, capable employees. He has a list of fixes to improve hiring statistics: agencies charged to support the jobseekers need to look carefully at outdated practices, like logos and marketing material that emphasize the disability, not the ability. "Many agencies still have wheelchairs or even Band-Aids in their logo. The message is that this is about the employee's limitation—what they can't do, not what they can." Linking employment with charity, as Goodwill has done for decades, sends a message to the entire community that their workers are unemployable elsewhere.

He also points to high school transition programs that too often rely on work around the school to teach skills. Ethan's school certainly did: he delivered mail interoffice, sorted recycling, cleaned library shelves and—his favorite job of all—helped the band teacher set up music stands. He also worked for a while at an in-school "coffee shop" where students made a pot of coffee, set out snacks, and left a box for teachers to put money in. Nothing wrong with these practice jobs, but making a pot of coffee and setting out a money box didn't realistically make him more work ready. DiLeo says the outreach to businesses needs to start with transition programs in high school that must make greater efforts to engage local employers, "not asking favors, but as an investment in the future labor force of their community." He is passionate, and still, after thirty years, a true believer in the mission of Employment First. "These people can work, harder and more effectively than anyone realizes. It's on us, folks," he says to a room filled with vocational coordinators, job coaches, and disability service providers. "We need to get out there more and work harder. We need to open employers' eyes. We need to make them *see* this."

As nice as it is to hear someone else taking the blame for Ethan's job struggles, I'm not sure he's right about this. Ethan didn't succeed at community-based jobs because working hard to fit in and doing the tasks he was asked to do wasn't worth it to him. Societal bias might have been a factor in the trouble we had initially in finding placements, but it's not why those placements didn't produce a job. Eventually, the employers were open and welcoming; they all seemed to like Ethan and enjoy his company. To this day, Ethan visits some of them to say hello and tell them how he's doing. He simply wasn't interested in the hard work.

Dileo concedes this particular challenge. "Any worker with a disability is going to have trouble fitting in because they're different, but these are solvable problems," he insists. In his speech, he told a story about a client named Danny, who had issues with swearing and spitting in public. He worked at a warehouse unloading trucks with seven other guys who didn't mind the spitting and swearing (they did it, too) but didn't like the fact that in between truckloads, Danny would read his car magazine. The solution was figuring out how he could look more like part of the team. He had to carry a rag, they suggested, and when the boss walked in, he had to get up and, with his rag in his hand, yell "Ho!" when a new truck came in. Danny loved all that. "When the job counselors enlisted the help of the other employees, it worked out much better!"

When Dileo tells this story, I wonder how many other parents ask themselves, as I do: What if my child does a little more than spit and swear occasionally? What if he likes to kiss people's shoulders? Or run lines from old Disney movies? Can you find ways to mitigate those behaviors? As the parent of an autistic child for two decades, I already know our answer: yes—if he wants to do something badly enough, you do what's necessary to stop his stimming (the self-soothing tics most autistic kids have) for the length of time required to participate. For Ethan, it was the high school musical, where we hired an extra aide at twelve dollars an hour to help keep him quiet backstage. When that wasn't enough, he got his iPad and headphones. But anyone who knows autism also knows that squelching those stims, especially in an exciting environment, takes a toll. It often doesn't work. Told not to make noise, Ethan will rock so aggressively he'll knock people over. Told not to bounce, he'll swing his arms like a pair of helicopter blades. Ethan is on the more physical end of the spectrum, but they all have these needs—tics and compulsions to ask the same questions over and over. What about this enormous group, for whom a rag in hand and instructions to say "Ho!" when the boss appears won't begin to address the trouble they have comporting themselves in a workplace?

In *Life, Animated,* Ron Suskind tells the story of his son Owen's first job trials and how they hired a behavior consultant to address stimming at the workplace. They initiated a behavior modification program that rated stims from 1 to 5, and set up a stim replacement plan where a less disruptive stim is tried to see if it will provide the same satisfaction. Hand flapping is replaced with fist clenching, for instance. Pacing or jumping with a short, intentional walk. At work they came up with a code word distinct enough to break through a stimming trance for the job coach to alert Owen to shift from a level 5 stim to a level 1 or 2. Their word was "bingo."

"For two weeks shoppers at Giant Foods might have felt like they'd wandered into a bingo parlor," Suskind writes. Owen was at the checkout counter bagging groceries while his job coach, Tyler, stood a discrete distance away calling out bingos. The important part of this story is Owen's motivation: he wanted the job enough to make these adjustments. He understood that his stims limited the friendly exchanges he wanted to have with customers.

His parents were lucky in this respect. Many people with autism aren't motivated in this way or fall somewhere in between like Ethan, who will say he wants to work, but doesn't equate moderating his stims to working with others. He'll nod and say yes, he understands that talking to himself is disturbing to the residents in the nursing home, and then he'll walk away and repeat the whole conversation he's just had out loud, talking to himself. As parents we could battle this tendency tooth and nail—which, for a long time, we did—or we could say, "This is Ethan." We can also let Ethan decide for himself where he feels comfortable and wants to spend his time. Perhaps unsurprisingly, it's not in the places where he's told over and over to stop stimming.

The insistence that every person with IDD wants a job in the community is one of the primary tenets of the Employment First movement. "Everyone is employable!" is a rallying cry I hear repeated often at the APSE conference. When asked a question about those with more severe disabilities, Dileo responds: "Every time I've tried to draw a line about what employable is, I'm wrong. I won't do it anymore because I've been proven wrong so many times." He has anecdotes: the man in the wheelchair who found a job checking people in at a gym; the nonverbal woman who busses tables.

I would argue that this insistence that the same universal goal applies to everyone leaves far too many people out. For parents who are managing issues like aggression and self-injury, such a rallying cry is both infuriating and ostracizing. This isn't a small subset of the population. One-third of people with autism are nonverbal; nearly half will wander or bolt from safety. By these measures, Ethan might be considered higher functioning. He can manage public busses, can walk into town alone, can buy himself lunch. Yet in most competitive job situations, he lasted less than a month. It's something parents understand and legislators may not. For many in this crowd, simply being in public is *hard* work. Reining in their impulses, their tics, their need to rock and talk to themselves. When parents say their child can't manage a competitive job, some Employment First advocates seem to assume this comes from narrow-mindedness—a failure to see their child's potential or imagine them as capable of something more. Or maybe it stems from fear. At the conference, I twice hear providers say, "Families have been our greatest obstacle." One elaborates, "They're worried about safety primarily." I hear the clear implication: parents don't get it. A lifetime of coddling our child with IDD has left us tunnel-visioned on one path, unable to let go and imagine another.

But most of the parents I know haven't pursued community-based jobs because *that isn't their child's goal*. We've learned the hard way about self-determination and we've been told repeatedly by vocational coaches, "*They* get to decide what they want to do with their lives."

As one transition coordinator told me, "There's a huge push across the nation for employment, but I will tell you that I have quite a few students every year where employment is absolutely not one of their goals. They want to be in a day program. They want a community and they want to go out, but they don't want to work. And I have to value their vision. I line up programs that mirror what they're telling me they want. I'll make sure they've tried the different day programs so we get the best match and make sure it really is what they want."

Bill Zimmer supported the philosophy behind Employment First when it was getting started in Massachusetts but was always concerned that it might become too narrowly focused. I hear similar thoughts from

other providers who asked to stay off the record: "The problem is so
many of our clients don't *want* to work, so if that's the only priority getting funded, what do you do? How do you offer enriching alternatives
when there's no money in that?" one tells me. Zimmer has been retired
for eight years and isn't afraid of being quoted, which isn't a surprise.
He was a maverick back in his DDS days—a hippie who still wore a
hoop earring even after his hair turned silver and began to thin. He
didn't much care what people thought about him back then and he still
doesn't. He cares about this group and solving the intractable problems
they face.

"I would argue that the valorization of paid employment as the only
dignified choice for adults is inherently devaluing of the large swath of
humanity who don't choose to do that," he tells me. In his view, this
over-romanticizes paid work and is a perfect example of ideology over-
taking common sense and preventing a necessary discussion. "Once we
adopt a policy about what is the right way to support someone with
disabilities, even fairly high-level managers aren't free to continue having a dialogue about whether that policy is correct. Everyone is concerned about jeopardizing their funding, so no one is willing to critique
or adjust any decisions that have been approved of." In his view, the result leaves families confused by a system that seems to say one thing
and do another. "We say that we prioritize choice, as long as you make
the choice we agree with. Truly informed choice should allow for the fact
that some people will make choices we don't agree with."

There's irony in the push by Employment First backers to put the
lion's share of federal funding into these supported-employment programs when, according to the National Core Indicators (2017–18) 71 percent of people with IDD weren't interested in community employment *at
all* and only 29 percent said that finding an integrated job was a goal.
Shouldn't those people get some of that money too, funneled into higher-
quality day programs, perhaps? Parents certainly haven't given up on
the idea of a full and productive life. They just don't believe that having
a job is the only way to achieve that.

....

Molly is a good example of a young adult who Employment First is tailor-made for. A charming thirty-year-old with Down syndrome, she carries herself with an old-fashioned primness born, in part, from the shows she loves to watch—British romantic dramas. Her favorite is *Pride and Prejudice* starring Colin Firth, but she loves them all. To me, she seems eminently employable; she's a good reader, enjoys desk work, filing, and alphabetizing. She also loves dressing the part of a working woman, in skirts and panty hose and button-up shirts. But no job she's tried has worked out. For a while she worked at Mercy Hospital, setting up patient trays and cleaning silverware. Then it turned out she was heat sensitive and working near the dishwasher made her faint. "Twice, her shifts ended with her going down to the ER to get checked out," her mother, Lee, tells me. After that, she interned at her favorite restaurant, Panera, but it never led to a job offer. "In restaurants, it's hard; they have to carve out pieces from other jobs—table cleaning, stocking— because there's a lot they're not going to let someone with Down syndrome do: take orders, ring up on a register, make change. It's hard for managers to figure out how to keep these employees busy. It just doesn't work for them."

Lee isn't bitter, just sanguine that this latest Employment First experiment won't really work the way people say it will. "When they talk about success stories, they're usually talking about an extraordinary job developer who spends all their time making community connections. Most job developers aren't like that. Most of them start your intake by asking if you have any friends or relatives who own a business and wouldn't mind hiring your child." It always makes Lee laugh. "If I had that, I probably wouldn't be sitting with a job developer, right?"

After leaving school and the internships that didn't produce any jobs, Molly went to Sunshine Village, a sheltered workshop in Springfield, Massachusetts, that sent enclaves to work in local offices. Molly worked about thirty hours a week in a Mass Mutual mailroom and on the other days, did mailings for Yankee Candle. She made between seventy and ninety dollars a week. She especially loved her days at Mass Mutual, where other employees included her group in office parties and other special occasions. After the state ordered the closing of sheltered workshops, which included her enclave work, Lee was told that Molly had been selected to join their competitive employment division. Molly was excited at the prospect of a real job until it turned out she would only get two hours a week of paid work, vacuuming stairs at a printing office. She only lasted three months. According to Lee, "They were vague about their reasons for letting her go, but I suspect it might have been a transportation issue. They were responsible for getting her over to her job and it was hard for them to organize—she was always late, which upset her. At any rate, she was let go, which she wasn't particularly upset about."

She's back at Sunshine Village, now primarily a day program, where she's kept busy, but Lee admits, "I sometimes wonder about the point of it all. Once a week, they go to a mall that's in the process of closing down and they have everyone fill out job applications in the few stores that are left 'for practice.' Everyone knows they won't get hired because the stores are all closing, but they keep going . . ."

"Is Molly better off with the closure of the sheltered workshop?"

"God no," says Lee, who is the retired director of Family Empowerment, a state-funded support/advocacy group in Hadley, Massachusetts. She knows this world well and knows that fighting government directives won't do much good. She sounds almost wistful as she tells me, "I think we've got to let this idea of competitive employment for everyone play out and once it does, people will see: it doesn't really work. There just aren't enough jobs for them, and there's not enough money for transportation and support. I don't think we'll go back to sheltered workshops, but I think legislators might consider different kinds of congregate work settings. They'll have to, since the reality is pretty clear—these folks are already spending their days in congregate settings."

A few sobering studies back this up. A particularly brutal one from Oklahoma tracked the long-term employment outcomes as sheltered workshops were phased out over a fifteen-year period and found that the vast majority of former workshop employees didn't find jobs. Instead, they went into vocational-readiness programs where, according to the study, "the staff pejoratively refer to their days as 'option quest,' indicating that there was a daily quest to find an option that would occupy each unemployed individual." Other analyses around the country have found similar results: In 2011, ten years after the closing of sheltered workshops began in Maine, the number of people in community-based day programs had more than quadrupled. The people who had found community-based jobs did earn more money per hour, but often worked significantly fewer hours so their average salary decreased.

Vermont, the first state in the country to close all sheltered workshops in 2002 is an exception to these dire findings. It has long been held up as a model, especially when their integrated employment rates soared up to 32 percent in 2009 which *is* a significant achievement, but there's also this: by 2016, the figure has gone down to 28 percent, and disabled employees in their integrated workplaces average only nine hours a week at their jobs.

As more studies come out citing statistics like these, more families and service providers are voicing their concerns. In the conclusion of his study on the impact of Employment First practices, educational psychologist Scott Spreat offers a stern warning to legislators: "We have an ethical responsibility to ensure that our social reforms do in fact leave people better off. . . . If Employment First succeeds in placing most individuals in integrated forms of employment and if most individuals with disabilities appreciate this, we have a demonstrably successful social reform. If those same individuals end up sitting at home watching television every day, we have grossly erred."

The most heartening stories I've heard come from the states that have figured out how to increase the numbers of people in competitive employment without closing down all sheltered workshops in the process. It's possible that Washington State has done this better than any others. In 2004, they instituted a working-age adult policy to support the "fundamental idea that all people with IDD have talents and ability to contribute in typical workplaces in every community." As one of the

For all the money that's been spent on vocational skill building and employment-related transition services, the vast majority of twenty-two-year-olds with IDD finish high school and go into day programs, if they are lucky enough to have a waiver or qualify for services right away. Study any graph chart and the curve looks the same: a thin band at the bottom of integrated work (representing between 14 to 19 percent of the demographic) and a huge mountain rising above it of people in "non-work day programs." The mountain reflects the growth in numbers being served, which has increased every year since the 1990s, and is now double what it was ten years ago. But few studies exist to assess either what these programs do or (more importantly) what they *should* be doing. Although it is called different names in different states, the goal of Community-Based Day Services (CBDS) is usually described in similarly vague ways like: "The provider may include volunteer work; continuing education; accessing community facilities such as a library, gym, or recreation center." No stipulations are given for how often these community outings should take place (once a week? once a year?). Presumably making specific demands on service providers charged with accommodating individuals with a wide spectrum of needs would be too onerous, but this leaves parents and providers in a quandary: What should a decent day program look like?

I return to Riverside five years after my initial tour and three years after the sheltered workshop closed, to ask this question and find out how they've adjusted their model. I start by telling the managers about the happy memory from my earlier visit and how sorry I am that the workshop closed. "You were obviously running a good one here. It seems like a shame—"

Kyle Scheller, still the admissions director, cuts me off before I can go any further. "I have to tell you, even though it was a hard adjustment at first, we all agree we've got a much better program now."

I'm shocked. I expect to hear a positive gloss—she is, after all, still in charge of selling the program—with an undercurrent of nostalgia, shadowed by a little resentment at being told by higher-ups what they had to do. There is none of that.

"In the old days, when we got a new participant in, we had to focus from the start on getting that person up to speed in our workshop. They had to fit in to what we had to offer. Were they strong enough for our larger machines? Did they have the fine motor skills for the smaller ones? We catalogued their skills according to *our* needs. Now, we get a new client and we can spend twice as long getting to know them. We can concentrate on finding out *their* interests and passions. We have a wider array of offerings so it's much more likely that we can honor those interests. If they're a dog lover, we can make sure they're volunteering at the animal shelter; if they like socializing with older people, we'll put them in Meals on Wheels. We can individualize a lot more than we used to."

Her enthusiasm is infectious. What they were doing before was an outdated model, she explains, based on securing contracts from outside companies for piecemeal work that was increasingly harder to get, thanks to new technologies and automation. "Maybe sheltered workshops in other states don't want to admit this as they're fighting for their existence, but our contract income had gone steadily down over the last ten years," Scheller says. "No one had a problem with our work, but companies had simply found other, cheaper ways to do the jobs." Toward the end, they had days when some employees had no work at all. "We filled their time with other activities, but their paychecks went way down and we felt terrible." Idleness also produced more "unproductive

behaviors." If people know they're doing busywork, some of them will
spend the day agitated, or unproductive, going to and from the bathroom. "Our bathrooms became busy places, unfortunately." She laughs,
and then sighs. "It was frustrating for all of us."

I certainly understand. Ethan had spent many school hours avoiding harder subjects and work by taking circuitous trips to the bathroom. Sometimes he traveled all around the building in order to say
hello to every staff person he knew. Not a crime, perhaps, but not very
productive, either.

"How many people have moved into community-based jobs?" I ask
Scheller tentatively. This is still the goal, of course—the statistic that
will, for many people, measure the success of sheltered workshop closure. I know these numbers are so low around the country, I hate to
even ask, but Scheller doesn't miss a beat. "We're working on that," she
says. The truth is basically as I suspect—they haven't placed too many
workers in competitive jobs yet—but they've used extra money from the
state to overhaul their vocational skill-building program, which she's
eager to show me. In a way, this is an evasion, but I'm happy to follow
her down the hall because this is what I really want to see—the tangi-
ble changes that employment statistics won't measure: Are the workers
more challenged than they were before? Has the bar been raised from
the old days of sorting and sealing Battleship game parts?

Their new vocational training program borrows a hands-on
Montessori-inspired teaching method in which the skills needed for the
graduates' most common jobs are broken down step-by-step, into task-
building activities that almost look like games themselves, with lami-
nate picture and word cards, stored in Tupperware bins. For grocery
store bagging, students need to identify which items are fragile, which
are toxic and which are refrigerated and should be packed together—
exactly the sorts of skills that might overwhelm a new employee into
making mistakes. A student categorizes and "bags" the photos of groceries, while timing themselves to gradually increase speed. The Montessori philosophy focuses on emphasizing the positive, so they are
going for improvement and personal bests. As they get better, they move

on to practicing with the real items and then, eventually, into a store, where they might at least have a better shot at one of the coveted bagging positions.

The job-training room is divided into four areas: grocery store—stocking and bagging; office work—folding, stapling, paper shredding, recycling; retail—clothes hanging, buttoning, folding; general cleaning—dish room, silverware-sorting, etc. This is a far cry from stringing large wooden beads onto shoelaces, which I had seen the last time I toured Riverside and is often the "skill-building work" that fills down time in sheltered workshops. Common as these activities are, I always wonder why they persist—along with tables of crayons and coloring books—when it makes adults look like they're sitting at oversized preschool tables. This Montessori job-training classroom borrows strategies from early childhood education but doesn't have that infantilizing feel at all. The focus is too specific. The teacher will ask, "When you're bagging two fragile items—chips and eggs—which should go first into the bag?" I'm sure Ethan's younger brother, Charlie, who worked as a grocery bagger for years, could sharpen his skills if he spent a day here.

There is also the famous Montessori spirit of positivity in the air. When the teacher takes the group to the grocery store, she makes a lesson out of best behaviors she observes: "I point out every time someone turns around to hold the door for another person behind them. That's a skill these students haven't been taught in a classroom, but it's important for customer relations. If they're taught, they can make it a habit and have a pretty rewarding exchange with a stranger."

I can't count the number of doors Ethan has blithely shut in my face. It's a hard skill for parents to teach without seeming screechy in the moment. "God, Ethan—you should hold the door open for your mother!" doesn't land on receptive ears when we've just walked into a grocery store full of exciting distractions.

Scheller tells me that they've kept data to track their success and have seen improvement on a wide range of measures: greater engagement, longer attention span, increased confidence. The specificity of the tasks also lends itself to transitioning into community-based jobs. Dileo might argue that "placing, then training" an employee is still preferable over a system that readies people indefinitely for jobs they might never get, but if the jobs don't exist in anywhere near the numbers needed, this seems like a promising alternative.

Perhaps an even better one tailors volunteer opportunities to individual interests, harkening back to Wolfensberger's plea to find "valued social roles" in the community, regardless of whether they are paid or unpaid. When I ask Scheller for her best success story following the workshop closure, she tells me about a young man who was "never a great fit for our workshop. He thought the work was boring and he was sometimes a negative distraction to other workers, so we'd have to give him warnings." When given the opportunity to volunteer instead, he started working with Meals on Wheels. "From his very first day, he seemed like a different person. He loved interacting with older people, loved meeting their pets. He was always friendly and appropriate and would leave his visits saying things like, 'Boy, we sure made her day.'" Scheller has seen this transformation with other volunteers. When the match is right, the fact that they aren't getting paid matters less. (Because this assumption has led to exploitation in the past, laws are strict about where this group can offer unpaid services, namely only in spots where the general population volunteers as well. After high school internships, no one in this group can volunteer to learn the ropes of a normally paid position.) Her stories include clients who've become enthusiastic real-world volunteers in ways that surprise both the Riverside staff and their own families. This isn't exactly what Employment First promises with its emphasis on paid work, but it captures an aspect of their philosophy—that with raised expectations, unexpected abilities will emerge.

Riverside has taken other steps to expand their enrichment offerings, quadrupling the size of the visual arts program, with classes in painting, crafts, weaving, and jewelry-making offered every day. This art program has long been a strength thanks to the professional artists who have studio space in their building and teach classes; the expansion means regular opportunities to sell work at shows during the year and regular craft fair visits.

After Scheller walks me through their renovated art rooms, she lets me see what I imagine is a reality at every day program: a room full of folks who, as she euphemistically puts it, "are on the longest path to employment." Some are doing puzzles, but many aren't doing much at all. One woman holds an ice pack to her head. Another perseverates with a chain, dribbling it from one hand to another. No one watches T.V, but three or four gaze out a window as if they wish there were a TV on the lawn. These clients are the hardest for providers to discern the best solutions for. Are they unmotivated to work because the expectations have been too low for too long? Presumably they've been offered other options than being in this room and they've chosen to stay here. Maybe their medications are titrated too high, maybe their families don't have much choice, maybe it's too late to plant ambition in a heart that has found peace watching clouds drift by. No one seems unhappy, it just seems a little empty.

I always worried about Ethan ending up in a day program where he'd glue macaroni to paper plates, but this group isn't even doing that. After I get home, I keep wondering: Can they be motivated to do more? All I know is that there are far more folks sitting in that room than there are workers who've found integrated employment in the community.

CHAPTER SEVEN

Riverside is proud of its visual arts classes, which it should be—they have the best art program for people with IDD in our area—but we've only visited this space briefly, after I've spent most of the day looking at where the bulk of its funding goes: the Montessori-based job-training program. Employment training takes precedence, even for those who express no interest in employment. It gets me thinking about programs that are much harder to find: ones that focus on the arts.

For Ethan and many of his peers with IDD, the arts are an effective and powerful vehicle for expressing themselves. His friend Christina, who has Down syndrome and is legally blind, has been a gifted painter since childhood. She paints with her nose inches from the canvas in electrifying sweeps of color. In high school, her work won an honorable mention in the Boston Globe Scholastic Art and Writing Awards competition and was regularly featured in the annual town-wide art show, not as the work of a disabled student, but as the ribbon-winning art of a talented high schooler. Whenever I visit her parents' house and see her breath-catching canvases adorning the walls, I think: *Why should someone like Christina spend four or five hours a day learning to bag groceries and only one or two hours a week in an art class, which is all Riverside is able to offer new participants?*

Ethan's artistic connection has always been to music. When he was still a toddler and couldn't put two words together in a sentence, he could sing whole stanzas beautifully, in perfect pitch. I've since learned that this isn't uncommon for autistic children, but at the time, whenever he did it, I'd break out in a damp sweat, and inch closer, heart clamoring, to sing along. When that stopped him, I learned to freeze and hold my breath. A child with an active vocabulary of thirty words sings "I love you, you love me, we're a happy family," you don't care that it's a Barney song. Let the purple dinosaur move into the house. Give him his own bedroom.

We started making up songs to encourage him to produce longer sentences. "I want more, I want more, I want more of my Rice Chex. . . ." I never got over my astonishment at this simple fact: Ethan could sing what he couldn't say. With so many roadblocks in his brain, music was a wide-open, eight-lane highway. Equally compelling to me was his passion for listening to music and the way he experienced it with his whole body, rocking, bouncing, and mostly: drumming. By the time he was a toddler, he was drumming on every surface, horizontal or vertical, that presented itself. His high chair, the wall beside it, the refrigerator covered in reminders and alphabet letters. The last was especially satisfying—the way it echoed and rained items down on top of his head.

Berkshire Hills Music Academy, one of the preeminent programs to focus on teaching music to young adults with IDD, opened in South Hadley—one town away from us—five years after Ethan was born. I first heard about it from one of Ethan's therapists who described it as "a college for young adults with IDD who love music. It's the only place like it in the country!" Ethan was eight at the time. We were beginning to understand he might not miraculously outgrow his autism and we would need to consider future options. BHMA looked like paradise, situated on a bucolic sixteen acres near Mt. Holyoke College, in a converted, century-old grand estate that had been remodeled to include a twenty-one-bed dormitory, classrooms, music studios, and a performance space. Even better than the view of rolling hills, in my mind, was the curriculum: substantive music courses like American Roots Music, History of Jazz, and Folk Ensemble, alongside practical life-skills classes like Banking—How to Use an ATM.

The first time we saw a concert given by the BHMA Performance Troupe, I was stunned: they were not only charming and charismatic performers, they were truly gifted musicians. The lead singer, Tory, had a dazzling smile as she belted out Kelly Clarkson's "Breakaway" and got the audience to clap along. The bespectacled drummer whose huge grin kept his glasses from sliding off his nose was so good I forgot he had a disability until a moment toward the end of a heart-stopping solo when one piece of his drum set inched away from him and he stopped playing completely, unable to figure out what to do. Everyone patiently waited while a staff member ran onstage and moved the snare and high hat back into place. He nodded his thanks and the song continued. It was impossible not to fall in love with the whole band. Their cognitive disability was only part of their identity. They were also professionals, effectively working as ambassadors to the rest of the world to convey a single message: *You think we can't do much? Just watch.*

Afterward, Ethan and I approached the drummer, a little starstruck. "You were so good," I said, breathlessly.

He smiled and nodded sweetly, as if to agree. *I know I am.*

We introduced ourselves and before I thought too much about it, I asked, "Do you ever give lessons to younger kids, Bret?" The idea came to me toward the end of the concert when Ethan had crept out of his seat to stand on the sideline, as close as he could get to this drummer and his magical, moving drum set. Usually when Ethan heard live music, he was in constant motion, bounding and pacing. This time was different. He stood perfectly still, transfixed. *Maybe he sees that they have more in common than a love of music,* I thought.

Bret said nothing but kept smiling. He looked confused so I asked again. "Drum lessons that we paid you for? Maybe you could just play together? I know Ethan would love that."

In adults with IDD, it's sometimes possible to watch the slower wheels of language processing play out on their faces. *Oh!* Brett's eyebrows seemed to say. He handed Ethan one of his drumsticks, as if to say, *Sure. We can play together.*

Ethan looked at me, stunned, as if Ringo Starr himself had handed over a piece of his kit. "Maybe not right now," I said. "Maybe we could set something up."

I called the school that afternoon and got the name of the music and human services director and asked if this was something they'd ever done before. "These guys are such good role models for younger kids with disabilities. Ethan doesn't get to see many examples of what's possible for him when he gets older."

About a month later, I began bringing Ethan to the BHMA campus for a weekly, half-hour drum lesson with Bret, who was sweet and patient and a little unsure what to do with a student as active and distractible as Ethan. I sat in on every lesson, redirecting Ethan's attention away from whatever else was in the room: other instruments, recording equipment, unplugged microphones.

"What's this?" Ethan would say, pointing to a knob on a piece of equipment.

Bret spoke Ethan's language, which is to say, a simplified one. "You turn the dial and it makes things louder," he'd say. Apparently, he wasn't sure of the real name, either. "That one makes it softer." He knew what he needed to know.

After a while, it became clear that Ethan wasn't a drumming prodigy like Bret. He was good at playing back a complicated rhythm—a drum conversation that I loved—but he couldn't manage doing two (or three) things at once: keeping a bass drumbeat with your foot and doing something else with your hands. When I sat down at the drum kit, I couldn't do it, either. Bret laughed good-naturedly at my attempts and shrugged, not sure how to teach something that came so easily to him. Our lessons became as much about Ethan talking to Bret as they were about drumming. Ethan still struggled so much to gather his words and get them out. I would prompt him through a story from our week and Bret would patiently nod and listen. Afterward, they'd have a drum conversation, which was easier for them both.

At the end of that year, Bret graduated from BHMA. He was from New Jersey, which wouldn't pay for tuition after he turned twenty-two. When I was told that he wouldn't be coming back, I wanted to cry. It was possible I enjoyed our sessions as much as Ethan had. Getting to know Bret never changed my initial impression: he was graceful, talented, and a true professional. We'd gone to a see a few more Troupe concerts, and he was clearly a calming presence for the other performers, especially a megatalent like Tory who could be high strung and occasionally talked too long at the microphone between songs. Bret would smile and do a *bah-dum* on his drums to move her along. Sometimes he made other jokes using a cowbell or castanet. "Oh, Bret," Tory would roll her eyes from downstage. "He wants me to get back to the music." They were a great combo—funny and a little flirtatious. I assumed Bret would find a band when he went back to New Jersey, but would he find one this good? Where they became mini-celebrities with every show they played?

It didn't occur to me that our lessons might have been as important to Bret as they were to us until the very end of our last one when Bret said softly, "I have a present for you, Ethan." He disappeared for such a long time, Ethan started guessing what it might be. "One of his drumsticks? An egg shaker?"

When Bret returned with a beautiful, tall red conga drum in his arms, I gasped. It was obviously expensive, possibly worth more than we'd paid him for all of the lessons. "My mom asked me what we should get you and I picked this," he said.

He knew Ethan by now. Some of their best drum talks had been on hand drums where Bret had showed him the whole range of sounds a slapped palm could make. That was the first time I understood that teaching had been an important step for him, and maybe Bret's parents worried as much about his future as I worried about Ethan's. His talent alone wouldn't necessarily fling open doors or smooth the rough roads that lay ahead.

I met his mother at his graduation. "You have a wonderful son," I said, hugging her and thanking her for the drum.

"So do you," she said.

We didn't talk long. She was busy with family. Maybe both of us were afraid of how much we had in common.

....

BHMA opened in 2001, the culmination of years of planning and fund-raising by a small group of parents who first met through a Williams Syndrome Association newsletter. Though it's hard to believe now, two of those parents—Howard Lenhoff and Sharon Libera—were among the first to recognize the unusual connection their children had to music. For Libera's son John, who was diagnosed with Williams at age three, it had been the most powerful teaching tool they'd found. Like Ethan, he sang whole songs before he could talk. Also like Ethan, music motivated him and sustained his attention in a way that nothing else could. For Lenhoff, whose daughter, Gloria, was diagnosed with IDD as a young child but not with Williams until she was in her thirties, it meant decades of being mystified by the surprising things his daughter couldn't do—tie her shoes, add two numbers, cross a street safely—along with the equally surprising things she could: teach herself to play accordion and sing opera in twelve languages.

Lenhoff and Libera lived on opposite sides of the country but connected through the newsletter after Lenhoff put in a notice asking for other parents interested in pursuing musical studies for their child. Together they hatched the idea to start a summer music camp for children and young adults with Williams syndrome. That first summer, about thirty students and their parents came, including Kay Bernon, mother of Charles and a professional fundraiser with many connections to Boston's philanthropic community. When Bernon saw all the ways that learning through music impacted her own son and the other children at the camp, she became interested in extending this model beyond a single week or two over the summer. Lenhoff had long wanted to create a residential music school where students could learn year-round. He enlisted Bernon and Libera's help in hashing out a plan. Because Lenhoff's daughter, Gloria, was older by that point (in her thirties) he pointed to the most pressing need as he saw it: creating a year-round educational opportunity for young adults with Williams syndrome and other developmental disabilities. Bernon and Libera agreed. They wanted to build something they'd never seen before: a college-like setting, with a degree-granting program, specifically designed for the needs of young adults with developmental disabilities. Students would learn how to be with each other as they developed their music skills. It took about four years from their early brainstorming meetings to raise the money and find a suitable location down the street from Mount Holyoke College in South Hadley, Massachusetts.

As they worked on building support for the project, Libera invited Oliver Sacks to visit their camp and consider writing about the extraordinary musical ability some of these students had. Mesmerized by the experience, Sacks wrote about it for the *New York Times,* which led to a flood of media attention. Gloria and John were featured in a *60 Minutes* episode called "A Very Special Brain," leading to more interest. As the word spread about the amazing, savant-like musical abilities of some people with Williams syndrome, a researcher from Canada made the surprising discovery: teenagers with Williams didn't actually score much higher than neurotypical peers on musicality and rhythmic memory. In relation to their other cognitive scores, these were standout strengths, but, with a few exceptions, they weren't close to the exceptional level of skill that some suggested people with Williams syndrome had. Rather, what stood out to researchers was their level of *responsiveness* to music. People with Williams weren't necessarily born with perfect pitch or a brilliant ear, they decided, they were simply captivated by music, far more than their neurotypical peers, a phenomenon that registered physically, in elevated heart rates, altered breathing, and visible emotion. Over half the test group with Williams cried when they heard Elvis Presley's "Love Me Tender." Their conclusion: though some people with Williams are preternaturally gifted, for the majority, their gift sprang from loving music so much they were motivated to work hard to play it well.

Reading this reassured me. After his lessons with Bret ended, Ethan decided that he was tired of drums and wanted to try other instruments. The devoted music teacher at his elementary school gave him a semester of piano lessons and after that, saxophone. Mostly he learned that he hated practicing and, even more, hated the awful-sounding music a beginner usually makes. Maybe we should have pushed him harder, but I worried that doing so might dim the pleasure music gave him. This study reinforced what I suspected Ethan was all along: a three-year-old who loved opera and could identify a handful of classical music pieces. A toddler whose favorite book was *Greatest Guitarists of All Time*. A prodigy at music appreciation.

By the time Ethan turned eighteen, BHMA was offering a transition day program, open to students from local school districts, which he was allowed to attend three days a week. At one of his early orientation meetings, Ethan described himself as "a really good singer." Mike and I rolled our eyes because this was only sometimes true. He did have perfect pitch and he could sing beautifully, but he often chose to play with songs, sing harmonies not melodies, or deliberately distort tunes in a way that pleased his ears but not other people's.

"He *might* be," we said, trying to sound optimistic.

Six months later, at his first open-mike performance on a Friday afternoon, I sat in the audience and held my breath as Ethan walked up to the front. To my knowledge, Ethan had never gotten near a live microphone without fixating on it—pursing his lips and blowing "*puh, puh, puh*" for at least thirty seconds. He also liked creating squeals of feedback by turning microphones on and off. I imagined him doing this for several agonizing minutes and never getting to his song at all. I readied the apology I'd make if he blew out our ears and laughed hysterically afterward.

Then—it didn't happen. The music started as he got to the microphone and without any other options, Ethan began to sing "Go the Distance" from the Disney musical *Hercules*: "I have often dreamed of a far off place / Where a great, warm, welcome will be waiting for me . . ."

He didn't miss a note, though admittedly, he chose different octaves to sing them in, seemingly at random. He'd hit the high, tremulous notes of the chorus and then decide, no, baritone is where I'm meant to be. The effect was a little unsettling, but it hardly mattered. He remembered every word of the remarkably apt lyrics and made it all the way to the end of the song without a hitch or any spray of spittle covering the microphone. I never cry at these kinds of things—the very idea seems embarrassing to me—but this time I couldn't help it. I wept.

I've since learned that BHMA audiences often leap to their feet after a first-year student takes a stab at open mike, but that day, it floored me to see the whole room rise up to their feet, as if they knew this was a triumph, and something Ethan had never done before.

....

For many years, Berkshire Hills Music Academy has stood alone in its mission—the only postsecondary school in the country for young adults with IDD to offer advanced music education. They could make their own rules and chart their own way because of Bernon's fundraising finesse and families who were willing to pay tuition out-of-pocket for the unique program they were offering. With a faculty composed mostly of professional musicians and trained music therapists (more of the former than the latter), students spend two years honing musicianship and performance skills and then are organized into a variety of bands and ensembles and sent out on the road. Their top-tier performing group—the Troupe—has a regular schedule of concerts, with devoted fans and supporters who invite them back year after year. For many people (including us), they are a first introduction to BHMA and a concert-length advertisement for the work they do. Over the years, though, I've come to think their second-tier groups—the ones that play in nursing homes and local schools—are doing work that's equally important and impressive. In general, they're made up of the slightly less polished, and more unpredictable, students. Their disabilities don't disappear when they're on stage, which lets the audience see the whole story. They might trip over a mike wire as they walk up to the stage. Teachers print up song lyrics so they can read what they can't remember. They're in need of a handful of supports—though not many—and still they always get through their shows, driven by a passion for the music that is mesmerizing and infectious.

They're often called inspirational, but for me the effect is something more subtle. At their twice-yearly concerts, every class and ensemble group plays one song. With their expanding student body, the concerts can get long, and not all the performers are of the same stellar caliber—some are even dreadful as Lenhoff acknowledged back in the early camp days—but they are invariably a passionate, supportive, and attentive audience for each other, and every performance is marked by an exuberance both onstage and off that you rarely see. It's a reminder of the gift they all have, even those without the technical ability to go along with it: joy in the magic of music and the connection it brings with other people.

Over the years, I've seen many shows at BHMA, with many standing ovations, many happy tears, many hugs. Still, the emotional tug I feel never goes away, even when I don't know the performers. Margaret Keller, executive director of Community Access to the Arts (CATA) in Pittsfield, Massachusetts, which brings high-level dance, music, theater, and visual arts programs to adults with disabilities, has a theory for why this is. When she attended her first CATA show, she was mystified by the wave of emotions she felt: Why had watching dancers with Down syndrome and actors with autism move her so profoundly, when she didn't have any family members with IDD? She now believes her response goes back to her earliest experience with disability and the warnings she always heard as a child any time she saw a disabled person: *don't stare.* A lifetime of such warnings, she posits, has effectively erased disability from our cultural landscape.

Just as people with disabilities were securing access to their rights as full citizens through ADA and other legislation, we were, as a nation, collectively being raised on the notion that when it came to disability, the most polite thing to do was look away. For Keller, this show was the first time she'd ever been invited *not* to look away and what she saw was a revelation: the excitement on their faces, the understanding of their material, the delight in themselves and in their performances. The next night, Keller returned to the show and brought her children with her "because it encapsulated so much of what I wanted to teach them about humanity and what connects us to one another. I realized what I was watching perfectly captured the power of art."

Founded in 1993 by Sandra Newman, a dance therapist working with adults with disabilities, CATA began with a simple idea of pairing professional artists looking for a steady income with people with dis-abilities. Instead of becoming a day program themselves, they part-nered with social service agencies to reach as many individuals as possible. Teachers traveled to schools and other venues to teach classes in dance, visual arts, textiles, drumming, acting, and others. They also partner with schools and other cultural organizations throughout the Berkshires to showcase the talent of their students in art exhibits, per-formances, and poetry readings.

At the CATA performance that I attended, the most breathtaking pieces were the modern dances, performed by a group with disabilities and without, a wide range of bodies striking lines and holding poses that left no doubt that these were trained and capable dancers. Another group performed scenes from Shakespeare with actors wearing elaborate Vic-torian costumes, while low-key assistants in black stood behind to help with lines if needed. At times, their faces lit up when they heard a line whispered behind them, as if they were remembering, all over again, how much they loved it. The effect was like watching Shakespeare be performed and processed at the same time. They laughed at a joke before they delivered it, scowled at a foe before they issued their threat. They certainly understood what they were saying, better, I daresay, than many of us who let Shakespeare's language wash over us. As I watched, I thought, many times, *Oh yeah, I forgot how funny that line is.*

I came away with a single thought: Why aren't there more day pro-grams for adults with IDD that focus on the arts? Why can't excellence in this kind of community inclusion be measured as a success? It's espe-cially frustrating when I think about the message hammered home to vocational providers at the APSE conference: *We have to let the world know about our talented students! We have to keep shouting, these people are capable!* What if one solution has been here all along: put them up on stage and let them show the world themselves?

The question is especially important when one takes into account how often the arts, especially performing, is a passion for children with IDD. This phenomenon has taken many parents by surprise as they watch their child rush for the spotlight or the karaoke microphone, and comes with an important revelation: *your child is less self-conscious about his differences than you are.* Some of Ethan's special-ed room friends learned to take deep, hand-waving bows before they learned the alphabet. One friend joked, as her son with Down syndrome took his third turn at karaoke night, "He doesn't know that he can't sing. I keep trying to tell him and he won't listen." Another friend once told me, "Every kid with Down syndrome I know has 'become a rock star' somewhere in their IEP vision statement. Either that or 'become a movie star.'" Putting themselves in the spotlight is such a common impulse that I sometimes wonder if they're making up for the half century their institutionalized predecessors were forced to live in the shadows.

After seeing the CATA show, I researched other arts-based programs for adults with disabilities and discovered, to my astonishment, how many more exist and thrive in other countries compared to the US. In the 1970s, as disability activists in the United Kingdom fought for school inclusion and access to public buildings, leaders of their movement argued that their fight wasn't just about ramps and lowered sidewalk curbs. It was also about taking back the narrative of their lives. For years, TV telethons (akin to Jerry Lewis telethons in the US) had painted people with disabilities as tragic figures, and they wanted the world to know the truth: with accommodations and the same opportunities as everyone else, they were *fine*—flourishing, even. Artists could convey this message better than anyone else, they believed, and demanded government funding for a disability arts council. They won both their battles—for access and for arts funding.

In the early 1980s, the UK Disability Arts Council supported the creation of numerous arts-based programs, including Mind the Gap, the first theater group devoted exclusively to training actors with IDD coming out of institutions. "Everyone was nervous because we didn't know what to expect from these folks," Mind the Gap founder Tim Wheeler remembers. "We thought it might help to create theater pieces where they were able to tell their own stories." Mind the Gap has thrived for over thirty years, producing contemporary and classic plays and touring the country and Europe, mostly to schools with discussions on inclusion and disability following the performance.

In the US, we do have some history for supporting the therapeutic potential of art and music. In the early twentieth century, Dorothea Dix traveled the country advocating for asylum reform and the moral treatment of psychiatric patients (who were often being housed side by side with the developmentally disabled). She advocated for arts, theater, and music as a way to restore the humanity of this forgotten population in the eyes of the public. In the early 1920s, Belchertown State School for the Feeble-Minded supported a thriving theater program run by the staff dentist who'd discovered some of the residents were musical and could sing in perfect pitch. In 1924, he directed a musical revue that toured to local communities and played shows for the Amherst Rotarian Club and other civic organizations and won rave reviews in the local newspapers. But with the advent of the Depression, the program lost funding, and by the mid-1930s the on-site theater was used for occasional movie screenings and little more. Learning this made me wonder: What if a performing arts program had been revved up again when the state school was moving residents out into the community? Could they have used performance in the same way Mind the Gap did, as a venue for residents to introduce themselves to new neighbors, tell their stories, and alleviate some fears?

"It would have been a great idea," Bill Zimmer, who helped oversee the closing of Belchertown School, concedes when I ask. "I've always believed the arts are the best bridge for people to find common ground. Unfortunately, that wasn't something that would have ever been funded back then."

By comparison, a wide range of disability arts programs have flourished in the UK since the time they began closing their own institutions. Since the inception of Mind the Gap, more than twenty theater companies working with people with IDD have formed. In 2011, Blue Apple Theatre in Winchester gained international attention by staging ambitious productions of Shakespeare and other classics, including a production of *Hamlet* starring Tommy Jessop, the first person with Down syndrome to play the title role in a professional production, along with five other leads who also had ID. His rendition of Hamlet's famous soliloquy became a viral YouTube sensation. When I googled Jessop, the biggest surprise for me was how much acting he'd already done before this triumph—a half dozen Shakespeare productions, a leading role in a BAFTA-nominated television movie.

It turns out successes like these breed more success. In 2012, the UK national Arts Council increased their investment in disability arts from 150,000 pounds a year to 2.2 million pounds to support international tours in every discipline: dance, music, theater, and visual arts. The goal was to become a world leader in changing the perception of disability around the globe and by all evidence, the effort paid off. There are now over forty disability arts festivals around the world and seventeen countries where disabled artists are able to produce work with government support. Belgium, Canada, Portugal, and Korea all make this list. The US does not.

Here in America, the National Endowment for the Arts has no designated funding stream, or even a separate office, to address the issue of access for disabled people to careers in the arts. Nor does it allocate money to help disabled people *see* the arts, though it has funded research that found people with disabilities were four times less likely to see a live performance in any given year than their nondisabled peers. The organizations that provide arts classes and programs for disabled students (like CATA and BHMA) have done so by relying on the largesse of individual families, on private fundraising, and offering fee-based services, meaning they are limited to people who can afford them and—as a result—are constrained in the scope of their offerings. Grants and state-funded initiatives are also available to some degree but one look at the stark difference between arts opportunities in the UK and America is proof enough of the difference prioritized federal funding makes.

The question of arts funding touches a nerve for Bill Zimmer. When he was the Franklin/Hampshire Area Director for the DDS, he believed that adult day programs should be allowed to include arts classes and that those classes should be properly funded to ensure the highest quality possible. "Riverside came up with this idea twenty years ago because they were sharing a building with all these artists' studios. It was a great idea, but it got a lot of pushback from my bosses because it wasn't aligned with the Department's increased focus on paid employment. The way I saw it, I don't want to live in a world without art and neither do people with disabilities. Then I started visiting the classes and I could see with my own eyes what a life-changing impact it had on certain people." The Riverside Arts program has produced artwork that has been on display at the Massachusetts State House and regularly sells at three popular shows a year. Even so, on my most recent tour of their facility, the arts room was our last stop, after we'd spent two hours learning about the prevocational program that trained everyone on bagging groceries. For participants who are passionate about art, it can only offer one to two hours a week in the studio. Unstated, but clear to me: the emphasis must be on developing work skills. I hear the echo of Zimmer's earlier words—*we say that we prioritize choice as long as they make the choice that we agree with.*

For arts-based programs like BHMA that began with no federal funding, the issue cuts deeper. They can continue offering a music-based education and keep their student body limited exclusively to those with families who can afford the tuition (approximately $80,000 to $90,000 a year) or they can broaden their program and accept local day students (mostly transition age eighteen-to-twenty-two-year-olds) and residential students who bring their waiver money from other states. "It wasn't really a big debate," Sharon Libera remembers. "Making some changes was the only way we could serve all the students who wanted to come."

With government money came government oversight, which took issue with two major components of BHMA's program: the absence of standard, vocational skill-building classes and the twenty-one-person dormitory setting. In 2014, when Medicaid established stricter rules to prevent money earmarked for community-based living going to any congregate settings, BHMA was put on "heightened scrutiny" by the state. Michelle Theroux had just come on board as executive director after some tumultuous years with several different interim directors. "The biggest problem, in the state's eyes, was the dorm," Theroux remembers. "They really didn't want us to keep that. Even though we're out in the community all the time and community comes here for concerts and events, they said it had the potential to isolate residents." She argued— along with founders Bernon and Libera—that dorm living is age-appropriate for a college setting where people are transitioning to independent living. Bernon believed that putting all these young adults in group homes at age nineteen or twenty would mean limiting their experience of navigating group dynamics and friend-making. "This is what people do when they get to college," she explains. "They have to enter a group and figure out which people they have the most in common with. Group homes don't offer that experience. Group homes mean the state dictates who you should be friends with and who you should share your life with. We wanted to give these young people more choice."

For now, the dorm that houses twenty-one students has survived, but a moratorium was put on building any new residential settings, which has been a blow. One thing the founders didn't anticipate is how many students don't want to leave BHMA after they graduate. They love the community, the classes, the regular concerts. Even those who aren't part of the Troupe or another performing group have found a home and want to stay. Initially, the founders responded with a plan to build transition cottages that new graduates could move into for a year or two and prac-tice living independently before moving into off-campus apartments. This is no longer a possibility. The desire to stick around hasn't changed, though, and in the last five years, over a dozen families have either moved to the area, or bought their child a home in South Hadley, to en-sure their continued place in BHMA's day program. Theroux also over-sees two small group homes, for those who have residential funding and state approval. The state won't permit the construction of any more group homes connected to BHMA in the same town. "Because they're allowing the dorm, they're stricter with us about anything else," Theroux tells me.

Heightened scrutiny also brought about another important change: a shift in their curriculum to put vocational skills and job development in a more central role. "Look, music is in our DNA and will always be part of the fabric here," Theroux says. "It's still the basis of our two-year program, but for the long term, it's not sustainable. We needed to diversify. In the real world, musicians have other jobs. So we're teaching them other jobs."

Andy Anderson, once the director of music at BHMA, is now the director of vocational services. Though I expect him to lament this change in focus, he sounds positive when I talk to him. He looks at the bigger picture, sees the issues that the state is trying to address, and thinks the changes are, overall, probably necessary. "The state has to ensure a level of quality control. You can't have service providers that put thirty people in a room, stringing beads and playing movies anymore. Providers have to be more thoughtful than that, and they also have to be accountable." At the same time, he is cautiously hopeful that they'll be able to sustain their core mission, as a provider of high-quality music education, with a strong vocational program as well. "We've been allowed to exist in this gray area and do what we do in a very unique fashion. So far, we've survived. I just hope we can continue to do so."

Though Anderson's background is mostly music, he's come up with several ideas to expand paid vocational opportunities, like a visual arts program where students can sell their work in an online marketplace. He's also become one of the most successful job developers I've met with. At this point, he's placed nine students out of about eighty in community-based jobs, from a local yoga studio to Trader Joe's. (By comparison, at the time of my visit, I only heard about three competitive job placements at Riverside, though undoubtedly they have more by now.) Perhaps this is a measure of the reputation BHMA students have in this relatively small, academic town: local merchants are familiar with their performances and are open to hiring graduates. Whatever the explanation, Anderson seems determined, as if he wants to prove that yes, BHMA can do both things—train musicians and get them day jobs—if the state is going to insist on this.

I still wonder, though, if something has been lost in making this shift from an exclusive focus on music to a generalized prevocational

program. The Performance Troupe still gives concerts and adds a regular influx of prodigies to their core group. Tory is still up front working
the microphone and charming the crowds. In all my conversations, I
hear many of the staff and teachers mention "balance," and maybe
they've found it. But it also has to be said: the fact that a program as
well-regarded as BHMA wouldn't be wholly embraced by the state—
would, in fact, be threatened with closure—sends a mystifying message. If the state is mandated to provide a choice in day services, why
pick on a program that is a first choice for many families and could be
considered the crown jewel of them all? The Troupe has performed at
Gillette Stadium, held fundraisers with legendary acts like Aerosmith,
and has luminaries like Luciano Pavarotti and Eunice Kennedy Shriver
on their Founding Board. A dozen families have bought property in
South Hadley to guarantee their child's spot. Clearly, they're doing
something right. Why not look closer at the places people are complaining about?

Bill Zimmer believes the problem boils down to a bias against arts-
based programs, which produce feel-good results that are also nebulous
and hard to measure. The government wants measurable goals so they
can track progress and have accountability. The arts don't offer this. But
they do offer something the government has seen a need for in the past.

In 2007, the President's Committee for People with Intellectual Disabilities, founded by John F. Kennedy, sent an unusual letter to then
President George W. Bush. Typically their annual letter offers advice on
their most urgent funding priorities—education, staffing, technological
assistance. That year, the tone was different. It was titled "Holding
Truths to Be Self-Evident: Affirming the Value of People with Intellectual Disabilities." In it, the group suspended making specific recommendations to emphatically remind the president that their constituents
are *people and fellow citizens*: "The committee was struck with the re-
grettable reality that people with IDD are too often excluded because
they are undervalued or believed less worthy of full citizenship."

The letter called on the president and members of Congress to raise
public awareness of "the inherent value of people with intellectual disabil-

ities." If you replaced that last phrase with any other minority group, you'd assume you were reading a historical document. They urged the president to "lead by example" and include "statements of support and stories of inspiration" in order to dispel long-held, demeaning stereotypes. The public needed to see a broader picture of people with IDD, they argued: they were better educated now, and more capable. They suggested establishing a "Disability History Week" to celebrate contributions of notable people with IDD. They pointed to Chris Burke, star of *Life Goes On*, a TV show featuring a central character with Down syndrome that ran twenty-five years earlier in the late 1980s. (No other examples were offered, presumably because there were none at the time.)

Though no disability-arts-specific funding ever materialized as a result, things have improved incrementally since then—shows like *Glee, Born This Way, Atypical,* and *Speechless* all feature central characters with developmental disabilities—but if the government once recognized the need to put the stories of these characters in front of a wider audience, why doesn't it support the programs to develop the actors who could play them? Tommy Jessop was able to play Hamlet because when he was a child, he saw a traveling performance of Mind the Gap theater troupe—adults who looked like him and made their careers as professional actors. At Blue Apple Theatre, Jessop has appeared in over two dozen plays. He's also acted in fifteen feature films and TV shows, was nominated for best actor at the Chelmsford Film Festival for his work in *Fighter*, and won for best actor in *Down and Out* at the Southampton International Film Festival. It would be an impressive résumé for any actor.

By contrast, arguably the most famous performer with Down syndrome in the US is Lauren Potter, who had a memorable, four-season-long storyline on *Glee*. Since the show's end, she's had a few TV appearances and, according to her website, now works primarily as a professional advocate, "to end bullying and raise disability awareness." I can't help wondering if Jessop, by continuing to work as a professional actor in a wide variety of roles, isn't doing more to raise the kind of awareness we need.

....

During Ethan's second year as a student at BHMA, Bret showed up in the audience at one of his holiday concerts. Ethan saw him first and bounced up and down from his spot on the stage. "Look who's here!" he called out to me, pointing. Though it had been a decade since we'd seen him, Bret looked unchanged—still grinning as his glasses slid down his nose.

"It's great to see Ethan again," he said to me afterward.

He had come back for a visit with his old friends, many of whom were still around. He hadn't realized Ethan was a student now. He was still shy, still a little hard to hear in the postconcert din. "I'm glad he got to go to school here. That's lucky."

"You were our inspiration!" I gushed. "Ethan's never forgotten his drum lessons!"

He laughed a little. "I didn't forget him, either."

"So what are you doing now?" I asked, suddenly worried this might be a weighty question. Tory was still at BHMA, singing with the Troupe; he was not.

"Different things," he said quietly, and with too much humility, as it turns out. Later, his mother writes me an update of his life and thankfully, it has been mostly successful and still has music at the center of it. He works as a music teacher for younger children five hours a week and has become a singer and performing ambassador for Best Buddies International.

For other graduates, it hasn't worked out as well. I hear a story of one young man who also had to move back home after finishing his degree at BHMA. He went from being a musician in one of their top groups to living with his parents and working a few hours a week at a Home Depot. In theory, this makes him a success story, a person with IDD holding down a community-based job; in reality, I'm less sure. I remember the groups of schoolchildren who once saw all these performers as role models and celebrities. I imagine him walking down wide cinderblock aisles with an orange vest on and it's hard to argue otherwise: it's not the same.

CHAPTER EIGHT

The first time we broached the possibility of sending Ethan to Prospect Meadow Farm, we didn't have high hopes. He was twenty-one years old and he'd already bombed out of seven different job trials. At some, he'd only lasted a day.

"His attention span is so short, he won't be able to work more than fifteen minutes at a time," I told Shawn Robinson, the director of the farm, at our first meeting. "He loves farm equipment, but he gets silly and unsafe around it."

I knew this from the previous summer he'd spent at Riverside in the hope of joining a landscaping crew, which never happened. "Unfortunately, he was silly and unsafe around the mowers," his final report read. Even though he mowed our own lawn and a neighbor's, I never questioned their assessment. I knew he probably *was* silly and unsafe when he walked into a shed full of mowers. Maybe he touched buttons he wasn't supposed to. This was a pattern at most of his job trials.

Then Robinson surprised me. "Why don't we try it out and see what happens," he said.

It turned out Ethan was fine mowing lawns at Prospect Meadow. Better than fine, even. He moved up the ranks and, after nine months, was offered a regular spot on their landscaping crew. Six months after that, he was taught how to use a zero-turn mower. It operated with levers and looked harder to drive than a car, yet the twenty-two-year-old who couldn't tie his shoes could not only mow a half-acre property, but could drive the mower up the ramp and onto the truck trailer at the end of the day.

This is the best argument that Employment First advocates make: people with IDD have been underestimated for far too long, sometimes most egregiously by their own parents, they say. Ethan is living proof that they're right. In our defense, I can only say, it's easy for this to happen. When our children were young, many of us dreamed big. Ethan loved classical music and opera at age three and we fantasized about the music career that might lie ahead. Marveling at your child's gifts and also accepting the reality of their limitations is a gradual process. You learn to do it slowly, adjusting expectations at every IEP meeting because you've begun to understand that your requests will be honored if they're more realistic. You lower goals and benchmarks in the hope that some will actually be met. When they are, you can all celebrate. You also know that insisting on overly ambitious goals can waste a lot of time and produce a frustrated malaise that's hard for your child to articulate and harder still to live with.

Twenty years of this leaves parents of new adults in a novel position—too often we're clarifying, in too much detail, everything we know our child *can't* do. At our first meeting with DDS to go over adult services, a coordinator offered a presentation on job exploration. After she finished, I said, "Okay, let's cut to the chase: he's done most of that already. It didn't work out too well." I suppose I was trying to lighten things with a joke, but I was also trying to say: *Let's not waste another two years putting Ethan in situations that frustrate and discourage him. No one needs that much practice at failure.*

I'm grateful that Shawn didn't listen to my nay-saying and even more grateful for his philosophy of getting to know workers on their own terms. His program was new enough—only five years old at the time— that the crews didn't have long waitlists, the way Riverside's did. If Ethan wanted to try lawn mowing, he could. Much to our surprise, without the build-up ahead of time, he got to work.

Launched in 2010 as the brainchild of Susan Stubbs, president and

CEO of ServiceNet, a residential and employment service provider, Prospect Meadow Farm began as a group home that came with a fallow farm and a few donated llamas in the back. Every time she visited, Stubbs noticed that caring for the animals was therapeutic for the residents so she added a few more, saw more benefits and began to hatch the idea of creating a working farm to employ the people they served. In the decade since, the success of Prospect Meadow has surprised even her. Within five years, it regularly employed about forty people with IDD and in 2017, they opened a second site about a mile away. They now employ about eighty people, most with IDD.

Much of this success is due to Robinson, who combines strong management skills with good instincts on how to meet clients where they're at. He's the first to admit that it hasn't always been easy. In the early years, the bias against congregate work sites was so strong that when Robinson spoke up in defense of them at the 2016 APSE conference, he was booed by the other attendees. "I was just trying to say, look people, let's not close off any of our options. Competitive employment is great but what about the folks who need more support and probably won't ever work in the community?" He laughs as he tells me the start of this story—he's such an affable, likeable fellow, it's hard to imagine him getting booed—but then he gets serious. "There are some leaders in this field who would say no program like ours should exist. They think if you're fighting for integrated employment, what we're doing undermines that goal. I get their point, but we serve a lot of people who've tried competitive work and it doesn't work for them. They might be a great worker three days a week and the other two they'll refuse to get out of the van in the morning. What employer is going to work around that on a regular basis? We can. We sit down and make a plan with the person. They're not going to get paid for the day, but they're also not going to get fired. We say, okay you're having a hard time today, that's all right, but let's try again tomorrow. Our folks need space like that."

The way he sees it, the overall goal should be offering meaningful work to as many people as possible. "A lot of our folks wouldn't be able to work in the community without prohibitively expensive supports, like a permanent job coach. If you've got a congregate work site, you don't need all those coaches. Our staff are trained to handle the issues when they come up, but for many of our workers, they don't come up that much. When you've got a looser environment that allows for stimming and self-talk, you don't get as much pushback, we've found. People are more relaxed because they can be themselves and still succeed."

For Ethan, who learned how to quit a job before he learned how to do one, this has certainly been true. In the three years that he's worked the farm, he's had occasional issues and more than a few bad days, I'm sure, but they're rare and usually relayed to me in an email at the end of the day. "Ethan seems to be having trouble with the heat," one said. "He's more agitated than usual and talking to himself a lot. Any suggestions beyond giving him more breaks and making sure he's drinking water?" In his job trials, a few days of agitated self-talk would have been a deal breaker. At the farm, they aren't. We all work together to make adjustments. After this note, I tucked a Gatorade in his backpack and told him to save it for the afternoon when most of his work was done. A few days later, I got another email reassuring me that Ethan seemed "back on track."

For us, the biggest revelation has been that, unlike his other jobs, Ethan has never once complained or said he doesn't want to go to work. There have been days, especially when the weather was either very cold or very hot, that Robinson has sent out a general email to all families suggesting that workers stay home if they don't feel like they can manage the extreme weather. Ethan has always chosen to go. "They need me," he says, in spite of Robinson's assurance otherwise. This represents something we weren't sure Ethan would ever develop: a sense of pride in his work, the feeling of being an important member of a collective effort larger than himself.

In trying to pinpoint why Ethan succeeded here and failed at so many other jobs, I spent a few days on site, observing how they operate. It didn't take long to see one explanation: The spirit throughout the farm is relaxed. Things move a little slower. There is a focus on work, but random conversation starters are also fine. Staff will stop what they're doing to help someone remember a song lyric or a movie line. I wanted to reach out and hug each one of them who indulged those moments. For Ethan, saying a line from *Shrek* in perfect Scottish brogue and having his coworker answer with Donkey's next line is worth more than any paycheck. But there's more to it, of course. As Robinson points out, the vast majority of his employees don't have one-on-one aides. Job coaches work with a crew of three to five farmhands assigned at the start of each day. For Ethan, who has grown weary of having a ubiquitous aide at his side, this freedom is a great boon. He can do his self-talk and his pacing away from the group and come back when he's ready. He doesn't have someone in his face all the time, as he did at school and on job sites, reminding him about "inside voices" and "quiet hands." It feels like a revelation: the freedom to be his scattered, random self has made him more productive.

....

The philosophical underpinning to Prospect Meadow Farm goes back over a hundred years and is another nod to Dorothea Dix's campaign for the moral treatment of asylum patients. In addition to urging the use of the arts, she also wrote extensively about the therapeutic benefits of farm work. Everyday tasks can "restore persons to a more healthy and satisfying function" without the daily stresses that often worsen their condition," she posited. William Gould, founder of the Gould Farm in Massachusetts in 1913 and widely considered the father of the therapeutic farming movement, expanded on those ideas. "All of us thrive best when we are in relationship with others," he wrote. "Creating a community where each individual has something to offer others is an extremely powerful model." In an article for the *New York Times* in 1921, Gould pointed out that a change of environment alone doesn't produce a cure. What people most needed was to "have the country interpreted to them by showing them where they fit into the scheme of things." In other words, people benefitted most when they had a job to do.

In a research study done for Smith College School of Social Work using Prospect Meadow farm participants, Frank Bayles found much evidence to support this theory. Most participants described their previous work as "boring," "depressing," and "unproductive." At the farm, work was described as "hard (especially in the winter) but also rewarding." One farmhand explained the feeling of satisfaction he felt after a hard day's work: "It's like imaginary people are tapping your shoulder, saying, 'Swell job.' This is the way I feel."

Bayles focused on one feature as especially encouraging to workers, which was instituted early on by Robinson: a system where some participants become "experts" at a certain task and are charged with teaching others, a gratifying experience for anyone with a developmental disability. "It's like we're all staff here," one said.

Reading this reminds me of Ethan coming home on the first day he learned to use the zero-turn lawn mower. "They say I might be king of the zero-turn someday," he told us. A few weeks later, he announced that it had happened. "I'm the king," he said.

We didn't believe it, frankly, until Miguel, his crew leader, told us a few weeks later, "It's true. He's really good at it. He might even be better than I am."

For months afterward, I heard Ethan, alone in his room, run through imagined conversations he might have in the future. Each time, he introduced himself the same way: "My name is Ethan and I'm a king."

Another finding in Bayles's research echoed a point Robinson had made to me earlier. It's critical to provide the regular opportunity to recover from bad moments or days. One participant said, "If I do a bad job one day, I don't feel as proud as I should maybe and I think about the next day—well what can I do better? I come here next time and I can do that instead."

"Each day is a new opportunity," is a theme that "nicely mirrors farming itself where change can be witnessed as well as experienced: sap changes to syrup, seed to vegetable, hay to food," Bayles observes in the preface to his study.

The opponents of models like Prospect Meadow Farm pose a valid question: Why bother closing down sheltered workshops if we're going to replace them with more segregated group work sites? Early on, Robinson attended two APSE conferences and listened closely to the concerns he heard. As he saw it, one of the main goals of Employment First was ensuring that the wider community was able to interact with these workers and see them in a more capable light. To address this, he made sure that the landscaping and wood delivery crews got instructions from customers and, as often as possible, navigated their own interactions. In 2017, he launched a farm store open to the public, with a CSA available for community members to pick up produce shares. Farmhands oversee the store and manage all sales and interactions.

To address another Employment First concern about hierarchical power imbalance, where neurotypical staff make all the rules, he established a system where farmhands who are particularly successful can work to become senior farmhands, with some added responsibilities and a walkie talkie. (Even with this appealing latter perk, Ethan has never wanted to pursue this path. The one time I asked, he said he didn't want to become a senior farmhand and leave his friends. I explained that it wouldn't mean this at all, but he still wasn't interested.) One farmhand has even become a job coach, which might explain something I notice every time I visit—the way all the farmhands share a sense of responsibility, regardless of whether they've been given a title (or a walkie-talkie).

"We got a hole in the pig fence," a worker told me the last time I was there. "It's too small for the big pigs but I gotta fix it or a baby might get out." He had some wire in his hand and a pair of gloves but no hovering job coach. I suspect he saw the hole and simply decided to fix it. "Trust me, you don't want to see what happens when a baby pig gets out." Whenever I see someone at the farm take on a task of their own volition like this, I hear the echo of William Gould's words: *people must see how they fit into the larger landscape.*

Because Robinson addressed the congregate setting concerns early on, Prospect Meadow was not put on heightened scrutiny in 2014, the same year that BHMA was. But in 2018, Robinson got a surprise when the Massachusetts DDS office issued new guidelines specifically targeting social enterprises created by service agencies to employ people with disabilities. By that point, Prospect Meadow had become the fastest-growing employer of people with IDD in Massachusetts, and Robinson was worried. "The way these new guidelines were written made it sound as if they were targeting us specifically. Like they were concerned that our success would get picked up and used by other agencies around the state."

In the end, he took the same approach he had from the start. He asked for a list of specific concerns and addressed each issue, one by one. Like Theroux at BHMA, he had to make some substantial changes. In the past, farmhands on off-site crews had been allowed to work up to six hours a day. This was a profitable side to the business but had high costs in transportation and could be unpredictable depending on weather. Because significant funding cuts were part of these new guidelines, Robinson had to scale everyone back to three paid hours a day, on site, which meant the end of Ethan's beloved landscaping crew and driving a zero-turn mower. I expected him to be devastated, but he wasn't. "Now I work in the pumpkin patch and crack people up with my jokes," Ethan told me. He shared a few of his recent wisecracks which, once again, made me grateful for the patient folks at the farm who laugh at jokes that aren't, by almost any measure, funny.

"Don't you miss the van rides and stopping at Cumby Farms after work?" I asked him.

"Nah," he said. "I'm a farmer now which means I do different things."

Robinson was nervous about these changes—work happens in the morning and in the afternoon, they operate as a day program, offering classes and running field trips—but like other service providers I've spoken with, he puts a positive spin on them. He points to the rising minimum wage, which in Massachusetts has been steadily increasing by a dollar an hour every year up to fifteen dollars. All farmhands earn minimum wage to start, which meant they were going to have to limit working hours eventually. There's also this discovery Robinson made: "By our measures, most of our farmhands seem happier since we started this new system. Attendance is up, behaviors are down. By pulling back on some of our business, we have less stress and we can be a little more relaxed. I have to admit, I'm surprised by this, but so far no one has complained about the lower paycheck they're getting."

His main concern is that the restrictions have made it almost impossible for other social enterprises to get started in Massachusetts. "The state gave us a pass because they know how popular this program is and they know I'm here fighting to sustain it. But these regulations make it pretty clear—they don't want to fund any new agency-sponsored start-ups like ours."

It's hard for the parent of a child who has struggled so mightily to find productive work to understand this logic, especially since some researchers have lauded agency-operated businesses as a solution to systemic unemployment. Scott Spreat, vice president of evaluation and research at Woods Research Center in Pennsylvania and one of the few researchers to analyze the impact of closing sheltered workshops on the employment rate of people with IDD, believes that they are an excellent stepping stone to widening opportunities for this group, especially for new workers who need flexibility and support. "If an individual doesn't want to work on a given day, the provider typically will have a pool of employees who could do the replacement work. Employee behavior that could not be tolerated in a more traditional employment setting is tolerable in a business operated by a vocational provider." I'm once again wondering why the state would target a program that families and researchers have validated.

Robinson sighs when I ask him about this. "If you're asking me, it's all about the congregate setting. The higher-ups really hate it. And the problem is, the workers really *like* it."

Robinson is right: most parents of twenty-two-year-olds entering a system that already has too few options don't see the problem with bringing a group of disabled people together to increase those options, but the policy makers—many old enough to have started their careers working in institutions—see a dangerous trend taking us backward to a time of mistreatment and criminal neglect. Which side is right?

Any parents fighting for a congregate setting should be obligated watch the exposés from Willowbrook or Belchertown to understand where the fear comes from. The abuse was unimaginable and not so long ago. But we also live in different times. Doctors no longer recommend placing infants in an institution "for the sake of the family"; people with IDD aren't scapegoated and blamed for society's ills. Our world has been changed forever by mainstream education. Is it naïve to believe that such dehumanizing treatment won't happen again? Robinson's comment points to the best argument for congregate settings: this is what Ethan and so many of his peers want. Being congregated with his disabled peers is the *best part.* It means the chance to voice every thought out loud and run lines from *Elf* to his heart's content. It means acceptance of his quirks and an audience to laugh at his jokes. It means being himself in the company of others. Is that so bad?

....

Forty years ago, Wolfensberger developed the concept of social role valorization (SRV) to address what he saw as the great failure of deinstitutionalization—former residents dumped into communities they played no part in. No relationships with neighbors, no genuine inclusion. A core concept of SRV is the idea that society identifies some groups of people as fundamentally different and of less value. He blamed the long history of negative images of people with IDD—portrayed as criminals, as sexual deviants, as eternal children—and argued that "re-imaging" was an important component of raising their social value. Traveling in groups emphasizes differences, Wolfensberger argued, as did allowing eccentric dressing habits and behaviors like self-talk and stimming. "Valued social roles for people need to be attained and preserved in order for them to become (more) positively valued socially."

Some of his colleagues disagreed and said this boiled down to an overly proscriptive set of goals based on appearance. Wolfensberger's approach seems to put the definition of "social value" in society's hands rather than with the person and says that "normalizing measures can be *offered* in some cases, and *imposed* in others."

Indeed, saying that Ethan shouldn't want to spend his days in a community of his peers—that neurotypical communities are always preferable—reminds me of the effort parents once made to fill their child's birthday parties and playdate calendars with neurotypical peers. We all did it because it felt like a victory, a way of narrowing the gap between our child and the world of first graders he couldn't keep up with. After a time, though, it was clear to most of us: those weren't real friendships and only one or two of them ever reciprocated, so where was the victory?

"People with disabilities should have the right to choose for themselves how they wish to live and to what extent they wish to emulate the pillars of society," Bert Perrin wrote in 1995, encapsulating the Scandinavian view of a concept called normalization. "Why would human service workers deny people with disabilities the right to be themselves?"

I would argue that the problem with Wolfensberger's social role valorization theory and the reason it hasn't stood the test of time is that this generation doesn't define themselves by the same societal measures that he does. These days, I take Ethan to a potluck dance at the Inclusive Community Center, our local recreation site for children and adults with disabilities. About fifty or sixty people come to these events, many in elastic-waist pants and Velcro-strap sneakers. Has society bestowed a valued role on them? Not really. Does it matter to anyone here? Not at all. Ditto for the prestige of having a job.

Ethan always walks into a room like this with both arms raised high, like Nixon flashing a victory sign just before his presidency collapsed. On this particular night, he sees one friend and starts riffing on a movie joke. "I'm gonna take you out back," he says, gangster style. "I'm gonna take *you* out back," the friend retorts. He's smaller than Ethan, but no one is worried about a fight breaking out. They hug and Ethan's glasses catch on his sweater. When he steps away, his glasses are dangling on the guys' chest. "Oh sorry," Ethan says, then laughs at the sight.

Everyone looks. Everyone laughs.

I usually drop Ethan off, but tonight I decide to stay and watch the evening unfold along with a half dozen other parents. The food is all potluck and no one's on a diet when there are frosted brownies and

SpongeBob cupcakes. They aren't particularly decorous eaters, but when one person stands up, he asks if anyone needs anything and brings back what people asked for: forks, napkins, an extra cookie. After years of hovering mothers helping them socialize, it's eye-opening to realize they have no need for us. By the end, I suspect we're not here to help, but to soak up what this group provides in abundance—happiness of self-acceptance; socializing without self-consciousness.

Of the fifty or so people at this event, I know only two who have "real jobs" in the community. One works at the Texas Roadhouse diner four to six hours a week as a hostess, another bags groceries about the same number of hours. A few, like Ethan, work in supported settings like Prospect Meadow Farm. Others go to BHMA or Riverside. As far as I can tell, no one mentions work or bosses or money they've earned. When a friend named Alex walks in with his hair newly dyed—half red on one side, half blue on the other—there is a commotion. Everyone gathers around to marvel at the change. They offer compliments and reach out to pat his new hairdo. "One at a time," Alex says, holding up his hands like a movie idol. "One at a time."

Later, after the hoopla dies down, Alex catches my eye, grins, and points to his head. "I'm the hair guy tonight," he says. "That's just who I am."

I've known Alex since he and Ethan were in preschool together. He has Williams syndrome, is a talented drummer, and is part of a band at BHMA. He also has an imagination that takes him in strange, funny loops. "I was a wolf in a previous life," he'll say if you ask him how he is. "I swear."

Behind him, his mom will usually roll her eyes. "She's asking about *this* life, Alex."

"Yeah, it's okay," he'll say.

Ethan has worn a beloved concert jacket tonight. After the excitement over Alex's hair dies down, Ethan stands up and announces that he is Bruce Springsteen tonight. "You can just call me Bruce," he says. No one does, but a few compliment his jacket. Ethan doesn't hear them because he's bounced up the hall, so pleased with his announcement that he repeats it a dozen times. In the distance I hear him tell some unsuspecting person coming out of the bathroom, "I'm Bruce tonight!"

It's not that they're childish, but more that their pleasures contain the childlike wonder of endless possibility. One of Ethan's favorite pastimes is running through dialogues of what he'd say if he met a celebrity. It's charming for a while, and mind-numbing after two hours of listening to him alone in his room say, "Hello, Jim Carrey! My name is Ethan! I can drive a lawn mower!" When his brothers grow weary and finally call out from their own rooms, "You're never going to meet Jim Carrey, so be quiet!" he stands his ground. "You don't *know* that, Henry."

How can we parents, lined up along the edges of an evening like this, not love watching it all unfold? As Jean Vanier, founder of the L'Arche community movement, wrote in *Community and Growth,* "A community is only being created when its members accept that they are not going to achieve great things, that they are not going to be heroes, but simply live each day with new hope, like children, in wonderment as the sun rises and in thanksgiving as it sets." Not everyone will agree with this sentiment, which seems to equate living in the moment with abandoning any hope of material success, but I think it's a useful reminder of the way Ethan and his peers define themselves and their own ideas of success. (I also love another quote of his: "To love someone means being prepared to waste time with them.") Mindfulness teaches us to look at what we have without pining for more. Ethan and his friends remind me to take pleasure in what's at hand. More importantly, they offer this affirmation to each other, a dozen times a day, in large and small ways. In prioritizing connections and living in the moment, imaginatively writing their own success stories, they model those things, too.

In *Father's Day,* a memoir about his son, Zach's, transition to adulthood, Buzz Bissinger writes about watching Zach with a group of young adults with disabilities. Born with both a developmental disability and savant skills, Zach is convivial and skilled enough to have worked in the mailroom of a law office since he graduated from high school. Still, Bissinger can see, it's not quite enough. "All Zach wants, all his friends want, is unconditional acceptance," he observes. "That is what they give each other. Unlike the rest of the world, they see no difference in each other and make no diagnostic distinctions. . . . They express neither pity nor self-pity; as Zach told his mother when he learned he was going out to dinner one night with a girl who was blind and deaf, 'That means I can order what I want from the menu.'" The story is funny, but it also underscores the relief young adults like Zach feel in being allowed to be themselves around each other. I'd wager most men, upon hearing that their date is deaf and blind would feel nervous about what they might say and do to fill an hour or so of conversation. It's perfect (and hilarious) that Zach doesn't fret this. In their world, some people don't talk, some people don't stop talking.

It occurs to me that saying Alex should, or ever would, measure his self-worth by whatever job someone has carved out for him at Panera Bread or Stop and Shop is silly. He's the hair guy tonight. Tomorrow he will tell me, conspiratorially, that he was a desert fox in a different life.

Wolfensberger's writings haven't remained wholly relevant because the society he describes—one that will only value and bestow a great life on those who've attained society's trappings of respectability—doesn't exist anymore. I would argue that too many young adults with IDD create their own pillars now, with parents marveling from the sidelines, because it feels freeing to watch people so confidently write their own rules.

In his book *Far from the Tree*, an examination of parenting children much different from ourselves, many with disabilities, Andrew Solomon puts it this way: "People don't want to be cured or changed or eliminated. They want to be whoever it is they've come to be." This is the pleasure that spending time in this community provides. It's the exhale of relief: we can all be whoever it is we've come to be.

CHAPTER NINE

The first thing you notice when you walk into Blue Star Electronics Recyclers in Boulder, Colorado, is the intense focus of the employees: seven men wearing goggles and wielding pneumatic drills with the concentration of surgeons. They are dismantling old computers; the work is exacting because no two units are alike. Precision is paramount, so no one uses a hammer or breaks anything open. It's all done carefully, by unscrewing equipment, piece by piece. They must study each one, find the joints and screws, separate each component, then sort it into large, waist-high cardboard boxes behind them. It's mesmerizing to watch and certainly not obvious that all these workers have autism.

I am visiting Blue Star Recyclers, founded by Bill Morris in 2009, to learn more about a growing trend of starting a business with the primary mission of hiring people with disabilities, without any government assistance—or interference. Because their mission is creating as many jobs as possible for people with IDD, they are, by default, congregate work sites. They pay their workers minimum wage or better (eliminating one of the primary arguments against sheltered workshops) and employ them an average of twenty hours or more a week, far above the six to twelve hours that most supported employees get in community-based jobs. With work sites tailored to accommodate employee needs, while also utilizing their strengths for a business advantage, I wanted to figure out: is it possible these businesses are unlocking the secret to more productive employment prospects for this group?

By most measures, Morris has been extremely successful. At the time of my visit, Blue Star Recyclers has grown from employing six people with autism and IDD in 2009 to employing forty across three facilities, in Colorado Springs, Denver, and Boulder. They've recycled twenty million pounds of electronics, and Morris has won a host of awards, including 2011 Colorado Recycler of the Year, ARC Employer of the Year, and Social Impact Business of the Year. He was also a finalist for the White House Champion of Change award, and in 2016 Mitsubishi awarded Blue Star a $50,000 grant to develop their model in at least two other cities. The first plant outside Colorado opened in Buffalo Grove, Illinois, in November 2019.

One of Morris's primary messages when he goes on the road is the business advantages to hiring people with autism and IDD. "The number one thing people need to know is that these are great workers who are amazingly reliable. In an industry with 500 percent turnover, I've got 0 percent turnover," he tells me. There's also this: "It's a business with an unusually high lost-time accident record, which drives up workers comp insurance and other costs. So far, our safety record is almost spotless. These guys watch a training video that most workers wouldn't pay much attention to and they memorize every step. They're inherently safe because they don't take shortcuts. They follow routines and don't stray from them. People with autism aren't just good employees, they're *phenomenal* employees."

I watch the team work for the better part of a morning, largely unsupervised by any neurotypical aides or coworkers. "Ian is the team leader," Zach Bowen, the plant manager, explains. "He's worked here the longest. If they have questions or problems, they go to him first. Usually they solve whatever problem it is themselves."

Ian is autistic as well, but his experience and willingness to stop and assist others has put him in charge. I watch him help someone loosen a stubborn screw. They work wordlessly and without any eye contact, and when the problem is solved, they high-five and return to their stations.

I think about the parents who've seen their child do very little without an aide at his side. Even those of us who've made independence goals every year understand that an adult will always hover in the background. After years, the message settles in: *he's not safe without constant supervision.* But now it seems clear: even around noisy drills and old computer parts being tossed into bins, these guys are fine. Bowen is in the back warehouse, administrators are in their offices. On the floor, Ian is in charge and everything is chugging along.

While they work, it's hard for me to tell if anyone struggles with communication. Ten minutes into their lunchtime, it's easy to see that they all do—at least when an outsider asks them a few questions. I had assumed they were all more socially adept than Ethan, but they answer my questions the same way he would: Is this your first job? "I don't know. You'll have to ask my mom." What do you like best about this job? "Everything!" Phrased a different way: "What's your favorite thing about working here?" "Hanging out with my friends!"

James, who has only been working for three months, is eager to tell me this is the best job he's ever had. Before, he worked as a janitor at a restaurant and it was horrible. "No one talked to me, ever. All they wanted me to do was clean up, clean up." He got paid more, but still prefers this job. "Here we're a team and we have a great time."

I ask James how working here feels like being part of a team. He thinks for a minute. "Well, at the end of the day we always have a dance party."

"Really?" I start to laugh and then stop myself. There are twelve employees in the Denver site that day, plus Bill and his wife, Janet, who is the finance director, and their two golden retrievers. Most of them don't say much or make eye contact. And they have a *dance* party?

As it turns out, they do. At the end of every day.

As they post the total number of computers each person has completed, everyone claps for their coworkers. Bowen turns on the radio—a mellow station that sounds like smooth jazz—and they dance for about ten minutes, exchanging high fives. Shane has the highest numbers for the day. The minute he sees this, he shoots off to the corner to stand by himself. He did the same thing earlier in the breakroom when Bowen explained why Shane had been chosen as employee of the year. "Shane goes above and beyond his duties every single day. He doesn't wait to be told what to do. If he sees a mess on the floor, he gets a broom and sweeps it up . . ." As Bowen ran through the litany of Shane's assets, Shane got more and more uncomfortable until finally he stood up and left the room.

I watch his face now, peeking up toward the board displaying his score. Then he does something that I'm guessing is uncharacteristic: inches a little closer to the writer who's asking questions. Pneumatic drills are easy for these guys; questions aren't. But he keeps coming toward me. "Congratulations!" I say when he gets close enough to hear me.

"Yes," he says.

"You're very good at this job," I say.

"Yes," he says, eyes trained upward.

"What's your favorite part of this job?"

"Recycling computers!" There's a hint of a smile I haven't seen before.

I suspect this is pretty talkative for Shane. I ask if he's ever worked anywhere before. "No," he says. "I went to a day program. I don't like my day program."

He left the day program three years ago but the memory still puts a cloud over his face. According to Bowen, ever since he started at Blue Star, Shane has worried about being sent back there. All of the employees get to work early, some of them arriving an hour before they need to. They hang out, make coffee, and get ready for the day. By nine o'clock they're at their stations. If Shane's bus drops him off late and he misses this early period, he frets most of the day and offers to turn in his Blue Star hat. "One of the reasons we made him employee of the year was to reassure him that he was doing a great job," Bowen explains. "But I'm not sure he'll ever believe it."

The atmosphere is so jolly and casual that both Bowen and Lorin Marco, business development manager, look puzzled when I ask if they had any experience working with disabled people before they came to Blue Star. No, they say. I've watched them all day and both are instinctively good at it—knowing when to gently joke around and when to back off. Mostly, they're full of high praise for their fellow workers. "Look, with these guys, you tell them to do something once, you know it'll get done," Marco tells me. "Sometimes you don't even have to say anything. They see something needs doing and they do it."

Bowen has to think for a minute when I ask what his strategies are for managing behaviors. "We don't have that problem too much. Here, we're a team of equals. Honestly, sometimes one guy will have a bad day because his bus got him here late and he hates to be late, so he'll be grumpy all day. Isn't that right, Kian?" he calls. Apparently, being late is unsettling for many of these guys. Kian smiles sheepishly. "Yeah, I hate it."

As they talk more about each employee's growth over time, it's clear that Bowen and Marco have made some accommodations, but they haven't thought of them as such. "A few of them took a while to adjust to busy surroundings," Bowen tells me. "They'd come in for an hour in the beginning and maybe work on one computer. Gradually they'd build up their tolerance. We have one new guy who's been staying for five minutes at a time. He watches for a while and then he goes home. He doesn't get paid for anything yet, but we're waiting to see if he gets interested enough to get over his anxiety."

Anxiety is a big issue for autistic young adults. Making transitions and navigating the unknown—like busses that don't show up on time— are particular challenges. As if Bowen and Marco have learned the best way to counteract this, the workers set the tone. In the lunchroom, their conversation is full of giggly laughs and recitations of lines from the latest *Avenger* movie. "Don't come work here if you don't like hugs," jokes Marco. "There's lots of hugs around here." Having come from a middle-management position in the health care industry where tensions got high on a daily basis, Marco says this is the best work environment he's ever been in. "It might not be for everyone, but for me it's good. You can feel it in the air when you walk in. We're all going to get our work done, but we're going to have a good time doing it."

Bowen agrees, and puts it a different way: "They probably don't realize it, but when you watch them being themselves, it makes everyone feel more relaxed. It's hard to be in a bad mood for long around here." /

Bowen and Marco may have never heard of Wolf Wolfensberger or social role valorization and yet they're living examples of the model, honoring each person for who they are and the value they bring to the community they share.

Though Morris's original mission was to serve as a training opportunity for employees to transition to other work, almost no one has. "Two of our best guys got jobs at a bigger recycling company, but they ended up in cubicle situations they didn't like. They missed the team and they both asked to come back here," he tells me. This is a comfortable, happy work environment and forcing them into an integrated employment setting wouldn't be their first choice. For many, it wouldn't be sustainable.

There is a catch, though. Morris's main message when he speaks at conferences is that hiring these workers is a business-smart decision, but this doesn't mean it's been easy or particularly lucrative. For many years, Blue Star operated at a loss, which Morris is quick to tell me, has nothing to do with his employees or model; it's a struggle throughout the industry. The cost of shipping materials to the recycling centers is astronomical and there's a ceiling on what businesses can afford to pay recyclers. For years, Morris resisted applying for nonprofit status because he associated that with the government assistance he was trying to avoid. After a while, he had no choice: declaring nonprofit status, which he did in 2016, allowed him to fundraise and apply for grants. After a decade in this work, and the opening of his first plant outside Colorado, Morris is allowing himself to relax a little about the future. "I used to worry a lot about what would happen to these guys if I couldn't keep Blue Star going. I've seen the day programs they'd go into and a lot of them—" He shakes his head. "Well, they're terrible."

Blue Star is profitable now—just barely—and Morris sees enough stability in the near future to achieve his ultimate dream of retiring and turning the business over to his employees. "These guys have earned that. In eight years, we've had almost no turnover, no absentee-ism, and no lost-time accidents. That's owner behavior. They deserve to be owners."

....

If Bill Morris has been an affable father figure in the world of social enterprises employing people with IDD, then Tom D'Eri and his father, John, founders of Rising Tide Car Wash in Florida, have been the media-savvy, hard-driving champions for the benefits of hiring autistic workers. They started in 2010, after Tom graduated from business school just as his father was researching ideas for businesses to employ his older son, Andrew, who has autism. They admired what Morris had done with Blue Star, but Tom didn't see it as an ideal model because by then it depended on its nonprofit status. "He'd always been *almost* prof-itable. He's managed that really well, but we didn't want to take that kind of risk," Tom tells me when I visit his site in Margate, Florida.

What they really liked about Blue Star was the way Morris had de-signed a systematic model that used their employees' strengths. Once they settled on buying a car wash, the D'Eris followed this approach. They color-coded the rags and cleaners. They broke down the job into forty-six steps that could, with enough practice, be completed in six minutes. In 2013, they opened their first site in Parkland, Florida, tak-ing a business that had been servicing thirty thousand cars a year to one that services a hundred and sixty thousand. Four years later, they opened a second, larger site in Margate. Both locations were profitable within the first year, a fact that Tom credits to the staff. "Neurotypical employees, I'm telling you, would start taking shortcuts and wouldn't follow the color-coded system. We'd have cars going out of here with streaky windows and exterior dirt all over their dashboard. With our guys, that never happens. Never."

They've made other discoveries: guys who have limited verbal skills can do all the communicating they need to in the loud environment of a car wash where people are used to following gestures: put your antenna down, foot off the brake, car in neutral. "We get a 125 cars through the tunnel an hour and most of those people don't realize that they're deal-ing with someone who doesn't really talk. Or drive!"

Andrew has now been working at Rising Tide for seven years. For his father, the biggest surprise has been the relationships he's formed. "It's not about the work for Andrew, it's about the friends he's made. Last week they all went to dinner and they did it on their own. They ordered their food, they settled the bill, all without any help. It's amaz-ing to me. They each have different skills—one can drive, one is pretty good at understanding money, one is a pretty good cook and loves food. I see it now—they can take care of each other. You put them all together and you have a highly functional unit."

Michael Alessandri, executive director of the Center for Autism and Related Disabilities (CARD) in Miami since 1993, liked what the D'Eris were doing and offered to come on board as a consultant. After years of helping families with younger children fight for a more inclusive educa-tion, he'd begun to think the most pressing need for families was finding options for the young adults aging out of the school system. He'd also started to believe that community-based jobs weren't always the best fit for people with autism: "People often make the mistake of thinking we have to prioritize inclusion and make all their social opportunities take place with neurotypical peers. But when you create an opportunity for similar individuals to be together in a work environment where they share a common purpose and a sense of being responsible to and for each other, you create connections we never saw before. Those relationships can extend beyond the workplace in a much more meaningful way."

Although he has worked on education inclusion for most of his ca-reer, Alessandri thinks it's a message that more professionals need to hear. "In academia, we constantly teach about making sure people with disabilities are meaningfully included with neurotypical peers, but I remember a young woman in a wheelchair once telling me, very elo-quently that 'my whole life people have been wheeling me into a room filled with people who weren't in wheelchairs and all I wanted was to find a room full of other people in wheelchairs.' We have to find a bal-ance. The voice of the people being served must be heard."

John D'Eri puts it a different way: "Parents bend over backward trying to get a job for their kids in an integrated setting. Usually that means they're inserted into a neurotypical environment and honestly, there's no level of real community." He believes that a business where the neurodiverse workers are the majority creates an atmosphere where more of them succeed. "Do they still have to deal with the neurotypical world? Of course! They're at work, they've got customers all day. They're interacting, asking questions, giving instructions and taking them, too. But they're strengthened by each other. It's organic. By creating the norm of atypical workers, we've also got all of them working more independently."

Now that Tom has been overseeing two successful car washes for seven years, he tells me his most surprising discovery is how much employees change on the job. "A few people came to us through a job coach who said, 'Look, I don't know if this will work because this guy has a real anger problem.' And then we never see it. They're an excellent worker. It makes me wonder if those maladaptive behaviors are an issue when the person is bored, because no one is bored here." He points to the group of about a dozen employees outside his window, bent inside of cars, vacuuming, and wiping. "You don't see any of those guys pacing and flapping and talking to themselves, right?"

In fact, it was one of the first things I noticed. Like at Blue Star, I tried to imagine Ethan working here, and couldn't: he would pace around too much and get distracted.

"Wait until they're off the clock." Tom smiles. "It all comes out. One group will start pacing in circles. Another will launch in on self-talk that we never hear during their work shifts."

I wait until the end of the shift, and he's right—a few of them go off to pace laps away from the action and one of them, who has been asked to stick around to talk to me, goes over to a corner of the breakroom to talk to himself for a while first. My heart leaps at these sights: even though we live three thousand miles away, I think, *Maybe Ethan* could *do this.* Absorbed in their work, these employees hardly seem autistic. It's reassuring to realize, yes, they are.

For Tom, his only disappointment in the success of Rising Tide has been the realization that their model isn't as replicable as he had hoped. Originally, he and his father dreamed about licensing franchises around the country—putting a real dent in autism unemployment, one car wash at a time—but in reality, it is an expensive and time-consuming start-up. To build a car wash from scratch can take up to two years. "This was a wonderful laboratory to explore what we wanted to do but it's not a great model to scale up quickly," he says.

Instead, Tom, who now oversees most of the operation since his dad's semiretirement, has shifted his focus to spreading the word in the business community about the advantages of hiring employees with autism. He's created Rising Tide U with courses online to help other families get started creating their own social enterprises, and partnered with CARD on a podcast called *The Autism Advantage*, talking to entrepreneurs who have started businesses with similar missions. He has been interviewed on the *Today* show, *ABC News,* and *Fox Business*, and appeared before the United Nations Assembly to discuss the possibilities of hiring neurodiverse employees internationally.

Maybe the D'Eris didn't start the movement, but Tom has become one of the faces out front selling it—and the movement is growing. In 2016, Amy Wright opened Bitty & Beau's Coffee in Wilmington, North Carolina, to employ her two children with Down syndrome, the coffee shop's namesakes. Rather than emphasizing the charity aspect like Goodwill has done (while paying workers much less than minimum wage using their sheltered workshop status), their employees offer up a feel-good difference in what would ordinarily be a routine exchange. For example, they hand out playing cards to let customers know when their order is ready. "I had a feeling you were the Jack of Hearts," says Bob, who has Down syndrome, grinning as he hands them their order. In 2017, Wright won CNN's Hero of the Year. In her acceptance speech, Wright said, "Two hundred million people around the world living with intellectual or developmental disability are not broken. What is broken is the lens through which we view people with disabilities." Since then, they've opened two other locations in North Carolina.

Arguably one of the most successful social enterprises of all is John's Crazy Socks, started by Mark and John Cronin, a father/son team. John, who has Down syndrome and has loved wearing colorful socks his whole life, is at the center of all their promotional activities. His face adorns the logo of their website that sells a wide variety of themed socks, and their motto is "Spreading Happiness," his favorite saying. They are savvy marketers who have seen their socks worn by George H. W. Bush and Justin Trudeau (they designed a special sock to honor the Canadian prime minister), and their business has exploded since they launched in 2016. They now have thirty-five employees, fifteen with disabilities, filling fifteen hundred to two thousand orders a day in a multimillion-dollar business.

What is the secret to success for these start-ups? After many site visits, the phrase I heard most often from employees was, "I feel like I'm part of a team," which reminded me of Wolfensberger: in order for inclusion to be genuine and successful, each person must have a valued social role to play. They must be part of something larger—connected to the shared mission of the company. I saw it at the dance party at Blue Star, and counting out the tip jar at Rising Tide. Michael Alessandri says, "One of the surprises we're finding in this push for community-integrated jobs is that the work we're able to find for these individuals is often far too isolating and far too disconnected from the bigger picture of whatever the company is doing." With a smaller company, this is more possible.

At Rising Tide, some workers were only minimally verbal and some were very chatty and forthcoming. Dee Dee Brodzki, twenty-two, told me about getting hired there after dropping out of an advanced physics program at Florida Institute of Technology. "I have Asperger's so the schoolwork was easy for me but everything else wasn't. School put me in a really dark place with depression and anxiety. Toward the end, I got really desperate. I had to drop out and I wasn't sure what to do." Her sister read about Rising Tide and suggested applying for a job while she recovered from what she called "a total nervous breakdown." It turned out to be the perfect fit for her. "It's structured. It's routine. There's a support network here that people in my situation really need on the job. If work gets too stressful, I radio in for help and the response is always immediate."

For Dee Dee, the last two years have been healing in many ways, especially when she came out as transgender last year. "They've all been really supportive. . . . I feel like I have people who will stand up for me here. I've never had to worry about my own safety, which is huge. The truth is, I could work here forever," she says. "I know I'm supposed to go back to school at some point, because obviously when you're good at physics, you probably shouldn't work at a car wash, but I'm not sure. It's been really great for me here." She's remarkably articulate, but here she hesitates, as if she's looking for the right words. "I don't know— we're a team here."

When I mention this conversation with Dee Dee to Tom—mostly to let him know he's done a good job supporting her—he says, "Yeah, we actually have two employees who've transitioned and it's gone pretty well. It doesn't take their coworkers long to adjust. Some of them hear it, nod, and from then on, they never use the wrong pronoun. It's the neurotypicals like me who make pronoun mistakes for weeks, sometimes months. I always feel terrible. And then I think this is what my neurotypical brain is bad at and these guys are pretty good at."

I'm guessing that Tom doesn't tell this story when he's doing his media blitzes and promoting the business advantages of hiring autistic workers, but to me, it represents an important aspect to the story. Full acceptance into a community has been the elusive goal of disability services for the last fifty years, since the early days when Wolfensberger and Nirje debated how to achieve it—and here is a quiet example of how true acceptance not only creates new lives but saves them as well.

CHAPTER TEN

Seeing the benefits of this teamwork in action—created when a group of people with IDD are intentionally brought together with a single mission—made me wonder if it could be put into motion earlier, during the transition period in high school, since isolated job placements have not had a great track record for producing long-term employment. Could students between the ages of eighteen and twenty-two be trained for higher-end jobs in congregate settings that would ease their transition into later job opportunities?

I'm not the first parent that this has occurred to. Yudi Bennett started Exceptional Minds in Sherman Oaks, California, when her son, Noah, who has autism, was still in high school but plateauing academically. He didn't care about keeping up at school; he only cared about a computer animation class he was taking after school. At the class she met a group of other parents of children on the spectrum in a similar bind. "We were nine desperate families who had no place to send our kids. So we said, 'Fine, let's we band together and start a school that focuses only on this.'"

They started by offering a three-year program with ten students to teach the exacting work of CGI graphics, visual effects, and animation. Soon after, they built a studio where students could work on real movies and get paid in the process. In the ten years since Exceptional Minds launched, the list of major movies they've worked on is eye-popping and impressive: *Avengers: Endgame, Black Panther, Captain Marvel, Ant-man, Game of Thrones.* Three years ago, they added an animation stu-dio and began a partnership with Cartoon Network to provide mentors and job training to twenty Exceptional Minds graduates specializing in animation. "We had a ten-year strategic plan that we got through in five years because the demand was so high," Bennett tells me when I visit their site. "Which says to me a lot about the need. The real problem is we don't have enough programs like this."

For Bennett, the biggest achievement of Exceptional Minds is the template it offers to other vocational-training programs. "Look—we've got an employment crisis out there for people with autism and IDD and this isn't going to solve it. There aren't enough jobs in the movie indus-try to employ all the people with autism who are capable of working and would like to. What we do is open people's minds to more possibilities." Bennett is focused on the larger picture. Her students have all gradu-ated from high school or earned GEDs, meaning most have no intellec-tual impairment. She thinks a lot about the full range of students with IDD, including those who haven't earned high school diplomas, and is excited to tell me about another program called Uniquely Abled, where she sits on the board.

Started in 2013 by Ivan Rosenberg, father of two children with au-tism, Uniquely Abled trains people with autism as computer-numerical-control (CNC) machine operators and programmers. "It's precision manufacturing. Lathes that make metal parts for every machine in the world from airplanes to space rockets to car parts. They need skilled workers—machine operators and programmers. We used to call these 'the shop' kids, but so few high schools offer 'shop' anymore that this is their first experience. If it's the right fit, they love it."

Bennett likes the idea that Uniquely Abled has flipped the model. Extraordinary Minds offers a path to employment that's glamorous—working on movies—but is also highly competitive. "UA trains students for work they might not have heard of before, but they're almost certain to get a job right after graduating." She also sees potential for replica-tion around the country. "CNC operators are needed in every state. And right now, they need them desperately. It's a sixteen-week program, you graduate and get a job making seventeen dollars an hour or better. A lot of these students are moving off of SSI and into their own apartments. Everything changes when they can be independent like that."

Bennett also sees the wisdom in the financing model Uniquely Abled uses by combining funding streams from the Department of Rehabilitation while the community colleges donate the space they need to hold classes. "The schools are happy to host a program like this because it taps a new market. The voc-rehab money means they don't have to spend all their time fundraising."

Extraordinary Minds has been able to fundraise enough in order to stay independent and focused on the mission that Bennett began with, but she also concedes that the nonprofit model may be too onerous to keep up in the long run. Their work doesn't come cheaply. "We chose to forego government funding—that was a conscious decision—but it means we have to go out and raise three million dollars a year, which is no picnic. I don't know if it's sustainable going into the future. We might need to find a balance."

In this way, Uniquely Abled is following a path established almost two decades ago when Erin Riehle started Project SEARCH, the longest-running and arguably most accomplished vocational training program for people with IDD in the country. Riehle, a nurse at Cincinnati Children's Hospital, got the idea when she noticed that her hospital frequently treated teenagers with disabilities but never employed them. She discovered that the greatest barrier to employment was the "hard skills" that they rarely learned in school—using a scanner for inventory, loading dollies, operating sterilizing equipment and floor buffers. The list of these skills went on and on, so she came up with a proposal: What if a group of students with IDD spent their final year of high school working at a hospital?

The core principles of Project SEARCH are simple. Interns are given substantive work, not fluffy, make-work tasks. They learn inventory skills, not just how to use a paper shredder, for example. They must train long enough to see if they can reliably succeed in the job and, in the course of what is usually a year-long internship, they must rotate through three different departments so they can make an informed choice on which area interests them most. Every Project SEARCH program is composed of a teacher who oversees the team, a skills trainer who instructs interns on job-related tasks, a department manager who will write a letter of recommendation, and a job developer who will help the intern find a job after completion. It has expanded across a wide spectrum of employers—banks, hotels, universities, manufacturing plants, and most recently amusement parks. By having interns spend the whole day at the job site (one to two hours of class time, four to five hours of work) the students also learn hard-to-teach soft skills like hygiene, social skills, conflict negotiation, punctuality. In the two decades since its inception, Project SEARCH has developed programs in over three hundred sites around the country, and 70 percent or more of Project SEARCH interns will obtain competitive, community-based jobs before graduating, or in the first year after.

One of the core tenets of Project SEARCH is that they aren't pretending to meet everyone's needs. They're here to teach people to *work*. Participants are not coddled; they must learn the rules that all employees abide by: productivity and professionalism. Coworkers need to see your contributions first, not your needs. The expectations are high but with them comes greater potential for growth, coordinators say. For the interns, higher expectations means more pride, more trust, and greater job security. It also means not every student with IDD is an appropriate fit, and not everyone will make it through the program. Candidates are screened carefully to find the ones with the highest chance of succeeding.

Like Uniquely Abled, Project SEARCH relies on a collaboration between multiple service agencies for their funding stream: the school system supplies a classroom teacher, a vocational rehab agency supplies job coaches, the employer donates mentors and classroom space, and a local DDS agency provides ongoing vocational support after the program is over. Project SEARCH gives each agency a role and a stake in the outcome and, at the same time, helps parents learn about navigating the byzantine bureaucracy of adult services.

An equally important part of their mission is teaching employers what people with IDD are capable of. Even for me, it's an eye-opener to visit a Project SEARCH site in Ronald Reagan Hospital at UCLA and see a young man with Down syndrome working an inventory scanner on a loading dock, and another navigating a cart full of heavy boxes down a crowded hallway. The employers who have hosted Project SEARCH programs say this is a reliable labor pool with low turnover, attention to detail, and something many have a hard time putting words to, though they all try: "They appreciate this job and they work hard to keep it," one employer told me. "It improves the morale of everyone around them."

The main downside to Project SEARCH is that, by its careful design, most work sites can only handle intern groups of approximately twelve, which means there aren't enough spots for everyone. Maria Ortiz, vice president of PathPoint, the agency that partners with Project SEARCH and runs the program at Reagan Hospital, tells me that it has been challenging to scale up in an impactful way. "Mostly the issue has to do with space, not with the people we're offering as interns. We need a designated room to use as a classroom. Some employers don't want to make that commitment for nine months. But we're getting more hotels on board. I'm also looking into starting something at the amusement parks. I feel pretty optimistic about that. Usually this program works best when someone at the top is really invested. Maybe they have a family member or they know the problem and they really want to help."

Virtually every entrepreneur I spoke with has marveled at the transformation they've seen in their employees and has looked for ways to expand. "You get hooked," Bill Morris told me. "You just want to go around the country and tell people: Look, this works. This changes lives." But they also all expressed a similar frustration as Tom D'Eri: "Okay, with my two car washes, I can offer jobs to eighty-five people with autism—but what about the other half a million sitting at home? I think about that a lot." Yuri Bennett told me, "Our program works great for the people here. But it doesn't solve the massive problem we have around this country."

As vice president in charge of Walgreens' distribution centers and the father of a son with autism, Randy Lewis was in a better position to change more lives than most. He initially got the idea of hiring summer employees with IDD while his son was in high school. He knew the online applications that asked for past employment, and that often included judgment questionnaires along with reading and math tests, wouldn't work for this crowd. Instead he started an intern-to-hire process, providing potential employees a hands-on chance to learn the tasks they'd need. If they could do them, they were hired. When it came time to build a new distribution center in Williamston, South Carolina, he began talking about tailoring it to workers with disabilities. "I felt like Chuck Yaeger, breaking the sound barrier," Lewis remembers, about going before his company's board, to convince designers, architects, managers, and employees to go along with his idea. Not only had this never been done by a major national company, it hadn't even been talked about before. The stakes were high. The board of directors reminded him: this was a business, not a charity. "Business is all about customers, product, and profit. It's not designed to take care of people, but to offer people a chance to take care of themselves."

Ultimately, Lewis's passion for the idea convinced them. The board committed to hiring people with disabilities as one-third of the employee pool, in order to provide "natural supports." Ultimately, it came down to determination and flexibility, Lewis believes. "We hired people and then figured out how to structure the job and/or the work site so they could do it." There were bumps along the way. Warehouses are fast-paced, complicated operations where time is money and speed is essential. They couldn't afford slower results or sloppier service and, at first, this happened—with many backlogged orders full of mistakes. The company adapted its HR policies, allowing an employee with a disability to bring an advocate to counseling sessions if they needed help understanding an issue. Lewis decided, "When a rule gets in the way of achieving success, let's go with what we are trying to achieve. We call that 'managing in the gray.'" He also discovered that he needed to let employees be themselves. "I don't think it's ever going to work to get these folks to look and act as neurotypical as possible. I don't think that should be the goal. The goal is teaching them the job and helping them succeed at it."

After making these adjustments, the results exceeded even Lewis's dreams. He echoes what other employers have said. Absenteeism went down, as did safety costs. "It's a workforce that shows up the day after Super Bowl and the first day of hunting season. We learned that performance comes in all different packages." Within the first year, managers at the South Carolina distribution center reported similar experiences as Bowen and Marco at Blue Star. Coming up with creative ways to accommodate employees who work differently at times, but are also dependable, conscientious, and happy at their job builds a greater sense of camaraderie among the overall workforce. In other words, when workers with disability set the tone of a company, that tone is palpably different.

....

At each site I visited, I started out thinking, *Ethan probably couldn't do this.* But by the end of the day, I'd met one or two workers who reminded me enough of him that I changed my mind. *Maybe he could,* I thought, over and over. *Maybe he could.* Every employee working an inventory scanner and steering a U-boat down a hallway paves the way for many more.

For parents who've trained themselves to narrow their dreams to a handful of possibilities that seem realistic, it's a thrill to add half a dozen jobs to the list. But for most of us, there is still a long road ahead. In our area, we have no Blue Star and no Rising Tide. Even Project SEARCH, which has satellite programs in almost every state, doesn't yet have one in Western Massachusetts. Does this mean every parent of a child with IDD will need to be a budding entrepreneur to ensure a productive life for their son or daughter? Hopefully not—though I suspect for the time being, they will need to be a fighter. When I return from my travels, I'm heartened to discover that an old friend from Ethan's preschool days, David, who also has autism, has been working for almost a year doing electronic recycling in Fairfax, Virginia, for a company that worked primarily on government contracts. I call his mother, Jenny Koprowski, to find out more. She tells me he loves the work and his team, but about a year after they started, the whole work-force was laid off due to a change in the federal policy on hiring proto-cols. For six weeks, the team has been attending a day program as their parents fight to get their contract reinstated. "All they do is sit at desks, miserable," she tells me. "They just want to get back to work." With the help of local legislators, Jenny and her husband, Dan, have put a bill before the Virginia General Assembly that will include language in gov-ernment contracts favoring companies that hire people with disabili-ties. As the largest single employer in the country, this feels like a commonsense way the government can help.

"The first job David and his team did when they started this work was taking apart all of Maryland's old voting machines," Jenny tells me. "There were thousands of them and they all had to be unscrewed and broken down, piece by piece. The government has tons of work like this and these people could be their best employees to do it. They just have to give them some preference in hiring because these aren't guys who are going to do great in interviews."

Later she sends me a video clip of David wearing headphones and working with the same fierce concentration as the employees I saw at Blue Star. Jenny was a powerful advocate back before our children even started kindergarten. In the days when I could hardly bring myself to tell anyone about Ethan's diagnosis, she wore T-shirts emblazoned AUTISM MOM. She taught me a lot about fighting for better services, and she's still doing it before the Virginia legislature.

I suspect this is how it will happen, as it always has—one battle at a time, waged on behalf of one young adult who will, by doing their job, open doors for hundreds of others to walk through behind them. As I watch the video of David at work, I think, *Yes—this will happen. Slowly but surely, change will come.*

O f course, employment isn't the only challenge that young adults leaving their school services will face. There's also the matter of living independently, having friends, a social life and a community, and, well—everything else. I think about the warning I got from Julia's mother just as Ethan entered high school. *Make sure he has a life before he graduates!* Every parent of a child in transition services will hear some version of this. *Get ready for the cliff! Put all the pieces in place before they turn twenty-two!* But no one answers this question: How exactly are you meant to do this?

When Ethan was still in preschool, I did many things wrong—I pretended his development was on track for far too long, I mitigated his issues to doctors and family. Once he was diagnosed, I tried to stage too many interventions myself—but there was one thing I did right: after he started preschool I began to meet regularly with a group of other mothers of children with disabilities. Those were the days when I ran into old acquaintances and still tried to pretend everything was fine. With these mothers, though, it was different. We shared a certain shorthand and we'd learned to seek each other out for playdates that wouldn't be politely refused. With them, I discovered that being honest about Ethan's delays was infinitely easier than maintaining the pretense that everything was okay. Sometimes we cried together, but more often we laughed. About the doctors who diagnosed our kids (I trotted out our chestnut about the *Rain Man* doctor), about the therapists we spent more time with than our husbands, and even, at long last, about our kids and their funny quirks.

"He's obsessed with railroad crossings," one friend would exclaim. "He doesn't really care about anything else. So we plan our whole day around when we'll park ourselves at a railroad crossing and watch the train go by. If we miss it—" She'd laugh. "Well, we never miss it. We don't really have that much else to do."

All our kids had these passions by then: for yellow trucks and sparkly pens, for Thomas the Tank Engine and Barney the dinosaur. Most of them were boys and most of them loved anything with wheels, so we all filled our days with outings that looked crazy and pointless because they were. Parking at construction sites to watch payloaders fill up with dirt, visiting fire stations once a week or more. When a child has been inconsolable through much of his infancy and is a hard-to-reach toddler and a mysterious preschooler without the same language his peers have, these passions are an essential clue to the monumental mystery of who he is. You do it because you love to watch his face staring at something he loves.

But it's also lonely. Especially if you never cared much about trains or dump trucks.

We talked about our children but we also talked about other things, like the jobs we'd given up after they were diagnosed. Meeting up with them sometimes felt like visiting our old selves, women who'd once had ambition and careers; mothers who never thought motherhood would define us so completely.

The first time Carrie McGee, one of these friends, mentioned her idea of starting an after-school center for children with special needs, I assumed she was wishing for impossible things the way we all did. If only there was a Starbucks next door to the office park under construction. Or a café combined with a trampoline park so we could relax while our kids tired themselves out. We were all sleep-deprived and obsessed with getting our children across the next milestone. Who had time to work on something more?

Carrie kept at it though, over a long, lonely winter. On chilly play-dates at the park, she'd fill in her vision. "It'll be like a community cen-ter. where we'll offer classes. Our kids can get movement therapy and we'll combine it with social skills. Maybe we can offer other classes, like art and music. And parents can sit in the lobby and talk to each other!"

I had to admit, that last part sounded nice. Eventually I agreed to go to one planning meeting and then, a few weeks later, I went to an-other. A few more people joined us: an older neighbor who'd once worked as a physical therapist at Belchertown State School, a gymnastics teacher who was terrific with our children and interested in the way gymnastics could help them organize their bodies. Carrie nudged us all along by doing the lion's share of work, finding a place to rent and get-ting estimates on the repair work it needed. When she applied for non-profit status and received it, the dream began to seem more real and we all started to share her idea that creating something productive and communal might be better than spending more time at home, alone with our children.

For me, the biggest revelation of starting Whole Children in 2004 was how many families emerged, seemingly from nowhere, to enroll their children. In our first year, we served thirty-two students; by the end of the second year, that number had quadrupled. Some families came with siblings in tow, some drove over an hour each way. Early on we made a point of introducing ourselves to everyone in the lobby, but after a time, there were too many, and we realized we didn't need to. They were talking to each other. Bonds were being formed and friend-ships made, for our children and for ourselves.

Our instinct that we could serve more children if we invited their parents and extended families to help—to join us in fundraising, on committees, teaching classes—turned out to be a smart one. We were building more than a place to take classes, we discovered; we were cre-ating a community. Andrew Solomon describes the powerful connection between families of children with disabilities as worlds "animated by such a fierce sense of community that I experienced pangs of jeal-ousy. ... Having a severely challenging child intensifies life. The lows are almost always very low; the highs are sometimes very high. It takes an act of will to grow from loss . . . but even as the downside wears you thin, the upside keeps on giving."

For me, Whole Children embodied this upside that keeps on giving. A place where Ethan could be himself and I could gradually shed the carapace I'd been wearing for most of his early childhood. Talking honestly about your child's deficits means you have a group to celebrate with when he overcomes one—a small audience who will give a standing ovation when he's finally out of diapers around his fourth birthday and again at age eight, when he masters a somersault.

Like so many other parent-initiated start-ups that I've visited, we began with the intention to go without government funding (or interference), but in our fourth year we saw the writing on the wall. To meet the growing demand for classes, we would need to raise four times what we had in the past. Our only option was pursuing financial assistance from the state. We filled folders with glowing newspaper articles, nervously laid out a tray of pastries, and invited legislators to visit our site and see what we were doing. We made our presentation to five state representatives who didn't touch the danish but were receptive to what we were doing. A few weeks later, we met with Bill Zimmer for the first time, regional director of what was still called the Department of Mental Retardation at the time. Though he politely flipped through our folder of materials, he was more interested in looking around and watching the classes in progress. He also wanted to talk to parents in the lobby, to shake hands with the teachers and volunteers. He knew what questions to ask and what to look for. At the end of that first visit he said, "I like this program. I like that you incorporate families and bring in so many outside volunteers. I like that this is a place people *want* to come."

He allocated a small amount of money to us that year and a little more the next. Every year he came back and made suggestions based on what he thought we were doing right. "You're using college student volunteers as mentors—it's wonderful!" he'd say. Sure, we thought. We have a dozen colleges in our area, many of which offer special-education programs for teachers. Of course we used those students.

"But you have young children volunteering, too! And grandparents!" These, too, seemed obvious. Retired teachers called us up, offering their time. Siblings volunteered because they liked being teacher helpers.

By the time Zimmer retired in 2012, Whole Children had grown into a multifaceted program that served six hundred individuals and their families annually, thanks in large part to his guidance and assistance. Before leaving, Zimmer found enough department money to help Whole Children move to a new location, four times the size of our original site. At his retirement party, held at our new site, he got a little dewy eyed. "This project was the most important thing I oversaw in my thirty years at the department," he said to the assembled group.

At the time, the group of founder-mothers looked at each other, a bit stunned. *It was? Our small center, created so we'd all have some place to go and feel less lonely?* As successful as Whole Children has been, I never understood why it was so important to him until I watched the documentary about the closing of Belchertown State School. My breath caught to see a thirty-years-younger Bill Zimmer on the screen, describing the Herculean job he'd been tasked with: finding homes for the residents who'd been institutionalized for most of their lives. In all the time we knew him, he had never once mentioned having had this job. But watching the documentary helped me understand why he loved Whole Children.

There was a glimmer of it in his eye the first time he visited our site. I remember him using the word "community" a lot, as well as the gist of what he said: community doesn't magically happen. It must be created. It must involve a sense of purpose, a collection of people working together, with everyone playing a part. The strongest communities make room for the widest variety of people. It must welcome everyone and must be a place where people *want* to come.

He knew what the absence of community had looked like and had too many memories of how misguided state care for this vulnerable population can go. He'd spent his whole career looking for solutions to a problem that money and power had not yet solved. "How do you build a community?" he explained to me later. "It doesn't just happen and the state can't buy it. It starts with families, reaching out to other families. Working together to create something bigger than any of them could have imagined or done on their own."

After Whole Children received state support, we began to think bigger. Our children were about eleven years old at the time—we felt energized and empowered, like anything was possible, even setting up a residential community. Carrie suggested taking a trip to Copake, New York, home of one of the longest-running Camphill communities in America.

The Camphill movement began in 1940 when Karl Koenig, a Jewish pediatrician, fled Austria along with a small group of children with IDD who the Nazis were targeting. A longtime follower of Rudolf Steiner, who argued for the sanctity and perfection of all human life, Koenig wanted to create a community that would not only protect these children but would demonstrate their value. From the beginning, his mission statement has had an extraordinarily contemporary feel, emphasizing acceptance over cures and society's need to develop accommodations for this group. Though their model depended on the commitment of a large number of families, teachers, and volunteers to support their community, they survived and eventually flourished. Today, there are over one hundred Camphill communities in twenty-three countries around the world.

After spending a day touring their beautiful grounds and talking with people who lived there, we all agreed: *anything is possible, except this.* How could we hope to recreate the bucolic setting, acres of rolling farmland dotted with charming cottages and winding roads wide enough for two golf carts to pass? The wooden street signs were hand lettered, the two work sites we visited—a seed sorting area and a weaving studio—were cheerful, light, airy spaces with artwork and crafts on the walls and workers engaged in their tasks. We shot each other looks as we proceeded through the tour. I could tell what my friends weren't saying: *Where would we find the millions it would take to pay for all this?* We knew about start-up costs and how hard we'd had to lean on friends and family just to pay for our early rent and renovations. This was six hundred acres, with the capacity to house 240 residents with and without disabilities.

The place had a certain international flair as well. Aside from the development director who took us on the tour, every assistant spoke with a European accent. At the textile studio, I asked where they were from. Germany in most cases, but not all. One family was from Denmark, as I recall, another woman from Sweden. They'd read Rudolf Steiner in school, a few explained. They believed in his teachings and, well, here they were. Another woman told us that she'd grown up in a L'Arche community and Camphill felt like home. It was a way to travel the world and live in different places for a year at a time. She loved the work, loved the people. "You can travel to foreign places and these communities feel very familiar."

I remember her saying this because I remember thinking, *To you, maybe, but not to me.* To us American suburbanites, it all seemed too idyllic and serene to be true, like permanent summer camp with outrageously good craft stations and the world's nicest counselors. On the ride home we talked ourselves out of hatching any real plans to expand our work into a residential setting. Our takeaway was that to create such a community, you had to have a guru with a following so loyal they'd give up their ordinary dreams—a home, a few cars, an IRA—and agree to live instead with our kids. Maybe in Germany it's easier to find people willing to make those long-term sacrifices, but we didn't know anyone like that. By the time we arrived home, we'd abandoned the idea altogether.

Twelve years later, I dig up the material we took away that day and it breaks my heart a little that we gave up so quickly. Two years ago, Maggie Rice, one of the mothers who was with us on our Camphill tour, revisited the idea of trying to start a residential setting for her son Cade, who is about Ethan's age and has Down syndrome. She lived in Northampton, Massachusetts, on an acre of land she wanted to sell, with neighbors on both sides who were interested in selling, too. She wanted to build a community of tiny homes that could be sold, affordably, to the general public and to families of adults with IDD. She didn't get too specific in her early planning because she wanted to leave room for families to decide what it would look like and how it would work: some residents might need a caretaker roommate, but some would not. There might be designated communal areas, but nothing too fancy. No swimming pools or gyms. Just a vegetable garden, walkable access to town, and an agreement that neighbors would look out for each other. Virtually every family she reached out to came to her planning meetings.

"This would be my first choice for housing," a mother told her. One family promised help with investing in upfront design costs. "This is the only option that makes sense to us," the father explained. "We want to see it happen." Another mother told her, "I really need this to happen. I've looked at everything else and I have no other options."

She solicited help from a development company that specialized in housing for people with disabilities and held two more meetings for families and other interested parties. Her living room filled with ten eager sets of parents and individuals hoping to secure one of her tiny homes. All said this would be their first choice for their child. There were still no building plans, no funds procured, no designs approved, but it was the best, and most viable, option they saw. But the second meeting ended on a discouraging note. Given the strict regulations in Massachusetts that oppose clustered housing for people with disabilities, there was no model to follow. The intention was integration, but would this be like cohousing? Or a retirement community? Nobody was sure. Cohousing sounded right—independent living with shared aspects; a community house or a center where residents could gather, but each person would have their own house with a kitchen, bedroom, and a bathroom. Our county in Western Massachusetts has supported four cohousing communities for two decades, so we weren't without precedent.

Then we hit the snag. "Who would live there with them?" the developers asked.

"We'd sell half the units to the general public and half the units to our families."

"But what about—?" one mother started to say and stopped. I knew what she wasn't saying. We know our children and the patience they require. The endless questions, the meaningless conversations, the fixations, the self-talk, the need to explain things over and over. Would a stranger buy a house that included a bunch of neighbors with all that baggage?

I went home from the meeting, did a little research and discovered that some disability housing developers are arguing—emphatically—that it is possible to market "support communities" to the general public. Micaela Connery, who describes herself as a "radical inclusionist," has gotten seed money from the Chan Zuckerberg Initiative to develop a housing model that centers on the idea that young adults like herself (she's in her early thirties) are part of the "inclusion generation," with a fundamentally different approach toward people with disabilities than the generation before, who never sat in classrooms, worked on projects, or played at recess together. She believes this familiarity means there's less fear, more understanding, and, for many, more appreciation for the benefits and joy of engaging regularly with people of all abilities. Her proposed development, called "The Kelsey" after her beloved cousin who died in 2018, will be a 115-unit apartment complex in San Jose, California, where 25 percent of the units will be reserved for residents with disabilities and all units priced below market value. There will be an on-site inclusion concierge to help residents connect with neighbors and the community. "The Kelsey's programs are for everyone because they benefit everyone. Inclusion and valuing diversity is not about helping certain people. It's about how we can all learn from each other and be better together," she argues.

In planning for what she calls a "radical community," Connery took time to visit other residential settings, in order to borrow from the best of the existing models. She loved L'Arche, but also wasn't as horrified as she expected to be when she toured one of the few institutions left in Connecticut, Southbury. In fact—like my first visit to Riverside—it was the opposite: "I wasn't expecting to encounter a music class, a dental clinic, or an accessible fitness facility. I wasn't expecting staff who had been there for thirty years and who could·recall journeying with residents (or "clients") through all the phases of their life. . . . I wasn't expecting to meet residents who seemed quite happy in their daily life," she writes.

For Connery, who has spent a decade advocating for inclusive housing, this was an eye-opener. She still believes institutions are not the answer but she wonders if focusing on avoiding congregate settings has been a mistake: "Perhaps where we're missing the boat is that we've spent so much time preoccupied with deinstitutionalization that we've failed to focus (or even hone in) on what it means to create communities, build life-giving places to live and thrive, and what we can add to the life of someone with a disability to make it a happy one." In a field where divisions run deep, Connery seems to understand how new we are to all of this and how little research there is to weigh our successes and guide us forward.

The Kelsey will be a more advanced version of what Maggie had in mind: inclusive, shared-living units, communal spaces, modest and affordable apartments. But who will underwrite development costs? Who will decide who gets to live there? What incentives will neurotypical residents have to buy units? Connery is honest about the challenges: "I think it has a lot to do with choices across all facets of life, meaningful and lasting relationships, intentional community identities, true connections to the people and places around you, and respect. The reality is that it's harder to define what you should do than what you shouldn't. . . . But, at the end of the day, that's where we need to put our focus."

For those trying to set up residential options, the biggest obstacle is often the government regulations that limit the size and numbers served to ensure that we aren't re-creating isolating, institutional housing. After half a dozen meetings with parents and developers, Maggie gave up. "It was impossible," she tells me now. "Maybe in another state it would be different, but in Massachusetts, it's not. I talked to a few people at DDS and I just got so discouraged—they all gave me a lot of reasons why this was wouldn't work. They all told me 'Watch out for this reg' and 'Watch out for that reg.' No one said anything like 'Hey, this sounds great. Let's help you make this happen.' Even when I had other parents with me, saying this was the only option they wanted for their child. They would much rather have everyone live at home with their parents than take a risk on developing any alternatives."

We might have started a thriving recreation and community center that serves hundreds, but a residential site for ten people feels impossible. This is the larger and more important question because this is the rest of our children's life and this will determine what happens to them after we're gone. We gave up because none of us saw ourselves as gurus, or capable of inspiring strangers to join us in forming a community that would support our grown children. But now that I learn more about residential options, I wonder if we didn't sell ourselves short. We thought creating a community like Camphill was impossible, but by most measures, what we were doing all along captured those ideals. In fact, I've seen these same ideals embodied over and over, around the country, at Prospect Meadow Farm, at Blue Star, at Extraordinary Minds, at places that began with a well-articulated mission and drew community in to join the work because they liked our young adults and liked working in an atmosphere defined by their differences, not one that would make them conform into sameness. Why does Zach Bowen at Blue Star call this the best job he's ever had? Why did Lorin Marco leave the pharmaceutical world to drive trucks and manage a warehouse at Blue Star? "It's these guys," Marco told me, smiling and shrugging, not sure exactly how to put it. "They love working so much and it's kind of infectious."

Sites that employ or host a largely disabled population have a disarming effect on a neurotypical visitor. At BHMA, a lobby full of greeters offers hugs and asks, randomly, what you've had for lunch. When my mother visited it recently, a new student from India bowed and asked, as he rocked on his toes and made no eye contact, "What are your plans for Thanksgiving?"

It was early September at the time. She said she wasn't sure.

"I'm not sure, either. Maybe we can spend it together." He was obviously nervous. He stared at the ceiling in the awkward silence that followed. "But probably not, I guess."

I knew what he wasn't saying out loud: he was far from home. India doesn't even have a Thanksgiving. It was confusing and he was at a loss for what to do. As it happened, my father had died about five months earlier and my mother was going to face every holiday from then on feeling adrift and unsure as well. I could see how touched she was by his odd offer. "I wish I lived closer and we could spend it together!" she said. By the end of the conversation, she took his hand and clasped it between both of hers. "It's been wonderful to meet you."

"You, too, Ethan's grandmother," he said, bowing again.

These moments don't play out once in a while, either. They happen all the time, five or six times a day. We've all worried at one point or another about what we'll do for Thanksgiving. For most of us, it happened in college or in our twenties and we remember feeling shy and tongue-tied about the matter. Surely this is a better strategy—a measure of bravery to go up to a random grandmother and fish a little.

"The gift of disability is that it cuts through the myths we weave around ourselves. It shows us that life is not about consumption, wealth, or power," Simon Duffy, disability rights activist and scholar, writes in a speech delivered at the University of Kent in 2011. "We are confronted by the needs of another human being and these needs place demands upon us and, at the same time, if we are prepared and really look and listen, we are also confronted with the real meaning of our needs: for connection, for contribution, for dignity and respect."

Creating community doesn't necessitate a charismatic leader; it depends on finding people who value these connections. Learning more about the current residential options and traveling to see them makes me wonder about this giant blind spot Mike and I have avoided discussing. For us—and I suspect for many other parents—this battle feels ominous, with uncertain goals. Living with our child sounds better than the gargantuan effort of finding an appropriate, happy alternative. On the sofa, at home, you know he's safe. After the stormy years of childhood, the peaceful balance you've found feels a little like a reward for the agony of his early years. There are pleasures to living with an adult who still writes Santa every Christmas and arranges a neighborhood Halloween party so people will stop by and marvel at whatever costume he's put together. If this sounds sad to any parents reading this, it isn't, I promise. It's a lovely reminder that your child is a bridge to kindness that you would never see otherwise. Having Ethan has taught us to take our eyes off the perpetual horizon of the future and live more emphatically in the here and now. Ethan will tell you he doesn't care where he lives in five years. He cares about what's for dinner tonight, what we're doing tomorrow, and what trip we might be planning next month. He loves pulling out our big white desk calendar with room enough to write his own activities in his misspelled scrawl: Potluk Socal; Wole Children Dance. He has taught us to string our way through a long winter, moving from one activity to another. At the end of each, he comes home, checks the calendar, and readies for the next. It's not exactly a Buddhist level of mindfulness, but it's in the arena. It's enjoying the possibilities you have before you.

In the last seventeen years, fewer than two hundred and fifty thousand people with IDD have received supports to move out of their family home. Three times that number—close to a million—live with parents or a caregiver over sixty years old. Fewer than half of those caregivers have a plan in place for where their child should go when they're not able to care for them any longer. This sounds like an unfathomably large number of people being shortsighted, but Mike and I aren't any further ahead in our arrangements.

The imperative is clear. Even if we make no immediate changes, we need to imagine what we want to see ahead. When asked, Ethan will say he wants to live "at home in my room" as long as he can. If I tentatively press further—"What if Dad and I aren't here anymore?" He'll say, "Then I'll stay here by myself." Of course this is his answer. How can he come up with any other when nothing else has been laid out for him? Yes, he sees his brothers going off to college and becoming independent but he knows, intuitively, that his dreams should be different.

There hasn't been enough research done, but what little I've found is clear: People with IDD who move out of their parents' home in their twenties live better, richer, more productive lives than those who don't.

D esiree Kameka, project leader of the Autism Housing Network, gets a little emotional when she speaks on this subject. "I can't tell you how many times I've had siblings call me up, frantic and scared, because a parent has just died or gone into a nursing home and they don't know what to do with their autistic brother. I start by asking them what state they live in and what kind of waiver they're on, and then they ask me, 'What's a waiver?' The system is so complex that oftentimes the principal stakeholders don't understand the main points they need."

In my academic town, many of my fellow special-ed parents are intelligent and well educated and still we are stymied by a system that seems impossibly byzantine, shaped by mystifying regulations that limit the options of people they serve. In the mid-1980s, as the federal government got more serious about deinstitutionalization, it began implementing a money-follows-the-person policy to ensure that individuals leaving an institution (or choosing not to enter one) would receive funding in the form of a waiver to support community-based living. The criteria around these waivers varies enormously between states, with a key point of contention being which housing options should qualify as community based. Early on, too much federal money went into overcrowded group homes that operated like the institutions they were trying to replace. In January 2014, with input from three self-advocacy groups, the Centers for Medicare & Medicaid Services (CMS) updated those guidelines by specifying housing types that shouldn't receive waiver money because they didn't promote community inclusion and individual choice. Farmsteads, gated communities, campus settings, and clustered neighborhood residences were all deemed ineligible. Though the guidelines weren't officially adopted, the suggestions had a chilling effect on every parent group or developer in the process of building any disability-specialized housing project. No investor wanted to fund a project that residents couldn't eventually use their waiver money to access. Many shut down before they got off the ground.

The self-advocacy groups that created these regulations did so with the best of intentions to address well-documented issues where group home residents weren't given choices in meaningful aspects of their life: their roommates, their schedules, their meals. They argued that federal money should only go to support true community-based residences which ensured privacy, facilitated inclusion, and allowed individuals to control their own schedule. In alignment with the Supreme Court's Olmstead ruling in 1999, which found that "congregate settings are segregation and segregation is never equal and never the goal," they also stated that the most important qualities of HCBS (Home & Community Based Services) were integration and supported access to the wider community.

These were all worthy goals. The problem came in determining which measurable factors were most important in offering people a life of their own choosing that was also as integrated as possible into the wider community. For years it was assumed that size was the critical determining factor, as institutional care deteriorated dramatically with overpopulation. Big was bad, small must be better, and thus the 2014 guidelines suggested that no group home should house more than four unrelated people. Most states accepted this as a suggestion, but Massachusetts made it a policy and stopped funding larger homes.

Julia Bascom, president of the Autism Self Advocacy Network (ASAN), one of the self-advocacy groups that helped write the guidelines, explained their stance in a speech she delivered at their 2016 gala: "We know that any time you round up people with disabilities and put them all in one place, the same thing happens. We've seen this before. We have a century and a half of history showing us that institutions, campuses, farmsteads—whatever we're calling them now (because when you line the descriptions up over time, the differences bleed away)—aren't safe. . . . Every time you take a marginalized group of people, put them together and isolate them, safety leaves the equation. Every time."

The problem with this argument is that smaller group homes offer no guarantee that residents will be safer. The same year Bascom delivered her speech, the *Chicago Tribune* ran a chilling three-part exposé on the level of unreported neglect and endangerment of adults with IDD being moved out of institutions and into group homes, identifying over thirteen hundred cases of documented harm and at least forty-two deaths linked to abuse or neglect in group homes in Illinois over the last seven years: "Residents fatally choked on improperly prepared food, succumbed to untreated bed sores and languished in pain from undiagnosed ailments. Some of the stories are unimaginably cruel: A man beaten to death for stealing cookies, a woman whose hands and feet were bound with duct tape." In many cases, the problem stemmed from inexperienced staff handling complicated issues for medically fragile people. A man missed medications one morning and later died from a seizure at work. A woman got in a bath of scalding hot water and died three days later from third-degree burns. Fingers of blame got pointed in many directions. Illinois hadn't increased reimbursement rates for group home staff wages in nine years, so even the best service providers were struggling to offer basic care. Houses intended for four residents regularly held twice that many. Food was rationed. Community outings were nonexistent. One newly transferred resident died sleeping on a moldy mattress laid out in a storage closet. At the time, Illinois ranked among the five worst states for adequately funding community options, according to studies by advocacy groups.

Unfortunately, Illinois wasn't an aberration. After James Taylor, the forty-one-year-old son of a prominent disability advocate, died in a group home when he was left unattended alone in a bathtub, the *New York Times* found that one in six of all the deaths in New York's state or privately run group homes—more than twelve hundred in the last decade—were attributed to either unnatural or unknown causes. In 2014, Gracewood, an institution in Augusta, Georgia, was cited by federal oversight agencies for repeated failure to ensure safety of 480 patients who had been moved into group homes. Over the course of that year, forty-seven of them died. That same year, the *Atlanta Journal* ran its own exposé and discovered the majority of the people being transitioned into group homes appeared to be no better off—and, in some cases, were much worse off—than when they lived in the state's dysfunctional facilities. Dispersed across the state, sometimes far from family members who might keep watch over their treatment, they had essentially been abandoned, the article concluded. "If disabled people were simply warehoused in state hospitals, as their advocates often asserted, now it is as if they have been placed in small, isolated storage units that easily elude attention."

The cash-strapped agencies overseeing group homes blame two factors: lack of money and inability to retain staff. In Illinois in 2016, the starting salary for a direct-care worker was $9.35 an hour, and staff turnover was 70 percent in group homes. "Staff turnover—it's like a cancer that affects care," said UCP Seguin of Greater Chicago CEO John Voit, who oversees a provider agency.

Amy Hewitt, director of the Research and Training Center on Community Living at the University of Minnesota, pushes back on that narrative. She says, "You will hear providers talk about the workforce crisis, and they use that word, but it's far worse than a crisis. Look it up in the dictionary—crises don't last thirty years. This is a systemic failure that we've been dealing with for more than thirty years."

The job of supporting and caring for people with disabilities is complicated and often requires managing complex behaviors and chronic medical conditions and navigating conflicts between house members. Ideally these positions should require extensive training, but most providers don't have the time or the resources to invest in educating a workforce that sticks around, on average, less than six months.

"I wish we had time to do real trainings on all the issues that come up in our work like de-escalation and conflict resolution," one agency director admits to me. "The problem is we don't. With staff turnover at just under 50 percent, we're always plugging holes and putting out fires. We need to do everything we can to retain the staff we have. One way to do that is not making them work double shifts without a choice, which is where we're at right now."

I speak with several agency directors who all ask me not to use their name. They seem torn between messages, the same way the Belchertown State School administrators once were. They want to show me what a good job they're doing with the resources at their disposal and also tell me the truth about the challenges they face. "The state needs to know how serious this problem is and Medicare needs to know, too," one says. Then she pauses to consider. "The thing is, they do know. They just can't figure out what to do about it."

Researchers project increasingly dire figures to come. With the rise in elderly living at home, the US Bureau of Labor Statistics now estimates that retirement and attrition will result in 7.8 million direct-care jobs that will need filling by 2026, and have suggested course corrections that might ameliorate the issue. All of them include raising the starting pay scale above minimum wage. If people have a choice between flipping hamburgers or helping vulnerable people through their days, it's hard to encourage them to choose the challenging, complicated latter. Doing this work well is a commitment of the heart and the compassion it requires must be rewarded in kind. Appreciation ceremonies, award dinners, and gift cards are essential for affirming the work that these employees do. But it may not be enough.

Ashley Woodman, director of the Developmental Disabilities and Human Services (DDHS) department at UMass, sees the lack of preparation as a big part of the problem. She tells me, "The status quo for staff these days is basically no training. You do have to go through some training to be a PCA (personal care assistant) but it's very administrative, about forms and logistics. They never really get substantive training on how to deal with clients. Nothing that addresses issues like supporting someone in autonomous decision-making or how do you talk to someone who uses a communication device."

In 2016, Medicare increased its state allocation for HCBS long-term support care by eight billion dollars, in part to address this issue of staffing turnover. It hasn't solved the problem. Of the four agency directors I spoke with, two admitted they are on the brink of closing group homes located in rural areas because they can't find staff willing to drive to those locations. If this happens, the residents will be relocated into emergency spots—most likely, nursing homes. This is the latest and most troubling reality of the escalating staffing crisis, a costly phenomenon of young adults with disabilities living in nursing homes. (If anyone wonders why the main character in *The Peanut Butter Falcon* is living in a nursing home at the start of the movie, this is the reason.) In Minnesota, fifteen hundred adults with IDD under the age of sixty-five are fighting against nursing home placements, and Texas is battling a class-action lawsuit brought by three thousand residents of nursing homes who transitioned out of institutions, but haven't been accommodated in group homes. Korrie Johnson, an otherwise healthy twenty-five-year-old with cerebral palsy, lives in a nursing home surrounded by people with dementia and other debilitating conditions because she can't get staff assistance to continue living in her own home. "This is no place for someone my age," she told a reporter in 2018. "I love these people, but I feel like I'm missing out on life every day that I'm stuck here."

....

The staffing crisis is a complicated one. This work frequently draws compassionate but inexperienced people and good intentions aren't enough to succeed, a truth I know firsthand. When I was nineteen, I got a job as a counselor at a camp for children with special needs in upstate New York though I had no experience. I wanted to be a teacher someday and I liked the brochure, which featured good-looking college students playing with smiling children in wheelchairs. It looked, well, fun. When

I got there and discovered that I'd be an education counselor doing one-on-one tutoring with campers to "prevent academic regression" over the summer, I sheepishly admitted to my boss that I had never taught before and she reassured me, "You don't need experience. Just get to know each child as an individual and you'll do fine."

Almost immediately, the job felt overwhelming. Some kids had academic goals they were already beyond; others blinked at me, stupefied, when I handed over a book and asked them to read. One girl with a note in her file asking us to work on math facts cried every time I pulled out a flash card. I swiftly gave up and instead, we listened to *Sesame Street* songs and clapped along. Within a week, it was clear that I was terrible at this work. Mystified by their silence and frightened of their tears, I became hopelessly awkward around the children. Other counselors could get them to laugh and cajole them into doing a little work while I struggled to fill every hour and hoped no one noticed how little we accomplished.

One of my campers was a boy with autism who never said a word. Judging by the fixated attention he paid to the window blind pulls and the tape player in the corner, I thought he seemed highly intelligent. I even wrote my parents a letter describing him: "No one has any idea what causes autism, but I think it happens when very smart babies take one look around at the world and decide they want no part of it." (This letter alone is proof that I could have used some training, or even just a pamphlet on autism.) All I remember now is how much this boy frightened me. With his darting glances and his unwavering refusal to acknowledge my presence—much less do anything I asked him to—I felt sure he understood exactly what a phony I was. Our goal was interaction so the stakes weren't high. We could roll a ball, draw a picture, anything, really, but for an hour every day, I failed at this much. I could never draw his attention away from the blinds and the buttons.

By the end of the second week, I wept every night as I replayed my futile efforts over in my mind. I soon requested a transfer to be a waterfront counselor, which, as if to confirm my worst fears, was granted almost immediately. I spent the rest of the summer feeling like a failure.

This experience haunted me whenever I met any new wide-eyed aide or teacher working with Ethan, enough that I would whisper preemptive reassurances: "It's not your fault if he has a meltdown. That just *happens* sometimes." Occasionally I'd offer what must have sounded like crazy, desperate tips: "If you click your tongue or whistle a little, it'll sometimes pull him out of a mood swing. He likes funny sounds." These were my tricks, but how was a stranger supposed to employ them in the middle of a school cafeteria with a child who was lying on the ground, refusing to budge? What would her supervisors say to tongue-clucking through a meltdown?

If the camp's philosophy came from Wolfensberger's ideas—the campers are people first, you don't need special training, just treat them like fellow human beings—I epitomized the shortfalls of that paradigm. I felt unmoored, like I was teaching in a foreign language I could count to ten in but not much else. Do you ignore a meltdown or bad behavior? Do you indulge incessant, nonsensical questions? If a child starts taking off her clothes and, when you try to stop her, bites her own hand, hard, what do you do? The questions go on and on until you finally land on this one: If you're nineteen years old-and only took this job looking for a little experience and a fun summer, how quickly can you get out of it?

I tell this story because it helps me understand why this problem of staff turnover is so intractable. The one thing I really learned that summer was that I never wanted to do this work again. Not because there was something wrong with the children but because it made me feel like there was something wrong with *me*. I look back now and can easily see the issue wasn't all me—I was offered no training or tools to fill in the gaps of my inexperience. For the most part, we didn't even know anyone's diagnosis. ("These are children, not labels," we were told, an okay philosophy until someone has a seizure midway through your lesson.) Back then, an optimistic philosophy dictated this approach. These days, workers are undertrained because training is an unaffordable luxury when three-quarters of them won't stick around more than a few months. If being unprepared sets you up for failure, we're in a doomed cycle.

To get a better sense of what direct support work is like now, especially for those working in group homes, I speak with Art Middleton,
who worked in group homes in Providence for over a decade. He was
even younger than I was when he started out as a CNA (certified nursing assistant) in a group home right after high school, supporting himself through college, and eventually becoming the manager of another
group home. The first place he worked was the most challenging, he
tells me, composed of six residents, five of whom were transitioning out
of a Rhode Island institution. "From the start, you were trained to be
vigilant about behaviors and prepared for the possibility of physical
threat," he says. He always felt badly about this because these clients
were only reflecting the history of their own treatment: "But yes, I got
hit pretty regularly. And yes, we had to restrain people." Few of his coworkers stuck around. "The longer I worked there, the more I saw them
bring in younger, more physically fit folks to do the work," he tells me.
"Unfortunately, those were also the people who burned out faster. The
younger they were, the less prepared they seemed to be for the reality of
the challenge."

Even so, he speaks well of his employer at the time, a nonprofit agency
that emphasized identifying goals for every client, usually around increasing independence and community interactions. The direct-care
staff met weekly with an occupational therapist to reinforce these milestones, which helped them recognize that even though they were working
with adults, the residents were always growing and changing. Their
work wasn't static.

It was hard, though. Community time was emphasized, but often
that meant a trip to Stop and Shop with little, if any, interaction with
anyone outside the home. "It wasn't exactly the warm, nurturing notion
of community that was probably intended. We'd try to create routines
where the person might be recognized but we didn't have very many
places to go. So we'd hope to wave to someone while they were picking
up their prescriptions. Things like that."

I quickly notice that Middleton calls the residents he worked with
"consumers." When I point it out, he laughs. "Yeah, that was the agency's

language. They were trying to emphasize professionalism. They wanted to make it very plain that we're getting paid for what we're doing and this was a business relationship."

I ask if that is a good thing when such intimate caretaking is involved. Middleton thinks so. Though it's clear from his stories that he cared enormously about the people he worked with, he recognized the need to keep these relationships professional. Otherwise, residents got overattached to staff members and then fell apart when that person went on vacation or quit. "I saw that happen a lot, especially later on, when I became a manager and watched staff come and go. I tried to warn people ahead of time about not letting people get too emotionally dependent on them. It might sound harsh, but I told new workers not to give anyone hugs until they'd been working there for a while, like at least six months." Respect and body boundaries were important to maintain—thus, consumers, not residents.

He left that work in 2011 to pursue a career in writing and teaching, but he still thinks about the people he served. As a group home manager, he emphasized maintaining professional relationships, but his reflections, in retrospect, sound anything but: "I think we do a disservice to a community of disabled individuals by preaching that our individualist society is always the goal and always the model that we need to follow. There can be something very beautiful about cohabiting space and learning how to engage in compromise. I saw someone move out from a group home, into an apartment on her own, and we saw her relationship with her self-care, housekeeping, healthy eating, everything go downhill. She had no one to hold her accountable. She would see her staff for three hours in the afternoon, but it wasn't enough—we'd arrive and she was still in her pajamas. She could do all the things she needed to do, but when she was alone, she didn't."

He sees this as a cautionary story about the goal of moving people, too quickly, into independent apartments. "There's a dialogue we might be missing about the importance of interdependence, and the sustaining impact of mutuality. We need to build a culture of care that emphasizes mindful commitment."

....

There's a coda to my disastrous summer at the camp. After I switched
from being an education counselor, I moved over to the waterfront,
where I met a pair of fourteen-year-old identical twins with cerebral
palsy. They both had learning disabilities as well, but one of them, Jonathan, was the opposite of the students who'd made me so nervous earlier in the summer. A nonstop talker and a political news junkie from
New York City, he loved to tell me stories about Mayor Koch and the
crazy things that happened in city government. He didn't like to swim,
so we often floated around in a rowboat, and lamented about the Demo-
crats' chances of winning another presidency in the age of Reagan.
Twenty years later, Jonathan showed up at a book reading I gave in
New York and asked if I remembered him. He still had a huge smile and
a funny way of talking. Of course I remembered him. He told me he and
his brother, Eric, still lived in the apartment they'd grown up in, but
their mother had moved out not long after they graduated from high
school. Though she only lived a dozen blocks away, she let them oversee
most of the major logistics of their lives. They both worked in the New
York City school system, Jonathan as an aide at an elementary school
for children with disabilities, Eric at a different school as a handyman.

Ethan was about ten years old by then and I was fascinated to figure
out how they'd managed to live so well, and so independently. I invited
them to visit us, which they've done a few times a year in the decade
since. When my kids were younger, Jonathan came up to share events
like Halloween or the Super Bowl. Most summers, he and Eric have
joined us for a weekend on our remote lakeside cabin, which puts Jonathan and me back on a waterfront, floating in boats and talking about
politics. To my relief, it also redefines my failure that summer. If we
were meant to relate with these kids, I found one to which I could, and
we've expanded each other's lives ever since. It's a friendship unlike any
other in my life: sweet, long-lasting, and occasionally exasperating, like
when he mixes up his bus schedule, or arrives with fifteen pounds of
chocolate for the kids.

But he's also given my family many memories we'll never forget, like a ten-hour walking tour of Lower Manhattan that culminated in a visit to the Ground Zero Memorial, where his friend, another school parapro-fessional, joined us. Both had been working in a downtown elementary school on 9/11. I'd never heard Jonathan talk about that day before. They each remembered needing to get a disabled child safely home, though no subways and busses were running. Both remembered pushing wheel-chairs up Broadway, navigating the crowds doing the same, unsure what their own lives would look like the next day. "I just kept thinking, I have to get this kid home," Jonathan said. It was the only time I've ever seen him cry. "I told myself, 'When he's home, I'll think about my own life and everything else,'" he said.

Before that moment, it had never occurred to me: he'd become what the world so desperately needs—a caring and committed direct support professional who was exceptionally good at his job. Certainly better than me.

CHAPTER THIRTEEN

'm now convinced that no one knows more about the current housing situation for people with IDD than Desiree Kameka of the Autism Housing Network and the Coalition for Community Choice, which is why I call her back a few times to get her to explain the ins and outs of the current situation. "Everyone keeps saying we're heading for a crisis but the truth is, we're living in the crisis already," Kameka tells me. One of her biggest pet peeves is the barriers put up by state and federal governments when a parent group proposes alternatives, as my friend Maggie did. "There should be *more* incentives for families to develop solutions so we can put a drop in the bucket of the demand that is only going to grow over the next decade," she says.

Eventually this will happen, she believes—because it has to. Group homes have long been the alternative to institutions, and for some people they are fine places to live, but when she considers likely trends over the next decade, she doesn't see much growth in group homes: "They're too dependent on a funding formula that's unsustainable and staffing that has proven too transient to offer a high level of care." The issue isn't only filling the job slots. "When people get paid like glorified babysitters, they act like glorified babysitters. There's no reason for them to go above and beyond, so they sit on their phones most of the time," she tells me. This is the reason she's seen so many parents rejecting group homes for their kids: "They might be fine with the idea and then they visit one and see the staff who'll be caring for their child and they see too much uncertainty . . . even the government is now talking very negatively about group homes."

To me, this comes as a surprise. Isn't this the hoped-for solution we've embraced for decades—smaller, more personalized, anti-institution? "Definitely not anymore," Kameka says. "Suddenly group homes have a lot of stigma attached to them, which isn't completely fair. There's many out there that do a wonderful job and have been for a long time." Her philosophy is that it's more important to protect diversity in housing choices than to swing dramatically from one model to another, which has happened a lot over the past twenty years. "I want to keep the choices we currently have and explore the new ones so that people entering adulthood have the widest number of options to choose from."

In March 2019, Medicaid rolled back the 2014 restrictive guidelines that ruled out specific congregate settings so that now the language is more general and focused on outcomes. Kameka is hopeful this will mean a change for the family groups and developers who'd put housing projects on hold for years, uncertain if individuals would be allowed to use their waivers to pay for them. Still, she's only cautiously optimistic. Every state is allowed to interpret Medicaid's guidelines on its own. So far, Massachusetts, for example, is sticking by the stricter policy—no intentional communities, no larger apartment complexes, and no homes with more than four people. In other states, though, the options have expanded considerably.

Two options in particular are growing in popularity, in part because they're more financially sustainable from the government's viewpoint. The first is called "shared living," though it goes by different names in different states. In this model, a person moves in with a family member or a roommate and, in exchange for a modest stipend, is supported as much (or as little) as needed. There's flexibility and a variety of possible scenarios here, but ideally, the support person acts more like a dependable, caring roommate than a staff member. There aren't necessarily set working hours, only the expectation that the shared-living provider will recognize what is needed and do their best to provide it. Many parents will still want stricter guidance, but I've seen enough shared-living success stories to be convinced that, with the right pairing, it works very well for some people.

When Penny Hanson was twenty-six years old and working in a disability service agency in Springfield, Massachusetts, she agreed to provide shared-living support for one of the agency's toughest challenges: Frank, a Belchertown State School resident since he was five years old. He was thirty-six at the time and had been evicted from three group homes for noncompliance and aggression. Shared living was a new concept when Frank first moved in, an ill-defined last resort when other possibilities had been exhausted. Hanson agreed to take him in for a year, on the condition that she could change her mind after that. Thirty-two years later, he remains with her still. When I marvel at this longevity, she's quick to tell me it wasn't always easy. The years of neglectful care and abuse had taken their toll. In the beginning, Frank wanted his freedom and refused to comply with basic boundaries she set. "He'd go out to bars and spend all his SSI money on drinks and cigarettes," Hanson tells me. After two years she gave him a choice: he'd have to move out unless he got a job and stopped drinking. Much to her surprise, he did both.

He has lived with Hanson through the birth and raising of her three children, and she is a firm believer that his behavior improved because she set higher expectations for him. "When he lived in group homes, he matched his behavior to the lowest common denominator. Staying with us meant he had better models. Not that my kids are perfect, but I could look at him and say, 'You're an adult. Don't act like one of the kids.'" Because he has been folded into the fabric of her family—he's gone with them on every vacation, attended every funeral, wedding, and major event—he stands as one of the best examples of shared living and community integration I know of. Yet when I ask Penny who his friends are, she laughs and says, "Oh the old guys from the group homes, mostly. I make sure he sees them once a week or so. Those are his buds." I suspect this is one of the secrets to how they've made it work. The more I talk to her, the clearer it is to me that she's maintained that high bar for him and she's also honored his needs, like helping him keep in touch with old friends and with what's left of his birth family. A few years ago, she drove him on a cross-country trip to Arizona to meet the biological sister he hadn't seen in fifty years. "She wasn't sure she wanted to see him, but I just said, 'We're coming! Get ready because he wants to meet you!' In the end, it went better than everyone expected. "Of course we only saw her for a couple of meals but still—he was on great behavior. His sister was relieved and I was proud of him and glad we did it."

Hanson has been compensated for the work she's done with Frank and the life she's helped him forge, but at a much lower cost to the state than a group home would have been. Reimbursement varies widely—most adult foster care providers receive between $700 and $1,600 a month—which means no one is getting rich doing this. Still, the money has helped supplement her income as a mostly single mom with three kids, all of whom say they benefitted from growing up in a house where Frank was loved and respected and treated like a part of the family.

Of course this isn't always the case, and for some families, shared living necessitates too much trust and too little oversight. Kameka tells me about another option that uses a twist on shared living. If families build an independent unit on their own property, they can use shared-living funding to pay a caretaker as well. Valle Dwight, a friend who lives in Florence, Massachusetts, is in the process of building an 840-square-foot two-bedroom house in her backyard. When it's finished, the plan is for her son Aidan to live there with a roommate and gain more independence skills. At some point, perhaps, she and her husband will move into the little house and Aidan can invite friends to live in the big house with him. Kameka sees more families gravitating toward this idea for a host of reasons: it guarantees that a person can stay in their home—and more importantly, their hometown—where they have a lifetime of roots. When their parents die, they won't be moved across the state to the first available bed, as often happens. It requires a significant initial investment, but it's a contained cost up front, not an annual expenditure down the line. More importantly, it frees families from the endless and stressful wait for government approval on residential funding. "With this model, you're in the driver's seat," Kameka points out. It provides a rare enough feeling, and one that helps me understand why more families are choosing this option. Many states now offer interest-free construction loans and have eased restrictions on in-law apartments and separate units because they, too, see the long-term benefit in allowing families some flexibility in caring for their family member over a lifetime.

For me, the stumbling block is imagining where parents will find the magical roommate who will patiently teach your child to cook and clean and care for himself in exchange for rent and a small stipend. Are there people with the skills and patience to do this well who are also willing to make such a commitment? "Sure!" Dwight says, without hesitation. Aidan has an older brother in his early twenties with friends who have graduated from college and are returning home, unsure what their next steps will be. Two of them have already asked about this project and told her they're willing to be Aidan's roommate. She also points out that having been part of an inclusive education program throughout his school years, Aidan has a lot of friends himself, also graduating from college and returning to town to look around for affordable housing. "If none of those work out, we'll find a graduate student," she says. In our academic town, we often talk about graduate students filling roles like this, but I've never been able to decide how realistic this is. Don't graduate students want to do things like date or occasionally host a party? Wouldn't they inevitably leave after a year or so?

Dwight doesn't see these issues as serious roadblocks. "Look, you start with some clear rules and expectations. They'll have four shared dinners a week, maybe. The roommate will provide transportation to a few activities and help in the morning. After that, we negotiate. If the person wants to have friends over, Aidan should be included, because it's his house, too. When it's time for the person to move on, we help Aidan adjust, just like he did when he got a new para or a new teacher at school."

There's a key message here: all of our options involve risk. If our children will have to adapt to other caretakers in their life, some of whom might come and go, perhaps our job is not to eradicate that risk, but to help them prepare for it. Having once thought this idea of finding a caretaker roommate would be prohibitively hard to navigate, I've discovered a two-year-old company based in Minnesota called Rumi that has been matching candidates online for two years. Individuals with a residential housing waiver can post a profile, and potential caregiver/ roommates do, too. Like other match-up sites, they can wave at each other to express interest, chat online, and meet up to see if they'd make a good match. It is overseen by Bridges, a service provider based in St. Paul, which provides background checks and helps people find apartments and iron out expectations and financial arrangements ahead of time. All caregivers in the state make about $12.50 an hour, but those who share their home pay no federal taxes. "That's a huge financial difference from a compensation standpoint that we hope will ultimately yield a higher quality of caregiver who is more experienced, more trained, more professional and more committed to staying in this arrangement for a longer period of time," Blake Elliot, vice president of Bridges told Minnesota Public Radio in 2019. The biggest difference for clients is choice. In the past, they've been offered a spot in a group home that they can accept or not. If they refuse, they go back to the bottom of a waiting list for another bed to open. Now they can take control over their housing in a proactive way. They can also decide what neighborhood they want to live in, if they'd like a pet, and agree ahead of time to their own rules—bedtimes, chore expectations, etc.

This sounds to me like movement in the right direction—especially for the families frustrated by waiting on ever-growing lists for funding of any kind. But this emphasis on support roommates raises a crucial question: What residential options are adults with IDD really looking for? Since the early days of deinstitutionalization, the assumed goal has always been independent living in an apartment of one's own, with initial support that will fade over time. Obviously, some will never achieve this goal and will stay with caretakers or in group homes, but the assumption has always been that those who are capable enough, should eventually "live fully integrated in the community." Art Middleton remembers this from working in support services almost ten years ago: "The goal was always getting people to the point where they had their own apartment and lived independently."

I have to admit, I've always been mystified by this. When Middleton describes working with a woman who moved from a group home into her own apartment only to regress on virtually every measure of self-care, I'm not shocked. So many people with IDD are social creatures and living alone can be—well, lonely. Acutely so, if you can't connect with, or regularly see your friends. Even Wolfensberger, the originator of this approach, declared, "Dumping them alone in isolated apartments around a city or town turns out to be the worst thing you can do to these folks." Without the proper support nearby, he said, people with IDD were more vulnerable, more victimized by predatory types, and more endangered by their own bad decision-making, often driven by their extreme loneliness.

Sara (not her real name) represents one example of a story I've heard many times. Often lauded by other parents as the highest functioning student with Down syndrome in her school, she was a terrific reader in elementary school and savvy about technology before any of her classmates with IDD, texting regularly with all her friends—disabled and nondisabled—throughout high school. With a passion for dancing and singing, she never missed a school event that included either activity. She was an early, passionate participant in Whole Children's Joyful Chorus and a regular at every potluck or dance party. To this day, she's the only disabled high school student I know who was offered a paid job from a school-based internship at a popular grocery store. She was a hard worker and friendly, with a sunny smile for anyone she hadn't seen in a while. After leaving school services, she kept her grocery store job and got another position working in a retail store. She moved into her own apartment and walked or took the bus to work every day. For years, I marveled at her pioneering spirit from afar and hoped she'd be an example for others to follow. Recently, though, I ran into her father and asked how it was going after three years. He said, "Yeah, that's been quite a saga. We're in the process of moving her out of that apartment."

Her mother, Jenny, thinks that in retrospect they might have jumped the gun. Sara had been on a waitlist for local low-income housing units for a year when one became available two days before Christmas. They were given a week to decide. Refusing it would mean going to the bottom of the list and possibly waiting another two to four years, so they said yes. Sara didn't want to move from the home she'd grown up in with so little notice or preparation, so they worked gradually, going over to the apartment during the day, making meals and eating there, then letting her come home to sleep at night. Eventually (with some bribery in the form of treats and extra computer time), Sara began spending short amounts of time at her apartment during the day alone, which eventually led to overnights with her mom and finally on her own. Though she'd always been a social creature, she was different there, her mom tells me: "She never talked to any neighbors. Even in the elevator if someone said hello, she usually didn't answer. Maybe that came from old rules we'd made about not talking to strangers, I don't know." It was hard for them to judge who she should trust in a building full of strangers, many of whom seemed to have challenges of their own, so they didn't encourage her to be friendlier. The real problem started with the arrival of vending machines in the basement community room and escalated when local bakeries began leaving day-old bagels and pastries in the apartment complex, too. "They thought they were doing low-income families a favor, but it was huge bags of pastries laid out for anyone to take!" her mom laments.

Within a year a half, Sara went from 160 pounds to over 200. A host of medical issues accompanied the weight gain. Her parents pleaded with the building management and then with the bakeries, to suspend the daily cornucopia of free carbohydrates, to no avail. They signed Sara up for weight-loss programs, but nothing worked. Eventually, they realized the uncontrolled eating and the weight gain was the manifestation of a deeper problem. "She was brutally lonely. Yes, she had two jobs in the community, but even when she was working, there wasn't enough interaction with other people. She'd become self-conscious, even with old friends from school. She'd see them at the grocery store, and wave hi but she wouldn't have a conversation." By then, they'd gotten her more paid support—twenty hours a week—to take her to activities and help her with chores. But these aides weren't real friends, Sara knew, they were people who got paid to stop by and spend time with her. It felt different. They were also unreliable and sometimes she would wait around all day for someone who never showed up, exacerbating the larger issue, which was having too many hours with nothing to do, alone in her apartment.

After three years, they discussed it with Sara and decided as a family: she tried independent apartment living and it didn't work. When Sara describes her ideal living situation now, it sounds to her parents like an intentional community. She wants her friends nearby, and places they can get to easily, walking or by bus. She wants to be able to make her own decisions, but she wants people she knows nearby to help her do so. Her parents are working on this—initially they were part of the group of parents offering to help Maggie develop her tiny-house project. Now they have found another group investigating the possibility of starting a L'Arche community in Western Massachusetts. Eventually, they want to find or develop a community where Sara would have friends to socialize with nearby. For now, they've agreed to a shared-living arrangement with a woman Sara likes. She'll be farther away from her parents but closer to BHMA. She has never taken classes or participated in programs there, but she's hoping that the proximity will help her come out of the shell she's developed.

Unfortunately, I've heard many tales like this. In *Next Stop*, a memoir of her autistic son's transition to adulthood, Glen Finland describes his experience with a program in southern Florida that promised to teach independent living skills by starting students from day one in their own in a rented apartment. When they dropped their son David off, the program director told the gathered anxious parents that now was the time to take off the training wheels. "Allow them to make mistakes—because they will—and then let them become the problem solver," he said.

Finland and her husband tried to follow that advice, but from the beginning there were problems. For the first few months, David lived on boxed cereal until he finally called home to ask how to get water hot enough to heat oatmeal. In one terrifying episode, he called to say a nice man had offered to drive him to the Everglades and he was in the car now. David survived those tests, but not the longer-term one. The classes were too challenging, he never figured out how to do laundry, he got fired from all his job placements. They finally decided the program wasn't working. As they packed his belongings into the car, his mother overheard a young girl next door tell her mother, "Do you see that? The retard is moving out." David left without saying goodbye to anyone and slumped in the car "like someone had let the air out of him," leaving his mother to wonder how many times he'd been victim to some other "casual crime against his spirit, other careless moments we would never hear about. Where does that pain go?"

These are the stories I hear most often, where the crux isn't abuse, exactly, but distance and suspicion that amount to cruelty. When people with disabilities so often have no choice but to live in low-income or subsidized housing full of families struggling to make their own ends meet, why do we suppose the neighbors will have the time to be kind?

"Autistic people are very social," one dad told me, as if I might not know this already. Ethan is indeed social—and can be painfully awkward in his attempts to express this. The father went on: "They just need help socializing. You put them alone in an apartment with a staff person who stops by for a few hours a day, you have a recipe for the worst loneliness imaginable."

....

The battle over what should define the best community-based residential settings is, if anything, even more vitriolic than the battle over sheltered workshops and employment. Policy makers and disability advocates have often insisted that integration is the best measure of success, while parents have pushed back and asked the officials to consider other metrics: interaction with neighbors, social opportunities, general health and well-being, even (gulp) happiness. Many parents have instinctively gravitated toward the idea of intentional communities without being entirely sure what it means beyond what we've been doing for our children all along—surrounding them with people who accept them as they are and want to be with them.

Author Michael Bérubé inadvertently stepped into the middle of this heated debate in 2016 when he published an op-ed in *USA Today* titled "Don't Let My Son Plunge off the 'Disability Cliff' When I'm Gone." Bérubé is a professor at Penn State and the author of two wonderful memoirs about his son, Jamie, who has Down syndrome, that focus on the ways having a child with cognitive disability has made him reassess his ideas about intelligence. He wasn't trying to stir the pot with his op-ed. "I was just a parent, pointing out that the residential options for young adults with IDD are shockingly limited," he tells me. Jamie was twenty-four when Bérubé and his wife, Janet, started looking more seriously at group homes, shared living, and supported independent living. None were a good fit for Jamie, who is social and independent in certain ways, but with more needs than many might assume upon meeting him. Group homes had too many rules and restrictions (curfews, bedtimes, limited family visiting, and vacation hours); shared living was too dependent on finding the right match; and independent living with support would require too many staff hours to be financially sustainable. "He wouldn't need help all the time, but when he needed it, he'd really need it, right there on the spot," Bérubé tells me.

When the whole family visited Camphill in Kimberton, Pennsylvania, they finally saw a feasible model that answered many of these concerns: built-in support close at hand, provided by people who've chosen to live in a shared, mutually supportive arrangement. "Because these communities involve long- and short-term volunteer coworkers who live in the villages, rather than rehabilitation professionals on work shifts, they integrate people with intellectual disabilities into communities in meaningful ways, twenty-four hours a day, seven days a week," he wrote, concluding—innocently enough, he thought—with a supportive plug: "It takes a village to keep Jamie and other young adults with intellectual disabilities from falling off the cliff. We must nourish and support these social arrangements; they are a powerful social good."

The backlash was immediate. Sam Crane, legal director of the Autistic Self-Advocacy Network (ASAN), explained in a response to Bérubé's piece in *NOS Magazine* that intentional communities may sound great, but by serving dozens or even hundreds of people on a self-contained campus, they are missing the goal of deinstitutionalization: "They are not really integrated or community-oriented at all. . . . In practice, they tend to be very isolating. They're designed so that people have no need to leave the campus on a daily basis except on group trips—people have their job, health care, and daily activities all clustered into the same campus. We're not opposed to people with disabilities choosing to live with other people who share common values or lifestyle preferences. What we are worried about is when people set up segregated, campus-style housing for people with disabilities under the guise of creating a 'community.'" Denise McMullin-Powell, an advocate with Delaware ADAPT, a disability-rights organization, put it more emphatically in the same *NOS* piece. "In these communities, staff are the only neurotypical people who live there. And neurotypicals are always in charge."

Kameka has been living on the front line of this battle for years. These disability advocates have worthy points, she says, but, like many of the parents she works with, she feels that there is practical side they are missing. "We're living in a post *Bowling Alone* society," Kameka says, citing the 2000 book by Robert Putnam. "Whatever the mythical idea of 'community' once meant—backyard barbecues and neighborhood get-togethers—doesn't really exist anymore."

Putnam's book became a bestseller and cultural phenomenon because it used extensive research by social scientists to examine a truth many people felt: Americans' civic engagement had dramatically deteriorated over the last two decades. People volunteered less and belonged to fewer organizations. Hand in hand with this trend was a diminished sense of community: people hosted fewer dinner parties, knew fewer neighbors, socialized less.

Putnam compares our current decline in civic engagement with the end of the Industrial Age when a sharp rise in immigration and urbanization carried most of society away from their villages and family roots. Between 1870 and 1900, America evolved from a rural, traditional society to an industrialized, urban nation with unprecedented wealth disparity that divided the nation into economic factions: "It was, in short, a time like our own, brimming with promise of technological advance . . . but nostalgic for a more integrated sense of connectedness." Between 1900 and 1920, the Progressive Movement addressed the division between the wealthy and the poor, the natives and immigrants, by creating community-service groups that would bring people together with a shared purpose. The list of organizations founded in that twenty-year period is staggering: the Lions, Rotary, and Kiwanis, the ACLU, NAACP, and League of Women Voters, 4-H clubs, Boy Scouts and Girl Scouts, and Big Brothers and Big Sisters. This club movement swept through the country, carrying the majority of Americans into its fold and lasting until the 1960s, when the average adult still attended twelve meetings a year around civic engagement. Another phenomenon of this period was the creation of "settlement houses," where idealistic middle-class young adults volunteered to work and live in urban slums to bring education and "moral uplift" to the immigrant poor. Hull House, founded by Jane Addams in Chicago in 1889, was the first; by 1910, there were four hundred such houses in cities around the US.

Progressives battled a nation's frayed social ties by creating new ways to build connections between citizens and galvanize a nationwide sense of civic engagement. Putnam argues we must discover a twenty-first-century equivalent of the old service clubs: "What we create today may look nothing like the institutions Progressives invented a century ago. We need to be as ready to experiment as they were." He concedes that "it is not yet easy to see what the internet-age equivalent of 4-H or settlement houses might be, but we ought to bestow an annual Jane Addams Award on the Gen X'er or Gen Y'er who comes up with the best idea." Is it possible that intentional communities are that new

incarnation—bringing disparate people together with the goal of raising one group's quality of life and the result of improving everyone's
understanding of each other?

Most families I know are drawn to the idea of intentional community because it suggests an extension of what we've been doing for most
of our kids' lives: fostering activities that will help them socialize. As
many of us have discovered, while our children might be awkward at
socializing, they're good at building the connections required to create
a community. I might even argue they're better than the rest of us. I've
noticed this at virtually every site I've visited. Standing back and
watching can teach those of us who spent the last decade staring at our
phones whenever we find ourselves standing among a group of strangers. For the most part, these kids don't do that. They reach out and offer
tidbits about their day. They ask you questions about your own. They
ask for hugs and give them in return.

This winter I stood in the Inclusive Community Center lobby when
a young woman I didn't know announced, "I'm really good at making
spaghetti sauce. Do you want to hear my recipe?"

"Sure," I said, looking up from my phone.

"I add a can of pumpkin to Ragú."

"Okay." I smiled and then I thought about it for a moment. I couldn't
tell if it was an awful idea or a brilliant one. "A whole can of pumpkin?"
I asked.

"Yes. Depending on your jar of Ragú."

"A big jar?"

"Big. Yes."

"Do you add anything else?"

"An onion if you're in the mood."

"What about garlic?"

"No. Definitely not. Maybe some herbs."

Suddenly it felt like we were neighbors exchanging recipes for Jell-O
salad. "I'm going to try this."

"You should. It's good. Do you have any spaghetti sauce recipes?"

I thought for a moment. "A jar of Costco pesto? Does that count?" I was trying to be funny. I love to cook but I don't have a repertoire of spaghetti sauces. In all honesty, this is one of my better ones.

She thought and shook her head. "Not really. That's a jar, not a recipe."

This unfailing honesty is one aspect I love about the folks at the ICC. They'll be the first to let you know when your roots are showing or your fly is unzipped. It's reassuring. Once when I went to fetch a nearly untouched loaf of zucchini bread I'd baked for a potluck, hoping to sneak a few vegetables into the sea of dessert offerings, a young man caught my disappointed expression. "That wasn't very good bread, but you're a very nice mom," he said, matter-of-factly.

If community means sharing the daily contents of our lives, the ups and downs, the "I got a new shirt!" and "My dog has fleas!" no group knows how to do it better than this one. They often seem to assume the best about people, which of course can be a dangerous quality and also a disarming one. "It's strange," one mom once told me, after we'd just spent twenty minutes hearing about a young boy's Halloween plans. He was going to dress up but not trick or treat because he hated trick or treating but liked dressing up. "I often come here in a bad mood about something, and after I sit here for an hour, I can't even remember what was bothering me so much." Community engagement takes us out of ourselves. It puts our thoughts on someone else, which invariably turns out to be a relief.

In the past, I would have said this bonding happens most in the settings where folks with IDD are most comfortable, surrounded by their brethren, but I've noticed something else as Ethan moves around the wider world on his own. After all these years, he's still terrible at conversation. He loves asking people questions and walking away as they answer because he's pleased with his own words—which he'll usually repeat—and uninterested in theirs. It's a rude habit that I'm always correcting and it's not until afterward that I realize how little it matters. When we walk downtown, he fist-bumps people I've never seen before. When I ask who they are, he'll say, "That was Jenny from third grade." (*It was?* I'll think. *How did he recognize her?*) Or my favorite: "I don't know who that is, but I see him sometimes." For most of us, there are a lot of people who fit that category, and we instinctively take a wide berth. Ethan goes in for a fist bump.

He's awful at conversing and fantastic at connecting. Just like Beth Simon in *Riding the Bus with My Sister,* who gave herself the job of accompanying bus drivers on their routes for the last twenty years, Ethan has given himself a role, too. "I tell people what songs I'm listening to," he once told me when I asked if he ever talked to anyone on his trips to town. "I say they should check them out. Sometimes I tell them what shows to watch." I'm guessing that most strangers aren't reshuffling their playlists on Ethan's recs, nor are they rushing home to watch the dated '80s TV shows he's fallen in love with, either. But we could all do with more of this kind of interaction. If he's talked to someone once, he remembers and says hello the next time they pass. He spins a web with these strangers and most of them seem to know him, too. "Yo, Ethan," a twentysomething skateboarder hollers as we pass. "Hello, Ethan, it's hot today," an older woman says, down the block. And it occurs to me: maybe there's a cumulative effect when you move through the world believing you matter. Maybe suddenly you do.

Putnam wrote *Bowling Alone* in 2000, before we knew the extent to which social media would reshape our definition of community and argues that the most critical social capital emphasizes bridging across differences. In his book *Tribe: On Homecoming and Belonging,* Sebastian Junger echoes that technological advances in modern society have spawned individualized lifestyles that seem to be "deeply brutalizing to the human spirit." Families are isolated from the wider community; personal gain has eclipsed collective good. He quotes anthropologist Sharon Abramowitz, who says, "Our tribalism is to an extremely narrow group of people: our children, our spouse, maybe our parents. . . . Our fundamental desire, as human beings, is to be close to others and our society does not allow for that." In her estimation, society is at its strongest—and best— when the collective livelihood is threatened and individuals rise to the challenge of helping, and even saving, the strangers around them. "The earliest and most basic definition of community—of tribe—would be the group of people that you would both help feed and help defend. A society that doesn't offer its members the chance to act selflessly in these ways isn't a society in any tribal sense of the word; it's just a political entity that, lacking enemies, will probably fall apart on its own." Have we lost our sense of collective responsibility because we haven't been offered enough opportunities to participate in it? Could intentional communities—which ask for a sizable commitment but perhaps offer an equally sizable reward—be one avenue for reclaiming it?

Intentional community is a broad term that could be applied to many models that already exist, from retirement villages to cohousing to student co-ops, where residents don't necessarily have any legal or financial obligation to each other, just a commitment to actively participate in caring for and planning their community. Many do establish expectations—of shared meals, committee participation, meeting attendance—but this varies. Opponents of the concept for people with IDD fear that it's simply renaming a slide backward into institutional settings, but many parents see it as a way to expand their child's world that narrowed so dramatically when they turned twenty-two and left school services.

By a looser definition, intentional communities don't even need to be residential. The work sites I visited foster community building as part of their mission. Rising Tide has regular team meetings and Dave & Buster dinners that have nothing to do with washing cars. Whole Children is now housed at the Inclusive Community Center that runs Milestones, a day program for adults, and hosts classes, camps, dances, potlucks, and other activities for all ages. If community means a place where people feel a sense of belonging, these have achieved that and created an atmosphere that is so convivial, families and friends want to come along.

Of course, intentional communities that provide long-term residential support have taken on a bigger commitment that depends on more unknowns. Will strangers recognize the value and benefit of living with people like Ethan? If they just try it as a lark for a year or two, will enough of them stick around long term?

To get a better sense of what a long-term intentional community is like, I spent time at L'Arche Boston North, started in 1984 by three families and Sister Pat Murphy, twenty years after the first L'Arche was founded by Jean Vanier in Trosly, France. L'Arche, like Camphill, did away with the "person-fixing" approach to disability long before the term "neurodiverse" was coined. From the beginning Vanier emphasized acceptance and inclusion, ideas that are so in line with current thinking it's hard to believe they were written more than half a century ago. People with IDD are not to be cured, but supported and celebrated. Daily goals are designed around making thoughtful choices and being present—having fun together more than accomplishing tasks.

L'Arche Boston North is composed of four group homes with seventeen residents and approximately thirty-five full-time staff. The houses, nestled into historic neighborhoods in a Boston suburb, look no different from the outside than the nearby houses. Inside, they feel entirely unlike other group homes I've visited. The exchanges are more intentional, more connected, more present. Food is cooked together. Unlike Middleton's experience in group homes where clients were "consumers" and staff was encouraged to keep a professional distance, L'Arche encourages the opposite. Hugs are a regular occurrence. Relationships are prioritized above other goals, so the emphasis is on finding meaningful activities. The residents with disabilities are "core members" and all staff (including administration) are "assistants." Work shifts are called "sharing time."

Because phones are discouraged at meals and personal interactions are prioritized, I saw more one-on-one engagement between visitors, staff, and core members than I have with my own family, where some nights we're lucky if we can stretch a dinner out to fifteen minutes. Here regular times of reflection and communal prayer are built into the schedule, along with a weekly "community meeting," attended by all seventeen core members and about thirty staff. It starts with readings from each house's "squawk box"—little notes that the community leader (and director of finance) Molly LeBlanc-Medeiros unfolds and shares aloud: messages, affirmations, questions, concerns. The week I visit, the notes are about 80 percent affirmations. "I like the way Sara has been helping in the kitchen." "Ryan is really funny and great at puzzles." "Devin is an awesome pizza chef!" Afterward, the piece of paper with each affirmation is given to the recipient. From there LeBlanc-Medeiros talks about upcoming activities that all are invited to join. One group is going to see Riverdance. Another is attending an MLK Day breakfast. With each announcement, a few people raise their hands to say they'd like to go along. Clearly, having four houses with more than a dozen residents and staff exponentially widens the choices available. How can staff in a three-to-four-person home ever hope to offer outings like Riverdance, which isn't likely to appeal to everyone, but will thrill three or four?

Later, LeBlanc-Medeiros goes over an event happening that weekend, something called "Visioning Day" where residents, their families, and friends are invited to give feedback on new projects: a day program, expanded housing options, and a community space. All are exciting measures of growth and change for this community. LeBlanc-Medeiros explains that the conversation on Visioning Day will get broken up into phases: Possibilities, Cautions, Commitments. I can see the wisdom in organizing the chat with people who have a range of participation skills this way. In the first part, they'll discuss what they want to see happen. Next, they'll talk about what worries them, and finally, how they'll commit to helping. For a population that is leery of change and often hates disruption of any kind (even good ones), this will help ease a transition that will almost certainly widen their world. One woman raised her hand several times to say that she wants to be part of the new day program because she doesn't like her current one.

"Good," Vanessa Henry, the director of community life and learning, said. "You can sit at my table and tell us what you want the new day program to be like."

"I think I really want to be in this day program. I don't like my day program now."

"That's why we're talking about this. We want your input."

"I just want to be in the day program."

Though the assistants I've talked with steer clear of overt criticism of the day programs currently available, it's clear that they aren't great. I hear a lot of core members complain that they're certainly not as good as living at L'Arche. One woman tells me she worked at Costco for a while but it stressed her out so much she'd have meltdowns and have to call Anthony, one of the assistants at the house, who would calm her down over the phone. "Didn't you have someone *there* to help you?" I ask. She can't remember. "I'm not sure," she says. "But Anthony is better. He's the greatest."

Anthony rolls his eyes at this. "I'm not sure about that. I'm okay. She's better at her job than she thinks. She just has to remember that."

It's a wonderful moment and just the right message to carry her through the next stressful incident. *You're better at this than you think.* An evening at L'Arche is full of these. Assistants give their attention fully to core members, which isn't always easy to do. In fact, it's hard work, as they can be hard to understand, their conversation random and self-focused. They can also be dramatic for the sake of attention. Toward the end of the meeting, one older woman raises her hand. She lives in an apartment with her husband, the only married pair in the group. They have support a floor below, but live by themselves. "I almost slipped in the bathroom last night!" she announces to the group, apropos of nothing. It's a classic conversation starter in this crowd. *I almost really hurt myself! I was scared!* In my experience, parents usually ignore these comments while strangers sympathize. This group offers something in between.

"You should talk to Michael," another core member offers. Michael Richard is the director of residential services; he manages DDS requirements and oversees medical needs of the seventeen residents. If anyone goes into the hospital, Richard is there. He's also there, apparently, if anyone almost falls in the bathroom. After the meeting is over, he bends down in front of the woman who almost slipped in the bathroom to hear the whole story. The exchange is muffled but at the end I hear him say, "Well, I want to make sure you have enough bars to hold on to when you use the bathroom at night."

It occurs to me: when folks are given plenty of attention, there's less of these attention-getting ploys. By the end, she's reassuring him. "Oh, I'll be all right. Thanks, Michael."

For me, the most interesting thing about this L'Arche is the way they started outside the government-funded system and have navigated their way into it, by being the highest-quality, most sought after provider of group homes in the area. After about twenty years of operating on precarious budgets, using a combination of private pay money, fundraising, and community charity, this L'Arche community became a DDS-approved group home provider.

Though the history of L'Arche is steeped in a Catholic call to service, they are officially ecumenical and welcome members of all faiths, as well as atheists. Talking to the young assistants, I'm reminded of current ideas about living mindfully. When I ask what draws them to working at L'Arche, they all mention the community spirit. "It has the feel of a family, but it's a really big family," one assistant tells me. "It's also a nice family, that talks a lot, prays together, and doesn't spend too much time on screens."

Vanessa Henry echoes this. She discovered L'Arche while working as a case manager for DDS in Washington, DC, and it was unlike any other group home she visited. "Doing work that emphasizes thoughtfully helping others means being surrounded by young people drawn to the same message. They're not interested in earning big bucks, they're interested in learning to live mindfully. Most assistants stay with us for two years on average. They value this experience and say they'll carry it with them forever, just like someone who does an internship to learn a marketing skill. Here, people are learning a life skill."

....

UK researcher Maria Lyons argues that it's time for researchers to take a closer look at intentional communities like Camphill or L'Arche that have been dismissed as too segregated or too insular to be replicable on a broader scale. She believes that these communities might achieve higher levels of inclusion than any other, in fact. It may be that "they have something to teach us about what makes for a real community where people can belong, contribute and flourish." She points to the growing body of research showing that people with IDD feel isolated living in scattered apartments and believes a mistaken assumption was made early on in the process of deinstitutionalization that "a sense of place and purpose will be an automatic by-product of living an ordinary life, surrounded by ordinary people. We know that this is frequently not the case. It's very possible for people with IDD to live in communities they play no role in." Her conclusion, published by the Centre for Welfare Reform: "Intentional communities like Camphill and L'Arche offer a different set of values and priorities. Instead of trying to fit people with ID into existing norms, they demonstrate that it's possible to celebrate their differences and *create new norms*."

I know, without a doubt, that Ethan would love living at L'Arche. He could raise his hand to go on every outing and spend his evenings consulting a big wall calendar that would be much fuller and busier than ours at home. He'd collect affirmations at community meetings and go back to his room and tape them all on the wall. At some point, he might even learn to write a few about other people. Even though we've never been religious, he'd like to go to church because in his mind, that's a free concert every Sunday where you can get a good seat near the organ if you go early. The rhythm of his days and weeks would have both the novelty of excursions and predictability of routine without depending entirely on one or two staff members. But we have no L'Arche or Camphill near us and aren't likely to any time soon. The Catholic parishes in our area are struggling to survive and without them, it's hard to imagine how we'd find enough twentysomethings to join in a service mission where faith isn't required but is the mortar that holds the foundation together.

Kameka believes this doesn't necessarily have to be the case. She tells me there are a growing number of intentional communities around the country dedicated to this sort of housing without religious ethos as part of their mission. Since the rollback of HCBS guidelines, she's hopeful that more states will approve funding for these communities in the future.

Chapel Haven in New Haven has almost as long a history and—in spite of its name—no religious affiliation. It was founded in 1972 as a two-year program to teach independent living and vocational skills by parents who were looking for a small, manageable city where their children with IDD could learn independent living skills while living away from home. Initially, the assumption was that all students would return to their hometowns after completing the program. But, like at BHMA, most graduates didn't want to move home. "They'd found friends and a community here that they loved. This is still true to this day. About 85 percent of our students stay here after graduating," Michael Storz, president of Chapel Haven, tells me, along with this startling fact: all the graduates who remain in the area live in their own independent apartments. Some have roommates from Chapel Haven, but no one has a live-in caretaker or shared-living arrangement, and no one lives in a group home.

"They do get support," Storz tells me. "But on average, our graduates only require four to six hours of support a week."

Wait a second, I think as Storz tells me the litany of things graduates do on their own: sign leases, pay bills every month, cook all their own food. All with *only four to six hours of support a week*? I haven't heard a figure this low before. Most people I know who live independently get about fifteen hours to help with transportation and community inclusion. The parents I've spoken to all talk about fighting for *more* support hours. Otherwise their child is alone in their apartment with nothing to do. Even Sara, who was independent enough to take public transportation to her jobs, had this problem, too. Her parents fought for and got her twenty hours of staff time a week. The mounting health issues connected to her weight gain helped their argument: "She can get herself places but she needs *company*," they argued.

I imagine Ethan living a two-hour drive away from us, signing a lease on an apartment and writing a rent check once a month. I can't. Which makes me assume—as I have so often—that these students were more independent than Ethan to start with. "Not necessarily," Catherine Sullivan-DeCarlo, vice president of admissions and marketing at

Chapel Haven, tells me on our tour. "Every parent comes here saying their child won't be able to learn these things and they're all shocked two-years later when they see their kids doing it all: grocery shopping, cooking, navigating their way around New Haven."

On one level, Chapel Haven seems to be a perfect compromise to those who oppose congregate-living situations. The majority of their graduates have their own apartments without live-in assistance, after all. But here's the crucial difference from the independent-living program that Finland's son attended in Florida: for the first two years, students *do* live in a congregate setting. As Storz explains it, "Most folks are eighteen to twenty-three years old when they come to us and all of them need some degree of twenty-four-hour supervision at first. Our dorms are set up as apartments. We have no cafeteria, so from day one they do all their own cooking. They learn kitchen safety, grocery shopping, making healthy choices, all of that. They also learn the map of New Haven and how to take public transportation."

Doesn't congregating eighty students in a single residence put them on heightened scrutiny with Medicare? "Sure," Storz says, grinning as if he enjoyed the challenge. "I told them bring it on! I was happy to have inspectors come in and look at what we do because they won't find anything that is confining, choice-reducing, or in any way institutional in any of our programs. Period. The only thing they're going to see is all the ways that our model works better. When our adults are done with our program, they don't want to live in group homes that are spread out and five miles away from their friends. For them, that would be way too isolating. Here we have a natural community. They're all nearby, within about a one-mile radius. They can walk to visit each other. They can take public transportation here. This is the life they've chosen and we're helping them live it."

The Hub is a key component of Chapel Haven's success, a place where they can all come for classes, meals in a small café, and a community-outings program on days they don't work. Another secret is their long history of building relationships throughout the town with employers and landlords who have come to trust and appreciate their students. "Landlords love us," Sullivan-DeCarlo explains. "We bring them young people who always pay their rent on time, who won't destroy their property or have loud parties. They also know if there are smaller problems—say someone bounces a lot or paces and their downstairs neighbors complain, we can figure out a solution."

She might call these small problems but they're not really. I've always assumed that Ethan's need to pace would be a deal-breaker for most potential roommates and certainly for any downstairs neighbor. Some mornings, he's up before six a.m., hopping and skipping across the floor. I once checked his phone and discovered that he averages eleven thousand steps a day, most of those on trips from one side of our living room to the other. But Sullivan-DeCarlo assures me, "By the time our students are looking for apartments, we've had two years to get to know their strengths and what the potential issues might be. We'd look for a first-floor apartment for someone who needs to pace, or more insulating walls for a self-talker."

Parents have a hard time wrapping our minds around solutions like these. Most of us can produce a laundry list of reasons our child might drive a stranger crazy (He plays with chains! She hums constantly! He doesn't shower enough!) As much as logistics and finances, I sometimes wonder if our fear of exposing our child to the world's judgment on those quirks isn't equally a factor in keeping them at home. Hearing Sullivan-DeCarlo describe how this hurdle works in her program—*we tell people he's a self-talker . . . she sings all the time, loudly*—is comforting. They are laid out as facts, not sources of shame.

The more I look around, the more I see how the success of the independent community–living program depends a lot on the dormitory-style congregate living early on. For two years, students have learned to cook a repertoire of reliable, favorite recipes. High schools often teach cooking, but many students end up with a narrow subset of skills. They can measure well enough to bake brownies and muffins from a mix, but opening a refrigerator and assembling a dinner from what's on hand isn't on many IEPs, yet it's fundamental to living independently. Ethan recently expanded his own cooking to include quesadillas that look like a hunk of cheese balanced between two lukewarm tortillas because he doesn't have the patience to cook them long enough. But he doesn't care and it's a start. For every parent who suspects their child could cook for themselves but never does, it's an eye-opener to watch Chapel Haven students wash their hands, pull out pans, assemble ingredients, and turn burners on. Yes, there might be an eggshell in an omelet, or too much salt on a pizza (that probably didn't need any) but the important part is: they've done it themselves. Just as the world needs to see more workers with IDD in a wider spectrum of jobs, parents need to see adults akin to their own child taking care of themselves in these ways.

Chapel Haven has produced transition program graduates who need fewer support hours than any I've heard of. They pride themselves on this figure, as they should. I suspect they achieve it by offering a lot of generalized support and easy-to-access, on-the-spot support for emergencies and tight spots. I also suspect their busy calendar of recreation and community-based day program is a big help, too. By having activities all week and every weekend for students and graduates to choose from, along with regular classes and get-togethers at the Hub—movie nights, dances, potlucks, etc.—everyone has a place to come and be sure they'll find friends. The day I visit, I eat lunch in the café with about a dozen other people, a mix of current students and graduates. Some are waiting for an afternoon exercise class, others are joining the community-outing group for the afternoon. There seems to be a built-in flexibility to their programming and enough folks around that every activity has plenty of participants. Sullivan-DeCarlo thinks the Hub is what keeps so many students in the area: "We have 185 graduates living nearby and most are here at least once or twice a week. It's a way that we can all check in with each other and touch base. When they come for their yoga class, they can tell us how their week has been and what's going on."

This also addresses an often overlooked problem. Chapel Haven has an impressive track record for placing graduates in community-based jobs, but most of these positions offer ten hours a week or less—anything more would threaten their social security income and their Medicare coverage. Working two or three half days a week is okay for most of these employees, but it leaves them with a lot of empty, unstructured time. For Sara, even having two part-time jobs left her with too much time alone to fill with the comfort of food. The buzz of activity around the Hub keeps everyone engaged. Twenty-four-hour emergency staffing is available to all graduates, but Storz says they use it less than you'd think. Most of their calls are about lost apartment keys (they keep copies at the office). Graduates also call if they're feeling sick and the nurse goes through a checklist to figure out how serious it is. Most of the time they just need someone to tell them how much Tylenol to take but if it's anything more, someone stops by and makes sure the person gets to a doctor.

Currently, CMS won't pay for their transition program, which costs about $65,000 a year. Most students get their tuition paid for by their school or their parents or some combination. Storz wishes CMS would take a longer view of what is a comparatively modest expense. "How many hundreds of thousands of dollars does a program like this save over a lifetime when we produce graduates who need so little support?"

....

Because each state has determined their own criteria for what qualifies as community-based housing based on Medicaid guidelines, there's a huge disparity in what has been deemed acceptable. Florida and Arizona, two states that pioneered the concept of retirement communities, have been more open to the idea of allowing similar developments for adults with IDD. The Arc Jacksonville must have taken any precautionary warnings in the 2014 CMS guidelines about including too many on-site amenities and thrown them out the window, because they're all here: a game room, a Jacuzzi, a community center, a movie theater, a gym, a pool, a kitchen for classes, a bank, a yoga studio. The cluster of houses with one- and two-bedroom apartments is designed to look like a charming New England village with the heat and sun turned up. Porches face the street, picket fences line the yards, everyone has a lawn and a garden. Residents are free to come and go as they wish, to work in the community, and take classes at the local community college. Jim Whittaker, the president/CEO, sounds a bit like Storz in explaining why the state has approved their model when speaking with Amy Lutz of the *Atlantic*: "What they're looking for is integration, control, and choice, and we meet and exceed those standards—we're off the chart on most. There isn't a group home in the country that's going to be less restrictive than our apartments."

Florida has struggled mightily with an ever-growing list of individuals waiting for waivers to provide services of any kind to adults with IDD. As is the case in many states, priority is usually determined by the age and the health of the caregiver, not the needs of the individual. Florida currently has the fourth longest waitlist in the country, with over twenty-two thousand names. Three years earlier it also had the dubious distinction of being number forty-nine in IDD funding. With such limited assistance available, proactive families looking to create residential options lobbied for a different kind of government subsidy: low-income housing tax credits for the creation of new residential communities. In exchange, they must keep their rents below market rate, which works well for families who are still waiting for waiver funding or fear they might never get it.

The Villages at Noah's Landing in Lakeland, Florida, the larger of two residential sites operated by Noah's Ark, has used this housing credit to make independent living for adults with IDD even more affordable. It might not have as many amenities as the Arc Jacksonville, but still has beautifully built, well-equipped apartments, a pool, community center, and a pedestrian-friendly layout with open spaces beyond the complex. While the estimated expenses for rent, food, and personal needs at the Arc Jacksonville are between nine hundred and thirteen hundred dollars a month, at Noah's Landing they've kept rent at an astounding $260 to $560 a month, per bedroom. Their goal was to create housing that would be sustainable on a resident's SSI income (currently about $740 a month) and by all evidence, they've done it. (In comparison, states join with Medicare to pay between $50,000 and $90,000 a year per resident in a group home.) Florida is funding this option for relatively few people but offering more options that parents and families can afford themselves.

Niki Johnson, the operations manager at The Villages at Noah's Landing, tells me how they began in 1997 as a small group of parents looking to expand residential options for their children. In 2004, the city of Lakeland donated fifty-six acres for the project, but it took another twelve years to raise the funding they needed and to win approval and the tax-credit support from the legislators. In 2016, they opened their doors to a model that's an example for other families interested in creating housing options that are affordable to people who have no housing waivers.

To succeed, they keep paid staff to a minimum. Community and parent volunteers run the bulk of the activity programs and also work regular shifts as van drivers, event planners, and teachers. Their monthly activities calendar has offerings every day, some as simple as a walking club or a movie night; others that involve some transportation, like bowling, golfing, or theater—but for the most part, no one gets paid to run these activities. "They do it because they have a family member here or they just love our folks. Some are retired special-ed teachers and they wanted to keep in touch with this group," Johnson tells me.

She assures me they also have some on-site resident support staff—including two who work overnight shifts to handle any emergencies—but for routine, daily support, families make their own arrangements through local service agencies or do it themselves. Two overnight staff for approximately 120 residents will no doubt seem like thin coverage to some parents. In Massachusetts, the laws are so strict that many group homes of residents with medical needs require two awake-overnight staff for every four people. Bill Zimmer believes the limited housing options in Massachusetts will never change until these onerous levels of required staffing are rolled back. But is it safe to do so? "What if more than two emergencies crop up in the middle of the night?" I tentatively ask Johnson. Seizures would be the primary concern, she tells me, and they have arrangements in place—emergency buttons, roommates trained to call for assistance. Technology helps a lot, with bedroom sensors that sound an alarm if a seizure is detected while someone is asleep. "So far those measures have worked fine. We haven't had any issues," she says. In fact, the bigger problem is new residents learning what constitutes an emergency. "Running out of Diet Coke is not an emergency," she jokes. "But every new resident makes a few calls like that before they learn."

What really happens with lighter day-to-day support is that they learn from each other, Johnson says, echoing what I heard and saw at Chapel Haven. "New residents watch the people who have lived here for a while and they pick up what they need to know. Some of these folks are very good teachers. They learn how to take public transportation to the stores—we have a bus stop right here. They also learn recipes from each other."

"But what if something comes up?" I ask.

"They have phones and they call us. We come over and help them out."

Just then I see a group of three residents get off the public bus, all with grocery bags in their hands, unaccompanied by staff. It's a surprise for me to see this, just as watching young adults cook their own meals was a surprise at Chapel Haven.

"Of course, we make sure staff go with them the first few times they do their grocery shopping, but after they get the hang of it, they're fine. Some residents really blossom when they become the teachers for new folks moving in. It's wonderful to watch their confidence grow."

Undoubtedly, there are challenges to relying on volunteers—if they're primarily parents, they're likely to be older and call in sick more, and they might be a Zumba enthusiast, not a certified teacher—but there's a plus side to giving them a role to play in shaping their child's community. I remember in the early days of Whole Children when parents taught many of our classes, including one called Recess Games. We all felt a little unqualified at first—the games now bear little resemblance to the ones we remembered—but the mission prompted us to visit our child's school at recess and learn the rules of the new games, which also taught us a lot about the minefield our children were navigating every day. Being a parent-volunteer means you aren't responsible for the quality of the program, but you still have a stake in it. I suspect it might mitigate what providers sometimes see as an endless stream of complaints from antagonistic families and remind people: *we're all in this together, working to create the best life we can for these folks.*

First Place, in Phoenix, Arizona, is a contrast to the idyllic (but slightly more isolated) Noah's Landing and Arc Jacksonville: a fifty-five-unit, four-story apartment complex in the heart of downtown, with walkable access to many amenities, next door to a light rail train station and on several bus routes. The building is exclusively for young adults with autism and IDD (with a few units for graduate students in this field), but the emphasis is on inclusion. "No one here is staying in their apartment all day," founder Denise Resnick says. Resnick is the mother to Matt, age twenty-eight, and she's been a galvanizing force of change for people with autism in the twenty-five years since Matt was diagnosed. After launching the Southwest Autism Research & Resources Center, she cofounded a residential transition program, similar to Chapel Haven's. First Place has been her primary focus and her most ambitious project to date. She began work on it about ten years ago, when she saw the numbers of autism diagnoses skyrocket while the projected government resources flatlined and realized that creating group homes for three or four people at a time would never accommodate the seventy thousand children with autism that would be soon entering adulthood every year.

By comparison to the communities in Florida, First Place apartments don't come cheap. A one-bedroom is $3,900 a month, which includes all utilities, activities, and initial support. In large part, this is owing to the early help Florida gave parent groups with the low-income housing tax credits. In other states, construction loans will have to be paid off over years and the rents will reflect this. Resnick is mindful of the families unable to afford a spot at First Place and is determined to figure out more ways to bring this figure down. To this end, she's launched the Global Leadership Institute to sponsor a yearly conference where others interested in setting up planned communities can come together to learn from each other.

Desiree Kameka believes this is the beginning of a trend that will only grow. "Parents are the most invested in finding long-term, sustainable solutions. They're the ones thinking outside the box. Government isn't going to take the risk of developing innovative housing models that don't have a proven track record of success. Parents need to study what's out there, find solutions that are feasible to them. Conferences like Denise's are going to help a lot of people break through the logjam."

Kameka points me toward a few other developments that might be called intentional communities, but are more integrated in their design. Four mothers in North Carolina have recently founded HOPE (Housing Options for People with Exceptionalities), with the goal to "transform the paradigm from congregate living to a supported, inclusive community which fosters a culture of belonging and reflects the natural proportions of the world around them—with 20 percent disabled, 20 percent elderly and the rest a mix of people interested in being part of a community that has made a commitment to care for each other." It will be an intentional community where the word "intentional" isn't downplayed. In fact, it's essential. Dotty Foley, one of the founders, is mother to Dylan, age twenty-nine, who has a housing waiver and lives in his own apartment in Chapel Hill. She'd hoped this would be his home for life, but she's learned that the reality of apartment living offers only the "illusion of inclusion." He doesn't know any of his neighbors in his one-hundred-unit condo complex. "The only people that Dylan is connected with are paid staff and family." It has been this way for years and now she's made creating a new, more inclusive community her life's mission.

The idea of integrating a retired population in the mix is not without precedent. In Easthampton, Massachusetts, there's Treehouse, a planned community that offers low-income housing to senior citizens and families raising foster children. The expectation is that all who move there will commit to supporting the families raising foster children, but at a fundraiser I attended, I heard as many stories about young people helping aging neighbors than the other way around. It's a simple idea with profound ramifications: we all benefit when asked to help others. Countless studies have shown the elderly and disabled populations at a higher risk for isolation, so why hasn't the idea of building bridges between them been explored more?

Ethan loves fetching things for his arthritic grandmother. At our summer cabin, he often lies on her bed, waiting to be needed. They have funny conversations that sound like they're both talking to themselves. They while away hours like this, killing time until dinner, the meal they both look forward to the most. Sometimes I interrupt, assuming she'd welcome a break from his company.

"No, I'm fine," she'll say cheerfully. "I've told Ethan it's time to stop talking now. He told me I have to stop talking, too."

Dottie and the other HOPE moms are mindful of the role they're playing in the arc of history for kids like theirs. "We are standing on the shoulders of parents whose children never had the opportunity for something like this because their kids were institutionalized. We're looking for a developer and a town who says we want to be an exemplar for a nation." Though they still might be years away from making this a reality, she isn't daunted. "We cannot wait for someone to knock on our door and say 'Hey I've got a place for you.' We have to take charge and change some things to give our kids some guarantee of quality of life. We are the ones we've been waiting for."

In recent years, part of Kameka's role at Autism Housing Network has been acting as advisor and cheerleader to families starting this process. Their website keeps an updated list of viable housing projects, large and small, being developed in every state which, she's happy to report, grows with every month. Kameka's most important first suggestion is: Do your research ahead of time. Know how your state interprets the Medicaid guidelines for community-based residences. In all likelihood, these will continue to change, but there are a few trends. For example, she tells me, "Medicaid wants to see proposals that emphasize a consumer-controlled model—where the individual is going to get as much choice as possible on how they spend their days and what activities are available to them. They cringe at the idea of service providers acting as landlords because they don't want one entity to get too much control over a person's life." She also suggests getting as much data as possible before going to any legislators or funders, because "If you can prove this is what people want, it's harder for them to say no." Solidify your vision ahead of time so developers aren't dealing with a large group of parents with different goals and priorities. Consider connecting with a cohousing professional who will know how to collect the information you'll need.

She cautions parents that the hardest part will be in the beginning when they have an idea and interested families and maybe even some land, but they won't get much financial help to work with architects and designers—exactly the spot where my friend Maggie gave up. Not only that, the government will want to see a "proven track record of some success," Kameka warns. But establishing that track record might be impossible without independent resources to put up the initial investment. "This is the big challenge, but more and more, I'm seeing it happen."

Last but not least, she tells families to be ready to work hard, but also to be patient: this will be a time-intensive project. The parent group behind The Villages at Noah's Landing toiled for twelve years between the time they secured the land and the day residents moved in. The Kelsey, Micaela Connery's project, is on track to move more quickly, but will still be seven or eight years in development. "In the future, we hope to cut those timelines in about half," Kameka says. "The more common this becomes, the easier it will be for everyone."

There's also a bigger picture to keep in mind: long-term financial sustainability. Family groups will need to have contingency plans for a future when government assistance might not continue at its current level. At a national conference for disability service providers in Ohio 2014, Nancy Thaler, former executive director of the National Association of State Directors of Developmental Disability Services, outlined the demographic shift toward seniors and people with disabilities over the next two decades and issued a chilling warning: by 2050, support for these two growing populations will drain Medicare and Medicaid completely. "At the rate we're going, with the level of services provided, *every single tax dollar collected will go to sustaining our elderly and disabled population,"* she told the crowd. Comparing it to climate change with two critical differences, she said, "It's happening faster and fewer people are talking about it."

The point of her argument was fairly simple: twenty-four-hour staffed residential options won't be sustainable, except for the most medically vulnerable. The options being developed will need to depend less on expensive staffing and offer more support for the people doing the bulk of the caretaking: the families. Of the 4.7 million people with IDD in the US, she estimates that 80 to 90 percent are living with or supported by their families, and the government must recognize that reality. "We need to figure out how we can partner with families and ensure that they're supported in their caretaking," she said.

Amy Lutz, the parent of Jonah, a twenty-year-old with severe autism, laughs when I read her this quote. When Thaler was the deputy secretary of the Department of Developmental Services in Pennsylvania, where Lutz lives, she wasn't exactly known for embracing parent ideas. "She said no to everything except three-to-four-person group homes. She's a very nice person and she means really well, but she's part of the old school that refuses to entertain anything that resembles an intentional community or a larger-scale residential model."

Lutz is an important voice in the debate. She believes it's imperative that the widest array of options be kept available. Her priorities for Jonah have little to do with employment or even community inclusion. Of course she wants those things for him, but without proper supervision Jonah is self-injurious and will hit his head until his retinas detach. If she can't ensure his safety, he'll suffer permanent damage and be left blind. The staff turnover and level of supervision provided in group homes simply isn't enough. "If you have four guys in a house and two staff, how does that play out? One goes for a walk with one resident that leaves the other staff overseeing three people. One needs help with his computer and that leaves Jonah alone, to injure himself." The stakes are too high. She would much rather have him in a high-quality larger setting, where many eyes are on both the workers and the residents.

As an example, Lutz points to Misericordia, which currently serves six hundred residents on a thirty-one-acre campus setting on the north side of Chicago. With enough staff and supervision to serve individuals with higher needs, they also offer an enormous variety of enrichment activities, including theater, dance, and choral programs, in addition to facilities that include a greenhouse, a swimming pool, a restaurant, and a bakery. Sister Rosemary Connelly, who founded Misericordia fifty years ago and still remains at the helm, has emphasized community-building and inclusion every step of the way. Many residents work during the day—in local grocery stores and restaurants around the neighborhood—and return to a wider range of activities than they could possibly access living on their own. Judging by the four-hundred-person waitlist and the $20 million Connelly raises every year thanks to an active and engaged parent board, they're clearly doing something right.

It's not hard to see why Misericordia gets under the skin of every activist working to oppose large congregate settings. The problem with this argument is that Misericordia doesn't take that much money from the government. Most individuals are funded through an older Medicaid benefit for intermediate care facilities—about sixty-five thousand dollars per resident (less than it costs to house a resident in a group home). The rest of their funding comes from the extraordinarily energetic fundraising efforts of Connelly and the families who have made sustaining Misericordia their mission.

Connelly agrees with Lutz that offering limited options for such a diverse population is not the solution. Since she started in the '70s, government officials have been telling her that anything big is bad. "They hate Misericordia because of the fact that we're big and we're not bad. We're good. And we're good because so many people believe in us enough to get involved. I don't think we're the only way. All I say is that we're a legitimate way."

Lutz wishes there were more options like this around the country. She represents a contingency of families who feel like they're in danger of being left out of the debate, and in January 2019, they formed the National Council on Severe Autism (NCSA) to address the issue. As she points out, this isn't a small subset. According to the CDC, a little over

half of people with autism are also intellectually disabled and 30 percent are nonverbal, and a 2017 study found that about a quarter of
autistic children suffer from aggressive and/or self-injurious behavior.
Critics have accused them of trying to put too much power in the hands
of parents, taking away decision-making autonomy from people with
autism themselves. Lutz wants to remind the world that the autism
spectrum spans a range of abilities and challenges. "We fully support
self-advocates pursuing the support that they need, but this is completely separate," Lutz says. "You have mildly affected people on one
end, who are college graduates and married with children. But on the
other end of the spectrum you have adults who have to wear helmets
and arm braces every hour of the day to prevent them from injuring
themselves." It's hard to take issue with her conclusion: one side
shouldn't rule out or eliminate options the other side needs. "There's no
single solution for a population that diverse."

For Lutz and the NCSA, larger residential settings with well-trained
staff are the safest options that also offer the potential for the fullest
life for Jonah. In 2015, she wrote an important article in the *Atlantic*
called "Who Decides Where Autistic Adults Live?" examining the debate around the larger residential settings being threatened in the
wake of stricter HCBS guidelines. She argued that the self-advocates'
focus on abilities and independence left her family and her son out entirely. He'll never work. He'll never live independently. Because he needs
supervision around the clock, he will also eventually need a residential
placement. Fitting him into the models that the HCBS guidelines left
for him in 2014—small group homes and life-sharing—would offer him,
at best, a lower quality of life and at worst, would be dangerous and
unsafe. She believes that thousands of families in her situation are being brushed aside by policy makers who say they're still working on
meeting the needs of the severely disabled.

I sympathize with her frustration; I've heard similar statements
countless times, from Employment First advocates and people opposed
to intentional communities. Once upon a time, this severely affected
group defined the whole population of people with IDD—as dangerous,

out of control, unable to take care of themselves. Now, it's as if the emphasis on the achievements and capability of some have erased this other group completely.

In our conversation, Lutz points out that policy makers will see the impact of this shortsightedness sooner rather than later, especially when inappropriate residential placements for the severely disabled begin taxing the emergency system to a breaking point. It's already happened in New Jersey, a state that proposed some of the strictest limitations on residential settings in 2014, cutting off many sites that were in development and threatening well-established congregate settings that serve a range of individuals with high needs. That same year, Tyler Loftus, a twenty-five-year-old with IDD and bipolar disorder, ran away from his fifth group home and was arrested when police found a pocketknife in his pants. Because there were no residential options left for him (he was difficult to supervise, a chronic wanderer), Loftus spent three weeks in jail waiting for another placement. Outraged families began organizing and advocating to protect the housing options their children had and to loosen the guidelines on what could be built. "It's very hard to get parents who are already exhausted to come out to meetings, but they did because they were so appalled by what was happening," Lutz tells me. "There were no residential options at all for their kids and the few good ones they had were being threatened with closure."

At one of those meetings in New Jersey, Lutz witnessed firsthand the power of parents. Of the approximately 250 people who came to the open hearing, only two speakers were in favor of the stricter HCBS guidelines. The rest spoke passionately in opposition, especially about the danger of closing down day and residential programs. ("It took eighteen years for me to find a place for my daughter. I'm seventy-two years old. I don't have eighteen years to find another!" one mother said.) Legislators listened and responded. The stricter guidelines were not adopted. "[The New Jersey legislature saw] the commonsense argument," Kameka tells me. "That choice is good and if families are willing to invest in something and the oversight is there, then there's no reason to suspect that people in a larger, intentional community setting are more prone to abuse than in a group home." Kameka now points to New Jersey as an example of the power of family advocacy. "They have a much more flexible approach these days. In fact, New Jersey has more housing projects going than almost any other state I can think of. It's pretty amazing."

....

Another group too often left out of the debate is the aging people with IDD. Now that medical advances have doubled the life expectancy of people with Down syndrome, we are learning they have a much higher risk of developing Alzheimer's at a younger age. Chapel Haven was the first site I saw directly addressing this issue with the construction of their first residential apartment building designed specifically for supporting older individuals. Because Chapel Haven has been around for so long, they've seen this issue come up before.

"It's heartbreaking," Storz says. "Some of our early graduates from the 1970s, folks who had lived and worked here for thirty-five years, had to choose between moving into a nursing home or leaving their community to return to their parent's house. It was a wake-up call to all of us about an unaddressed need."

Chapel Haven's Schleifer Center is designed to meet the needs of the aging adults with IDD. I toured the as-yet unfinished building, which has the feel of a high-end assisted living facility. Every apartment has a full kitchen, but every floor also has a community kitchen designed to encourage group activities around healthy eating, along with a lounge. Residents will be invited to come out of their apartment and cook or watch TV together. Another difference from an assisted living facility is that while the building is designed with older individuals in mind, it is open to all community members, including those who are younger, like recent graduates who want more support early on. On my tour was a woman in her mid-forties who'd graduated from the program and had been living with roommates in her own apartment for ten years. Now she wants her own space but with more support so her parents feel comfortable with her staying long-term.

All of these settings could be called intentional communities and all challenge the assumption that allowing adults with IDD to live collectively by choice is a dangerous mistake. As Lutz points out, "We are all part of many communities and the government is generally not in the business of legitimizing some over others." Of all the stories Lutz tells, I'm especially haunted by one about Micki Edelsohn, an energetic mother of an adult child with autism, who thirty years ago began creating housing options for adults with autism with her foundation, Homes for Life, based in Delaware. Over the last three decades, she's built over twenty-five houses and raised enough money to underwrite two apartment complexes that are integrated enough to meet the strictest interpretation of the CMS guidelines. These are the options the government has prioritized for the bulk of residential funding—individual apartments in the community—but what is her final verdict? "Community integration is a myth. My homes are in nice neighborhoods—do you think the neighbors are asking the residents over for barbecues or to go to the movies? Of course not. There has been no real interaction between the neighbors and the people living in the homes besides the occasional wave." Edelsohn told Lutz, "Before I die, my son will be in an intentional community."

CHAPTER FOURTEEN

E very independent living option necessitates assuming some degree of risk. Only a handful of these residential options have existed for more than ten years; most have been in operation for less than five. When Amy Lutz argued that an intentional community or larger residential settings might be more appropriate for someone like her son, Nancy Thaler told her "in the nicest possible way" that she was being "overly optimistic about the potential for good in congregate settings and really naïve about the potential for evil." Older policy makers who began their work in institutions have never forgotten the inhumanity they witnessed, but many parents today have a hard time picturing anything like that. The world has been changed by the mainstream education their children received, and they're mystified by that level of fear.

The question of risk management has been a thorny issue ever since deinstitutionalization began. In the late 1960s, Robert Perske coined the phrase "the dignity of risk" when he argued that "Overprotection can keep people from becoming all they could become. Many of our best achievements came the hard way: We took risks, fell flat, suffered, picked ourselves up, and tried again. Sometimes we made it and sometimes we did not. Even so, we were given the chance to try. . . . The world in which we live is not always safe, secure and predictable. . . . To deny any person their fair share of risk experiences is to further cripple them for healthy living."

As Ethan worked his way through school, I took my cues from his teachers on determining acceptable levels of risk. In elementary school, he loved visiting the school secretary in part because she was a boisterous, friendly personality and in part because her name was Ms. Champoux (pronounced *shampoo*), which made him howl with laughter. Delivering attendance sheets to her desk—accompanied by his aide—was a reward he earned once a week. When he was in fourth grade and pining for more independence, I asked at an IEP meeting if he might be allowed to deliver the attendance sheets by himself. I pointed out that he was actually good at navigating the school hallways; when we came for school events, he usually led us to the correct room. The worst thing that could happen would be that he might poke around a bit—find the music teacher to say hi, or the janitor with his beloved floor buffer. Would that be so terrible? Even as I asked, I wasn't sure. To their credit, the teachers gave it some thought. They weighed the plusses—it would give him a "real" job to complete on his own and a sense of accomplishment after he'd done it. Still, they worried. *What if he took too long? What if he got lost?* Then, the gym teacher, who saw Ethan once a week and didn't know him well, said, "What if he disappeared completely?"

The discussion froze. This concern wasn't based on anything rational. Ethan still had regular meltdowns at school, but he never bolted from safety. His teachers knew that. I knew it, too. Still the note of uncertainty shifted the conversation. "Let's wait on that idea," his lead teacher finally said. "We'll keep it in mind as something he's working toward."

Over the years, we revisited the possibility. In middle school, he was allowed to walk up the hall by himself to get a drink of water, though an aide stood in the doorway and watched him the whole time. He was not allowed to go the bathroom, around the corner and out of sightline, by himself.

Most parents would never dare to complain about too much staffing. Having an aide largely gave Ethan *more* freedom, not less. In high school, it meant he could participate in general-education classes with his peers, like art, music, and drama. But alongside the opportunities that having an aide by his side gave him, it also confirmed a powerful assumption for his teachers, his peers, his parents, and himself: he wasn't safe alone. Ever.

He was eighteen when we finally revisited the question of allowing Ethan to move around the school by himself on occasion. We were more emphatic and this time it was allowed. Just as we expected, it meant he took a few detours to say hello to his favorite people. Early in the semester, his brother Charlie, two years younger, told us a story about sitting in an English class with a new teacher he both admired and was intimidated by, when Ethan leaned in the open door with a big pinwheel wave. "Boy Howdy!" he called to the teacher. The teacher stopped his lecture. "Boy Howdy!" He waved back. A moment later Ethan was gone and the teacher resumed his lesson, still smiling, and said, "I love that kid. He's a buddy of mine." It was an important lesson for Charlie and for his parents. Apparently, when given some freedom, Ethan formed connections to people we never expected.

We had never considered the school's emphasis on safety over all else as an issue until his first year in high school when we signed him up for chorus. Participating in his middle school chorus with a wonderful teacher who found ways to include students with a wide range of abilities had been a highlight of Ethan's two years before. We assumed it would be the same in high school. Our first clue that it might not be came early when the teacher sent me an email saying, "I wonder if Ethan really wants to be in this class. Much of the time he doesn't even sing."

She was probably right, I knew. He hadn't always sung in middle school chorus because he loved listening to the harmonies around him. I'd watched him in concerts where he waited for his favorite parts and stopped singing entirely so he could rock and listen, grinning wildly. Was that so bad? I wrote an email back: "He very much wants to be there. He loves all aspects of music, making it and also listening. Participating in chorus is his favorite part of the day—a great seat at a concert of wonderful music." I was laying it on thick, appealing to her vanity. Over the years, I'd learned to approach some teachers with humor—making a joke about Ethan to let them know, it's okay, we can laugh about his quirks. Others, the more earnest ones, I approached this way.

We'll see, she replied.

Determined to stick it out, we threw ourselves into a fundraising effort for the end-of-the-year chorus trip to New York City. The middle school chorus group had also gone on day-long field trips to Boston, once a year, and the outings had been thrilling for Ethan, something to tell the extended family about for months afterward. Mike rolled his eyes and accused me of trying to curry favor by buying more pounds of coffee and bars of chocolate than we could possibly need. "I'm making *a point*," I said sternly, though I wasn't sure exactly what that point was: *Ethan can be a valuable part of your community, too?* It was a strained relationship right up to the spring concert when I asked a parent sitting next to me when the New York trip was happening, and she said, with some surprise, "They went last month. Didn't you know?"

After I learned that all four special-ed students in chorus had been left out of the field trip, I dropped my fawning facade and called a meeting with the teacher, the principal, and the special-ed director. "I worried about their safety," the chorus teacher explained. "New York can be a very busy and dangerous place. I didn't think it was appropriate for those students."

The principal looked away. He knew the bigger picture: IDEA, the education law for students with disabilities, guarantees that no students will be denied access to an outing like this. Safety can be ensured. Aides can go along, as they had the year before when these same students went to Boston with the middle school chorus.

The teacher admitted that it had never even occurred to her to include these students, which was why she hadn't been in touch with us to discuss the matter. "I believed it wasn't safe. I assumed parents would agree," she maintained.

For me, it was an important glimpse into a mindset I hadn't yet encountered because Ethan had always been included on similar trips before. In fact, they'd often been the most successful part of his year. As other opportunities for inclusion narrowed over time, field trips were one of the few chances for him to spend time with his classmates. But it was more than that. I leaned forward and said: "If he'd been allowed to go, he would have talked about it all year. He would have had a story he could tell at Thanksgiving and Christmas. He would have taken a trip without his family. It might have been his last chance—ever—to do that."

It was hard to tell if my words landed. The teacher rolled her eyes and offered an apology, kind of: "Well, it was one field trip. I made a mistake. I'm sorry."

What I learned from this episode is that citing concerns about safety is, and has always been, the easiest way to exclude this population. Parents are naturally hesitant to take risks. I would have been easily cowed if Ethan and these same peers hadn't been to Boston the year before. It was hard to tell if the others at the meeting understood the larger message I was trying to convey. This was years before so many job internships refused Ethan on the basis of safety issues, but a shift had taken place in my mind. I saw a barrier I hadn't considered before. For Ethan to participate in the wider world, we might have to push past people who told us it wasn't safe for him to do so.

....

As a parent, it's almost impossible to decide how much risk to allow for when we've seen so few examples of adults with IDD take any risks at all. Ironically, the first time Ethan walked into town by himself only happened at the urging of his aide from school who insisted he was ready and Charlie who downloaded an app on our phones that let us track his progress up the street. Without this, I'm sure we never would have allowed it. He was nineteen by then and still, we were consumed by fears we couldn't name. *What if something happened?* is the doubt that makes your chest go tight even if it's not clear what specifically you're afraid of. There were about seven streets for him to cross, all with crosswalks, the busy ones with lights to stop traffic. He knew how to do this just fine. He also knew not to get in any car or talk to any strangers for too long.

Still, Mike and I held our breath as we watched the little blue dot of his phone make its way up the street. The farther it got, the faster my heart beat. I wondered, irrationally but genuinely, if a police officer might see him and give us a call. Twenty minutes later, he was home, soda in hand.

Over the next month as Ethan made the trip more often, we did get some calls from well-meaning neighbors to say, "I just passed Ethan walking into town. Wanted to make sure you knew." By that point our attitude had shifted dramatically. It was a point of pride. "That's right! He's walking into town by himself now!"

....

Every residential option we pursue includes weighing the risks involved, and Thaler might be right. Communities begun with the best of intentions by involved, loving families could degrade over time. Funding might get cut and parents might get too old to properly oversee the quality of care their child receives. This, of course, must be weighed against the other option—remaining in their childhood home with aging caretakers they will eventually outlive.

This uncertainty comes just as a new study gives us all something shocking to feed our fears. According to a 2018 US Department of Justice report, people with IDD are seven times more likely than the general population to be the victim of sexual abuse. NPR broke the story of this report as part of a five-part series that became a wake-up call to parents, educators, and service providers as more statistics came out. About half of those abused will be the victim of repeat offenses, only 37 percent will report abuse to an authority and—the grimmest figure of all—fewer than 10 percent of perpetrators will be arrested. Fewer still will be successfully prosecuted, leaving abusers free to do so again. Sheryl White-Scott, a New York internist specializing in treating people with IDD, told NPR that the absence of sex education for people with IDD has too often left them without the language or vocabulary to understand, or report on, what had happened to them. As a result, she believed the abuse rate is probably higher, around 50 percent. With a sigh, she added, "It could be as high as 75 percent."

"If this were any other population, the world would be up in arms," said Nancy Thaler, on the NPR report. "We would be irate, and it would be the number one health crisis in this country." Thaler calls this an open secret in the field of disability providers, one that remains unaddressed because the issue seems unsolvable. "People with IDD are the perfect victims," she explained: taught to be compliant and trust adults, and they spend the majority of their lives with rotating staff in settings rife with opportunity for abuse. NPR interviewed Stephen DeProspero, serving forty years in prison for sexually assaulting a ten-year-old boy with IDD who lived in a group home. He said he regrets his actions now, but partly blamed the intimate nature of the job, the proximity, and the lack of oversight. "I could have stayed in that house for years and abused him every day without anybody even noticing at all. It was a predator's dream."

Here is a genuine, terrifying risk that every parent needs to weigh before deciding on any residential arrangements. We all know our own child's unique vulnerabilities—their love of adult attention, the unguarded way they approach strangers. Many of them have spent their whole lives in a protective bubble of special-ed oversight, and have only known adults who are kind, patient, and well-intentioned. How do we prepare them for the reality that some are not?

One logical place to start would be better sex education at an earlier age for special-ed students. I had assumed that the transition initiative that uses federal funds to support older students with IDD in preparation for adulthood—with vocational experience and independent living skills—also included a mandate on sex education and was genuinely shocked to discover: it does not. In fact, the federal government has no mandate on providing sex education in public schools for *any* students, with disabilities or without. Though it offers some recommendations and guidelines, any mandates are left up to the individual states. Currently, only thirty-eight states require sex education and of those, thirty focus on abstinence-based curricula or something called "abstinence plus," which also teaches about STD avoidance. Only eighteen states require a discussion of birth control, and only nine require that LGBT issues be covered in a way that is inclusive and affirming. (Seven states specifically prohibit this.) Only one state in the country—Oregon—requires that a sexuality curriculum be provided for students in special-ed programs.

In the other forty-nine states, school districts—and most often, individual special-ed teachers—are left to decide for themselves how, and when, to teach this topic. The result is haphazard; sometimes students are included in early lessons about body changes and puberty, sometimes they aren't. Usually there's little, if any, follow-through, so it's unclear how much of the material they've retained. Andrew Maxwell Triska, author of *Sexuality and Intellectual Disabilities,* believes that, in the absence of coherent policy or recommendations, sex education for students with disabilities tends to be provided *re*actively rather than *pro*actively, meaning it most often happens in response to an emergency. A teacher walks in on two students in a bathroom stall, a student repeatedly touches himself in class, or a nonverbal girl is discovered to be pregnant. The teachers are ill prepared, and the message gets muddled by panic and uncertainty. Students walk away with a vague sense that this must never happen, which doesn't exactly align with the message they are getting on TV and in movies, where sex happens all the time, and everyone seems to like it.

By contrast, in 2017 the UK enacted a law requiring relationships and sexuality education (RSE) take place not only in all secondary schools, but in primary (elementary) schools as well. Younger students start at age six with one or two lessons a week on antibullying, friendship-building, and empathy, while older students cover a wide variety of topics including consent, healthy and unhealthy relationships, LGBT issues, gender stereotyping, harassment, and using social media safely and responsibly. The government argues that starting early and building the topics into the curriculum every year sets up a strong foundation for the more complex subjects later on, and this mandate not only includes special-ed students, but also modifies curriculum for them and adds appropriate, visually enhanced supporting materials. On the BBC educational channel, it's possible to watch elementary students with IDD pass around an anatomically correct doll as the teacher talks about body parts. For older children it's possible to buy books with cartoon illustrations called *Things Ellie Likes: A Book About Sexuality and Masturbation for Girls and Young Women with Autism and Related Conditions.* There's also a version called, *Things Tom Likes. . . .* We have no equivalent available in the US.

Brian Melanson, a sexuality educator with Pathlight in Hadley, Massachusetts, fears that in the US, the topic has become so controversial that a silence has grown around it. Parents hope the schools cover it, the schools hope the parents cover it, and everyone's unsure how to address it directly. One of his main messages is that schools won't teach it unless parents ask for it, and students won't learn it unless it's taught in an appropriate sequence with supporting materials over time and reinforced by families at home. "I tell parents: you have to bring it up, the earlier the better and really insist on follow-through. This is a complicated topic that can't be addressed in a few sessions and in all likelihood, the schools aren't going to suggest it themselves," he says. But what should parents ask for and what exactly should schools be teaching?

About four years after we opened Whole Children, Maggie Rice, co-director of the center and one of the founding mothers, began to notice a change in the atmosphere in the classes. "It was like the kids were all going crazy at the same time, wrestling in the hallway, crying in the lobby. For a long time, we couldn't figure out what we were doing wrong and then it occurred to us: they were all hitting puberty." She laughs at the memory. She went to her son's school and asked the special-ed teachers how they were teaching students about body changes and what to expect. The teachers shook their heads sheepishly—they were only addressing the topic to individuals on an as-needed basis at the request of parents. "I'm guessing that meant they helped girls with their periods if parents asked for it, but for the whole group, there was no plan in place. We knew we had to do something."

Without a widely accepted curriculum on the market, Rice consulted with some professionals and began to develop her own. Most of it was done by trial and error. "We had a lot of errors in the beginning," she jokes. But she also made a lot of important realizations, like this one: "Parents can make some pretty serious mistakes, especially as their child gets older but still needs help around things related to grooming. My son was fifteen and I was still chasing him around to wipe his nose for him and clean his face off after he ate. Then finally someone pointed out: every time a parent insists on touching a child, even when they resist, they're reinforcing the dangerous message that their child has no control over their body." Rice shakes her head. She's not laughing anymore. "You're telling them they can say no, but it won't matter, adults will do what they want anyway. You're grooming them to be a victim."

This revelation sends a shuddering wave of recognition around the parent group I sit with for a presentation on Whole Selves, the sexuality and relationship curriculum Rice and Melanson have developed over the last eight years as they've expanded the initial class offerings and taken it out to school districts around Massachusetts. "What should we do instead?" one mother asks.

"Tell them their face needs cleaning. They can either do it themselves or you can help. Let them decide."

In the first classes she taught on puberty, Rice did an experiment. She taped out a circle, divided it into pie pieces and had each student sit in it. She said, "This is your space, and no one can cross a line without your permission." The result was revelatory. "None of the students understood how to ask permission and even more surprising: no one in the room knew how to say no. For years, they've been trained in compliance. It's really ingrained and it's dangerous for them." They redesigned the class to focus on issues of self-esteem and confidence-building. "We had to teach them that *they matter and what they think matters*. They have control over what happens to their body."

They got creative to figure out ways to teach these abstract concepts. Early on, they had students stand up and read confidence statements aloud. "I am different and I'm fine the way I am." "I am ready for a challenge!" "I am me and I am awesome!" Though it sounded hokey, Rice marveled at the change she saw in students as they learned to do this. "In the beginning they all said these things with question marks at the end, like they had no idea if it was true or not." After a while, that changed pretty dramatically. They were saying the words and hearing them and *meaning* them.

As Rice and Melanson have developed the program, they've become convinced that self-esteem—and self-knowledge—are not only essential for self-protection but are also the first building blocks of good relationships. Another early exercise asks students to identify likes and dislikes. This way they begin to recognize what it means to have things in common with another person. Melanson points out that lots of people with IDD are fixated on finding a neurotypical boyfriend or girlfriend. He thinks this might spring, in part, from what they've seen on TV, where all the relationships are between people without disabilities. After they've completed exercises about finding someone they have interests in common with, they start to consider potentially more appropriate matches.

Whole Selves is a comprehensive K-12 curriculum that parallels the philosophy of the UK programs: start early. Unlike other sex-ed curricula which begin in high school, this one starts around first grade, with exercises that teach basics of self-esteem, respect, empathy, and healthy friendships. Later, it teaches body changes, puberty, and hygiene at the same age as general-ed students, but offers more frequent reinforcement of the material covered. Ideally lessons should be at least one hour a week in elementary school and then, by high school, two to three hours a week to give them a chance to cover all the core curriculum but also branch out into the topics students want to discuss.

To parents who fear that introducing the topic will spark curiosity about an experience that their kids will not be able to participate in, Melanson points out that most of them have spent their whole life watching the same TV shows and movies as their neurotypical peers. Sex is everywhere. "It shouldn't be a bombshell when I tell parents, look, they already know that sex exists. That genie is out of the bottle." The biggest problem he sees comes from the silence around the topic. If students haven't heard adults speaking matter-of-factly, they make assumptions based on a confusing combination of what they've watched on TV and what they see around them at school.

He tells me a story of an eighteen-year-old with IDD who'd been prohibited from making physical contact with anyone at school—no high fives, no hugs, no handshakes—because of an issue where he'd been asking neurotypical girls to hold his hand while they walked down the hallway. The girls felt badly for him and agreed, but it made them uncomfortable. After a while, they complained to the administration, who responded with the no-touching-in-school edict for this student. (For everyone else, it was still allowed.) In one-on-one sessions with the young man, Melanson discovered the problem: the student wanted a girlfriend and he believed that holding hands was the only way to get one. Melanson says, "About 90 percent of what we teach in these classes is around relationship-building, not sex. The nuts and bolts of sex comes at the end and is usually a surprisingly quick lesson. Sex isn't the complicated part. The hard part is putting together all the pieces of a healthy relationship."

With the young man who tried to hold too many hands, Melanson went over a lesson about getting to know someone. "I told him that all the people he sees holding hands around his school have done a lot of steps before that. They've talked to someone at school, they've called them on the phone, maybe they've gone out to dinner or a movie. That was all completely new information for him."

Melanson stresses the point that these early steps are often missing. I think about Ethan, who has twice come home to announce—seemingly out of nowhere—that he has a girlfriend. The first time, we were surprised and delighted. It was an old friend he'd grown up with and she had invited him to the Best Buddies prom. He said yes and assumed, without much discussion, that this imbued them both with a new relationship status. He bought her a corsage, wore a suit, and, from what I could tell, seemed like a fairly attentive date. After that night, he talked a lot about his girlfriend to family members and proudly showed everyone their prom picture. When a *Lilo & Stitch* DVD came with a free, cheap necklace, he saved it to give to her. The relationship continued for over a year, but any time I suggested calling her on the phone or going out to a movie, he wasn't interested. "Nah," he told me. "That would be weird." We weren't shocked when he came home and announced without too much emotion that they'd broken up. "She said she just wants to be friends."

The next time around, he was older and perhaps as a result, seemed more serious. "We're going to get married," he told us about a week after we learned the name of his BHMA classmate. "I should buy her a ring."

Ethan was grabbing at the scraps he understood about relationships. First you get a girlfriend, then you get married. "Shouldn't you go on a date first?" his brother Charlie, asked. "Or get her phone number, maybe, and call her?"

Ethan looked confused. These suggestions sounded daunting. "You don't *have* to, Charlie," he said. "There isn't any law that says you must call someone before you marry them. You can just get married if you want."

Charlie had to concede that no, technically there wasn't any law about this.

This relationship did seem more real—they laughed a lot and held hands between classes. At a final BHMA recital, they sang a duet, and when the sheet music blew off of their stand, they laughed so hard they had to hold on to each other to keep from falling down. It was endearing, but still wasn't enough to entice Ethan into the ominous trenches of a real date, where he'd have to talk the whole time over dinner. "No thanks," he said when I suggested it. "I'd rather go out with you guys."

At the end of that year, his girlfriend's funding was cut. She had to leave BHMA and he hasn't seen her since. My takeaway lesson is that Ethan may never decide that the awkward first steps of dating are worth the wedding he enjoys imagining, but also that he does think about these things, and he wants to have some version of the adult relationships he sees on TV.

For Melanson, this is a crucial component of the curriculum they're developing. It's one thing to teach children about self-protection and it's quite another to help them navigate their way into healthy relationships. "Lots of parents and teachers will agree that we need to teach the basics of sex-ed for self-protection and safety, but there isn't enough talk about sexual expression, being a human right. It's something everyone should have access to if they're interested."

A sex-ed curriculum for special needs students that encourages sexual exploration with healthy parameters around it? Triska points to the UK and other countries that have taken this approach but fears it might be a tougher argument to make in the US where transition IEP plans often focus exclusively on measures of independence. Sex ed goes unaddressed, because sexual expression furthers no career or educational goals. "In the view of independence-minded clinicians, [sex ed] is useless," he argues. This means goals unrelated to self-sufficiency, "including such not-readily quantifiable goals as happiness and enjoyment are sacrificed."

In the US, sex education is agreed upon as a necessary component of abuse prevention which tends to make the focus exclusively on language like "Good Touch/Bad Touch" and overly simplified lessons about stranger danger. Melanson sees this as a problem because it doesn't focus on relationship-building. For starters, an abuser is far more likely to be someone a student knows and can even be someone they consider a friend. He wants to focus on helping young adults with IDD decide for themselves what a healthy relationship looks and feels like. "In a healthy relationship, people don't make you do things you don't want to do or make you feel bad about yourself. That's an important lesson for everyone."

There's another challenge in their work that can't be overlooked. It's estimated that 30 to 40 percent of these abusers are people who have IDD themselves, and at least some of them fall into a category known as "naïve offender," in which the perpetrator isn't aware that they've violated any laws or mores. This is one piece of a larger problem most parents will recognize. Leslie Walker-Hirsch, author of *The Facts of Life . . . and More: Sexuality and Intimacy for People with Intellectual Disability* writes, "A lot of children with intellectual disability get hugs from the teacher when other children don't get hugs. When that student grows up, and they've never learned who is or is not appropriate to hug . . . if they're working in a store and run up to a customer, or another employee, or worse yet, a child, they'd be out of that job so fast their head would spin."

This issue can quickly extend past a problem of inappropriate hugging. Rice tells me a story about being called in for an emergency consultation by a school district after multiple complaints were filed about a seventeen-year-old boy with IDD getting too close to certain girls, touching their hair or their arms, making them uncomfortable. The boy got a warning that he might be expelled from school if it happened again. It did. His teachers said they had tried everything to get it to stop—rewarding him when he went a few days with no incidents, talking about it from a "feelings" perspective. "How would you feel if someone kept doing something that made you uncomfortable?" Nothing worked. Afraid of the gauntlet the administration had set down, his parents went in for a consultation and discovered that one part of the problem hadn't been previously mentioned by any of the teachers or administrators. When he got near the girls, he developed an erection that he didn't understand or recognize. Because he always wore sweatpants, it was noticeable and scared the girls. "He literally had no idea what was happening. He didn't know what an erection was, or why it was such a problem for him to stand near girls."

Melanson did some individual counseling. He went over all the basics, explaining how bodies respond to attraction and how, when he is in a private place like his bedroom at home, it is okay to masturbate. He taught him about tricks for hiding erections in public. Last but not least, he gave him a booklet they'd written explaining how to masturbate "to completion." Clearly this was all new information to this seventeen-year-old. When they asked if he'd ever "seen white stuff come out of his penis, the boy said no."

After these sessions, the school saw dramatic changes. The student was less aggressive, "less frantic" according to his teachers, and never had another incident where he made girls uncomfortable. Rice sighs at the end of this all-too-common story. "This poor kid had no *idea* what was going on and how to cope with all these new feelings in his body. No clue." For her, it's ironic that some parents are afraid that learning this information might be dangerous and make their child behave in sexually inappropriate ways when the danger is the opposite. "It's ignorance that makes some of them act in scary ways."

Both Rice and Melanson think teaching some basics around masturbation is important. "Many of them have discovered that touching themselves through their pants pockets feels interesting and good, but they haven't figured out anything else yet, so they keep doing it in inappropriate places. In some classrooms, this is a chronic problem," Rice tells me. A friend of mine remembers working as an assistant teacher in a classroom for autistic children where the teacher cut out paper hands and taped them to desktops. At the start of every lesson she would say, "Public hands! Show me your public hands!" My friend laughs at the memory. "In retrospect I'm not sure that was such a great solution."

Equally important, for both of them, is introducing concepts of sexual and gender diversity. Some studies suggest that gender fluidity and homosexuality occur in a higher percentage in people with autism, though no one knows why. Because students with IDD have such a strong desire to belong, studies have also shown that they can sometimes imitate the worst behavior they see in neurotypical peers. "They've been the victims of stereotyping themselves, which means they can sometimes—with surprising relish—say homophobic or surprisingly offensive things. They've been the victims of it, for sure, and they want to test what it feels like to dish it out," Melanson says, and argues these kinds of mistakes can be as ostracizing as inappropriately touching themselves in public. "They reflect the same problem: they haven't learned the building blocks of how to show respect and empathy."

Melanson has indeed seen a higher-than-expected number of transgender students with autism, and teachers who are unsure how to address this issue, afraid they might complicate what is already a complex subject. When they hit puberty, many of these students encounter depression, aggression, and a plummet in many hard-won skills. In a few cases, the incidences escalated to a crisis and hospitalization. But when one of those students returned to class and was allowed to express their preferred gender, with their chosen name and pronoun, the change was dramatic: "Like night and day," Melanson recalls. "Other kids were very accepting because the bigger change they saw was that this kid wasn't hitting people any more or lashing out."

I think about the two transgender employees I met at Rising Tide Car Wash and how quickly their coworkers adapted to using their preferred pronouns. It's a similar revelation that parents often have: *My child can learn what I once might have thought was too complicated for him.* For our kids to gain the independence their government says it wants for them, they deserve an education that will give them the tools and protection they need.

....

I suspect many parents might feel as Mike and I did for many years: grateful this didn't seem to be a pressing issue for Ethan, who loves the idea of girlfriends and marriage, but has never been interested in being alone with one long enough to do anything more than hold her hand. In fact, he's always seemed allergic to the idea of learning more about sex. Any time characters in a movie engage in any kiss longer than a peck, he leaves the room; any time his brothers tell an off-color joke, he'll put his fingers in his ears and say, "I don't want to hear this!" And he seems to mean it. There are some subjects he *really* doesn't want to hear about. Even watching *Springsteen on Broadway* with his beloved Bruce telling stories about his childhood with an occasional expletive made him uncomfortable. Maybe it was the swear words, or maybe it was the fact that Bruce had once been poor and made fun of in school, which didn't make any sense to Ethan. Whatever the reason, he couldn't watch for long. Honest, chatty Bruce wasn't the Bruce he knew and loved.

Then *Leaving Neverland* came out. I warned Ethan this one might make him uncomfortable, but instead of heeding my caution, which he's generally done in the past, he watched with us, wide-eyed and slack-jawed. I had heard the NPR report a year earlier and knew this might be our best chance to explain something that would be hard for Ethan to imagine. When he finally asked, "What are they saying about Michael Jackson?" I didn't flinch. "It seems like maybe even when he was making great music that everyone loved, he was also inviting young children to Neverland and hurting them. He was touching them without their clothes on. They trusted him and they also weren't old enough to say, 'No. Stop. Don't do that.'"

Was it a good strategy—introducing him to a danger and at the same time, giving him the words he can use if a similar situation arises? I don't know. All I can say is that his response surprised me. He didn't do any of the old things he used to do when he felt uncomfortable— laugh inappropriately, leave the room, plug his ears. Instead he thought for a while. "What about when he was making 'We Are the World?'" he asked. "Was he doing it then?"

"Maybe." I nodded.

Another long pause and then this: "They must be feeling so mad at him now. All of them. Quincy Jones, Stevie Wonder, Bruce. Are they all mad?"

Ethan has long processed emotions by asking us what other people, often celebrities, are feeling. Sometimes he uses his stuffed animals instead of celebrities. "What are my ponies feeling about this dessert menu?" he'll say, grinning in a restaurant after we've told him, yes, he can order one. Usually we roll our eyes and make a joke. "They're feeling very excited but also like you should pick one out and order it nicely from the waiter."

This time, I wasn't sure what to say. "Maybe. I don't know how they're feeling," I began. Then it occurred to me that this might be a first: he wasn't asking what other people were feeling, he was guessing for himself. "You're probably right," I said. "They're probably feeling mad. And maybe a little sad, too."

When I told another parent this story, she was shocked that we'd let Ethan watch the show. Her son was a lifelong Michael Jackson fan, too. I told her that a year ago, I probably wouldn't have. "Now I feel like it's a good idea to talk more about these subjects." She went quiet but nodded. We'd all heard the story by then. We were all haunted by the voices of victims, using childish terms to describe the adult crimes that had happened to them.

Not talking about it didn't seem like a choice anymore.

CHAPTER FIFTEEN

By any measure, 1990 was a huge year for the advancement of disability rights. Not only did the Individuals with Disabilities Education Act (IDEA) pass, guaranteeing that these students could attend the same school as their typically abled peers, it also marked the passage of the Americans with Disabilities Act (ADA), ensuring access for people with disabilities to all public buildings, outlawing discrimination based on disability, and—crucially—mandating that employers provide reasonable accommodations for employees with disabilities. In signing the legislation, George H. W. Bush made a special note of this last facet: "They want to work, and they can work, and this is a tremendous pool of people who will bring to jobs diversity, loyalty, proven low turnover rate, and only one request: the chance to prove themselves. . . . When given the opportunity to be independent, they will move proudly into the economic mainstream of American life, and that's what this legislation is all about."

Thirty years after this glorious prediction, however, the employment figures for people with disabilities aren't much better than they were in 1990. For people with developmental disabilities, the numbers have remained particularly stubborn. Mary Johnson, author of *Make Them Go Away: Clint Eastwood, Christopher Reeve and the Case Against Disability Rights,* argues that the ADA might have seemed groundbreaking at the time, but was ultimately toothless—it didn't punish noncompliance sufficiently, and had too many loopholes. Employers didn't have to make accommodations if they cost too much, nor were they obligated to employ someone if their disability posed an undue hardship on the company.

In pinpointing why the ADA made promises it was unable to deliver, Johnson points to the battle to pass the legislation. Though some called the ADA the second great civil rights legislation of the twentieth century, disability activists hadn't waged anything like the public fight that led to the Civil Rights Act of 1964. In 1977, they held a twenty-five-day takeover of the San Francisco Department of Health, Education, and Welfare. In 1990, they staged a protest that became known as the "Capitol Crawl" where hundreds of wheelchair-users pulled themselves up the eighty-three steps outside the Capitol to draw attention to Congress's lack of progress on the ADA. With these notable exceptions, though, the general population saw few public demonstrations. Rather, the campaign was largely fought in courts, away from the spotlight, between individuals and companies.

"The disability rights movement was very good at getting laws passed—better it seemed, than gays or women's groups—but the movement shied away from public discourse. It seemed afraid to open up the issue of disability rights to public debate lest it lose the debate," Johnson observes. She concludes that the ADA might be the law of the land but "its major philosophical underpinnings had never really entered the national consciousness." In the end, she believes that the law has been undermined as a result: "A law cannot guarantee what a culture will not give."

Ethan was born in 1996—only six years after IDEA guaranteed him an education in the same public school as his brothers. He, and the millions of young adults now aging out of the system, are part of an ambitious experiment: the first generation of kids with IDD to be given a proper education and, equally important, to grow up alongside neurotypical peers who are less likely to be mystified by or frightened of his disability. Schools have invested significant resources teaching students who were, less than fifty years ago, excluded from public education entirely. So why haven't their prospects changed?

In a speech delivered to the Autism Self Advocacy Network Gala in 2016, Ari Ne'eman, president and one of the founders of ASAN, made a similar argument about the history of disability activism and the strategy activists used to get legislation passed. He called it a hidden-army approach—a tactic in which very few people (including the legislators sometimes) understand the details of the laws they're enacting. By keeping the public in the dark, activists can forge bipartisan bills on the general idea that they're "doing something good for disabled people." Ne'eman said that for years this was the only option: "We couldn't galvanize our people into huge marches or public displays. It was better to work behind the scenes, tinkering with policy until we settled on something and asked our advocates to put it forward, which they did."

It may have been effective, but the result was a cultural understanding of disability as apolitical. "The danger of this is that people with disabilities might not seem as vulnerable as they are because they haven't marched on Washington and showed their vulnerability," Ne'eman added. But he also warns us that doing so will be necessary sooner than we expect: when funding for support services gets slashed, or if Medicare is cut by turning to block grants. "We've never built a mass movement because it's scary to speak to the American public and realize they may just not care what we have to say. . . . It's scary to admit that maybe we've been lying to ourselves about the strength of our movement."

My favorite portion of his speech came at the end. "In Washington, the last thing you want to admit is that you might not be as powerful as you think you are, [but] there's also a unique strength in that acknowledgement. The moment we stop lying to ourselves is the moment we can start building the power our community has the potential to build. The majority of people with disabilities and their families have yet to be activated politically. . . . Our role is to build a strong foundation so the next generation may take for granted the simple and obvious fact of their humanity."

I like the idea that speaking honestly about vulnerability can be empowering. I also agree that many families with disabled members are not activated politically for a variety of reasons: self-consciousness, exhaustion, uncertainty about what we should expect or ask for. The issue has another layer, though. Even as the ADA was being systematically chipped away at and undermined in court decisions over the years, few people protested publicly. In the 1970s and '80s, as disability activists fought to get precursors to the ADA enacted, the Black Panthers and workers' unions brought food and supplies to the sit-in. In later years, there was no sign of solidarity like this. Mary Johnson argues that a fundamental difference of philosophy had begun: people believed that racial minorities, gays, and women faced discrimination that sprang from prejudice and animus. No one felt that toward people with disabilities. Their problems, it was assumed, were essentially private, medical issues that government and society couldn't do much about. "Policy cannot make people with serious disabilities move as if they did not have them," the *New York Times* editorial board posited in 1979.

When Christopher Reeve was injured in a horseback riding accident in 1995, he became, arguably, the most famous—and most sympathetic— disabled person in the country, but in the years following, he chose to make his fight—and his platform—about finding a cure to help him walk again, not about increasing access or accommodations. "I'm not interested in curb cuts and ramps," he told ABC's *20/20*. "Some people are able to accept living with a severe disability," he told a congressional committee in 2002. "I am not one of them."

The debate between medicalizing disability—emphasizing cures and prevention over support and accommodation—has been central to the autism community for almost as long as Ethan has been alive. ASAN, founded by Ne'eman, has persuasively argued that far too much of the limited government funding for autism has gone toward researching causes and cures, rather than supporting access and quality of life. Autism Speaks, the most powerful fundraising arm for people with autism, has also come under fire for their disproportionate spending on research for cures rather than supporting the daily needs of the community. As Autism Speaks has belatedly begun to acknowledge this point, the new questions become: What should the money be going toward instead? What are the best ways to support this population? Many seem to agree that the most vexing problem for people with disabilities, especially those with IDD, is lodged in society's limited vision and lowered expectation of what they can and should be doing. But can money help solve this problem?

In a keynote address given at the University of Washington in 2019, disability activist John Kemp asked if their work needs to be more public, the way it was a generation earlier in the fight for basic access to schools and buildings. "I think our movement has gotten too timid," he said. "We have to be stronger, louder and in their face more. But we also have to win over hearts and minds. It's hard to find a balance, but I know we had some kick-butt people in the '60s who would chain themselves to busses and climb on their knees up the steps of the Supreme Court and you don't see that anymore. It makes me wonder—have they thrown us some crumbs and we're scared of losing those crumbs so we don't say anything?"

This question is haunting especially when the crumbs Kemp mentions aren't even available for half a million new adults with IDD, sitting on waitlists, not receiving any services at all. Some activists lament the distance between disability groups, especially when all are being adversely impacted by competition for limited Medicare funds. The physically disabled don't want to be lumped in with the cognitively disabled, those with hidden disabilities resent the support others receive and they have to fight for. The more I learn about the movement, the more I sympathize with Kemp. It would be inspiring to see a unified protest march against this frightening new trend of nursing home placements for young people who don't have any other options.

Sarah Triano, an organizer of Chicago's Disability Pride Parade, believes the problem stems from feelings of inferiority and internalized oppression: "The sense of shame associated with having a disability has, indeed, reached epidemic proportions. Disability rights movements in different countries have made many gains in the area of civil rights over the past decade, but what good is the ADA if people will not exercise their rights under these laws because they are too ashamed to identify as being disabled?"

For Harriet McBryde Johnson, the answer to this issue of internalized shame starts with encouraging more people with disabilities to
share their stories. Johnson, born with a degenerative neuromuscular
disorder that left her unable to walk, dress, bathe, or eat independently,
was also an outspoken lawyer, disability activist, and writer. She died
in 2008, and is perhaps best remembered for her appearance on the
cover of *New York Times Magazine* in 2003 along with her essay,
"Unspeakable Conversations," about her debate with Peter Singer, a
Princeton-based philosopher, who argued for legalizing a parent's choice
to euthanize babies born with severe disabilities. "The widespread assumption that disability means suffering feeds a fear of difference and
a social order that doesn't know what to do with us if it can't make us fit
its idea of normal," she said. "When we seek what we need to live good
lives as we are, we come against that wall. Why bother? the thinking
runs; all they can do is suffer."

For decades, the disability rights movement has been mobilizing to
make demands, to fight for the accessibility and accommodation that
the ADA has so frequently failed to deliver. Now it's time to do more, she
argued. "In the face of these powerful social forces, I believe that living
our strange and different lives, however we choose and manage to live
them, is a contribution to the struggle. Living our lives openly and without shame is a revolutionary act. . . . We need to confront the life-killing
stereotype that says we're all about suffering. We need to bear witness
to our pleasures."

Four years after Johnson issued the challenge to "bear witness to
our pleasures," Mel Baggs, a disability activist and blogger with autism,
made a nine-minute video, *In My Language,* that garnered over a million views. The first half of the video shows Baggs humming and
stimming—though Baggs never names those activities. The second half
is a "translation" of Baggs's world and thoughts for the world of nonau-
tistics. I recognize every gesture and tic, all of which defy description,
though we've given them names: hand-flapping, rocking, finger-flicking.
Throughout there is a soundtrack of Baggs's hummy droning that Ethan
could harmonize along to happily, for hours on end. Baggs (who identi-

fies as gender nonbinary and uses gender-neutral pronouns) is, technically, nonverbal, so using a computer-activated voice, they make the
argument that theirs, too, is a valid form of communication. "My language is about being in a constant conversation with every aspect of my
environment. I can sing along with whatever is around me." In 2010,
Baggs took up McBryde-Johnson's challenge to testify to the pleasures
of a life that might look difficult to others in an essay written for *Disability Studies Quarterly*. Addressing a man who pitied such an existence, Baggs writes, "I wonder if he is capable of looking around and
seeing shapes and colors instead of objects and of mapping the patterns
of those shapes and colors. I wonder if he understands my kind of beauty
or only that which comes from a different sort of perception. . . . I wonder
if he understands that with any pain that comes from jerking-around
fluctuations also comes a rhythm and beauty." Baggs's death in April
2020 drew national attention and a reminder of this essential message
that all language—and all forms of communication—should be honored
and respected.

It's also a reminder of McBryde-Johnson's challenge. To impact the
hearts and minds of those who don't know disability, we must all tell
our stories—those with disabilities and those who love them—but a directive like this is easier said than done. When Ethan was younger, it
was impossibly hard for me to talk about our life and I spent what now
feels like an inordinate amount of energy minimizing his issues and
keeping our struggles as private as possible. I told myself that I didn't
want people to feel sorry for us. Pity wouldn't help our situation and I
assumed it was the only response we would get. Surely parents hustling
children between soccer practices and music lessons would never understand how those simple activities eluded my child, so what was the
point? When I finally started writing about our experience—and putting into print what I rarely had the courage to say openly—one of the
biggest shocks for me was how often I heard from people whose children
weren't disabled. They wanted to tell me how a point I'd made struck a
chord. Opening up a dialogue that was honest and straightforward
didn't mitigate our problems; it wasn't as simple as saying, "Oh, now I

recognize all children struggle to one degree or another," because as any parent of a child with special needs will tell you, there's a difference between a shy, quirky kid and one who is autistic, just as there's a difference between one who struggles with math and one who is cognitively disabled. But talking more openly reminded me that stories are powerful and people are interested in hearing them. Usually their response was not pity (my greatest fear), but curiosity about Ethan's quirks and interests. Once they were given a little information, it was easier to get to know him, and other parents surprised us. One couple invited him to a classical musical gathering at their home, a string quartet where Ethan was the only non-adult present. He was about nine, and by that point, I'd written a few articles about our experience. Most of the attendees understood why he rocked and bounced as he listened. Afterward a few marveled at the fun of watching him process the music. "My kids wouldn't even hear it, but he really did," one father told me. And he was right: Ethan was good at this.

There's a balancing act, of course. Some parents might press too hard and insist their child be included in occasions that aren't appropriate, for the child or others. But most parents I know err on the side of caution. We always did. Unsure if Ethan might disturb others, we left him at home. Even when we knew he would love an activity or event, if we heard the slightest hesitation from the organizers, we backed off. No need to push him into any situation where he might not be wanted, we reasoned. I wish I'd pushed a little bit more. It doesn't get easier as they get older, and over time, their options will narrow dramatically.

This new generation of young adults with IDD will need to take their rightful place in our world, and our new battle, not just as parents but as a society, is to think imaginatively and bravely about how to help them do this. In 2006, Jason McElwain, an Indiana high school basketball team manager, became arguably the most famous autistic person in America. After years of serving as manager and cheering from the sidelines, he was, for the very first time, allowed to play in the last minutes of the team's final game his senior year. In those four minutes, he scored twenty-two points, three baskets and four three-pointers. A video of his extraordinary feat—along with the crowd in the stands cheering him on—went viral. In the weeks following, he appeared on *Oprah*, *Larry King Live, Good Morning America* and the *Today* show. At the end of that year, ESPN gave him the ESPY Award for Best Sports Moment over Kobe Bryant.

To my mind, the most important part of McElwain's story isn't that an autistic kid made twenty points in the final minutes of a basketball game. The crucial part came long before, with a mother who saw her child's passion and climbed over her own fears to ask if he could have a role on the team. With a coach who said yes and found jobs for him. With a team who moved over to make a place for him on the bench. With a community who allowed themselves to try something that hadn't been done before. In doing this, they helped countless others see: if you open your house, your job site, your classroom, your basketball team, you will widen your world. Yes, you will face challenges but you'll also be part of the solution to a global challenge.

Arriving at society's true and meaningful acceptance of this group will necessitate that all of us—myself included—tell our stories more, live proudly and publicly, and show the world that Ethan's life is not a tragedy, and helping him through it is not an unmanageable burden. It means delineating for ourselves and others the unique, and real, pleasures it offers. The stories we tell must be honest and include the hard parts, because if there's anything we've learned, it's that the greatest struggles offer the richest rewards. In sharing our stories, I suspect we'll be able to see them better ourselves and put them into a continuum with all the world's fight for connection and community.

As Ne'eman points out, there's a unique strength that comes from telling your story and acknowledging your vulnerability. In his book, *Fully Alive: Discovering What Matters Most,* Timothy Shriver, Eunice Kennedy Shriver's son, suggests that his aunt, Rosemary—and his mother's decision to go public with their story—had a profound impact on the other siblings and was, perhaps, an explanation for the family's legendary political skill. He remembers a story his uncle, Ted Kennedy, told about being at a pool party and watching his brother Jack leave the people he was talking to and sit down beside his sister: "Whatever shame her siblings felt about Rosemary when they were growing up had found its counter in an empathy that took root deep in their souls, an empathy not learned in school or politics but triggered by countless moments when their sister was alone and the only response that made sense was to sit by her side. They were asked over and over again to look out for that sister, but in being asked to give, they had received something too, hundreds of moments when they were alone with her, sitting with someone they loved, by the pool, legs dangling in the water together, saying nothing."

In his inaugural address, Kennedy challenged the country to "ask not what your country can do for you—ask what you can do for your country," galvanizing a nation to rediscover community spirit and commitment to public service it had found during the Progressive Era and later, during the war years. Where did his certainty that people would respond come from? "I will never be able to prove it, but I think it sprang from the family and the faith that taught him to give himself to Rosemary and the unspoken happiness that he received from her in return . . . [in] caring for her, they all gained the confidence to believe that they could ask others to give, knowing the joys of giving . . . They learned to believe that peoples and nations could cross boundaries of fear and intolerance to join together in peace and friendship," Shriver adds. In her own way, he says, Rosemary had the most influence over public life of any member of his family: "This is a hunch, an intuition. What I know for sure, though, is that the unique combination of love and loyalty and anger and empathy that Rosemary inspired in her family would also give rise to a global movement."

He's talking about the Special Olympics, but I wonder if this idea (and the Kennedys' influence) might ultimately generate a movement toward living more communally, in every sense of the word. As we watch more of these communities spring up, I wonder if there might be a ripple effect, easy to see but impossible to measure. I wonder if a world of employers who are more open to hiring a person with IDD—or at least less afraid of its unknowns—might discover the advantages other employers have been so struck by. "Disability rights hold the power to change the trajectory toward a cookie-cutter society," Matthew Diller, professor of law at Fordham University, writes. "It has the potential to transform society itself."

Mary Johnson argues that the fight for access and accommodation is, at its core, a battle for the "increased humanizing of society." Small wonder this goal is hard to write into policy. It manifests in everything unmeasurable: in mood, in pace, in atmosphere. We are a society raised on the idea that achieving goals faster is always better. A growing industry on mindfulness teaches people how not to do this. So, too, does being around people with IDD.

It's easy to fall into a sequestering pattern, especially as your child gets older. We leave Ethan behind from some situations because I've thought it was wrong to impose him and all his attention-drawing oddities too much on his brother's lives. They tolerate a lot of it, and they're usually good sports, which makes me want to be mindful about not overdoing it. But I'm learning—slowly—that maybe I shouldn't always follow this impulse. Recently we all went on a college visit for Ethan's younger brother, Henry, who loves theater. We were meeting Braydon, an older friend of his, for lunch, a megatalent who had starred in many shows with Henry. He was a lowly college freshman now, but to Ethan still a celebrity, and the sort of person who can inspire Ethan to nervously dominate a conversation with silly talk. We'd planned to sit separately in the college cafeteria so Henry could ask his questions in peace but, of course, there weren't enough tables and we had to crowd together. Halfway through lunch, Mike leaned in and said, "Ethan has two questions he'd like to ask Braydon."

I raised my eyebrows at Mike—*Do you know what they are?* He didn't.

"Okay, Eth," I said. "It's your turn. But remember this is Henry's friend and we're going to mostly let him ask the questions."

Ethan geared up by rocking wildly. "Do you have a school mascot?"

I was pleasantly surprised—it was reasonably appropriate. They did have a school mascot, as a matter of fact. "Good job, Eth! What's your next question?"

He considered for a long time, It started to seem like he might go to one of his reliable ones: Have you ever heard of Bruce Springsteen? Or Mr. Rogers? Not terrible questions, but he asks them a lot and they've become a nervous habit. I don't think they get him to the conversations he wants to have. He looked at Henry. "Do you have a family weekend where people can visit?"

Braydon smiled at Henry, as if even he saw what was behind the question. Ethan is worried about what life will be like after Henry leaves. "Yeah, we do, actually," Braydon said. "They're fun. They have a lot of activities and things to do. You should definitely come. We can all hang out."

It was a small moment but it reminded me, once again, of all the ways that Ethan gives people a chance to demonstrate their kindness, and more often than not, they do. Community building necessitates legislation, infrastructure, and money but more importantly, it requires a lot of moments like these. Moments that come when families remember to keep pushing their child out into the world.

In the end, of course, the most important part of telling our stories is letting our children tell their own stories—and listening, however they communicate, to what they say. Naoki Higashida, a nonverbal, autistic thirteen-year-old, made publishing history with *The Reason I Jump: The Inner Voice of a Thirteen-Year-Old Boy with Austism,* an account of his life, spelled out on an alphabet grid. In it, he writes about visiting America and finding a country where people "understand autism" better than they do at home: "Even at a museum, a guard allowed me to follow a fixation without forcing me to obey the rules that other visitors had to." He's talking about being allowed to be himself in public. I'm especially touched because museums have always held a special fascination for Ethan, too. I picture every velvet rope Ethan has leaned across because he wants to look at some painting in his own way— through peripheral vision, past the tip of his nose. Maybe he wants to smell the thing. Who knows? I always hover close to him and watch the worried looks he gets from guards. I whisper, "I'll make sure he doesn't touch," so they know what I know: he won't touch. He knows that rule.

Recently, Ethan's been asking to go back to Washington, DC. "Remember the Smithsonian? Remember seeing Mr. Rogers's sweater and George Washington's coat?" Those items, randomly placed not far from each other in the Smithsonian Collection of American History and Culture, are extraordinary. But perhaps more extraordinary is the fact that he remembers them from the last time we visited, which was thirteen years ago. I have to wonder now if they made an impression because he was allowed to see them his own way.

For me, the most reassuring thing Higashida offers is acceptance of his own limitations and a peace with his autism. He wants the wider world to understand that autistic people don't act out of selfishness or ego or a desire to cut themselves off. His book is a testament to the opposite, in fact. It lays the groundwork for connection, the scaffolding for a bridge between parents and the stranger their own child might sometimes feel like. We are more alike than you realize, his book reassures, even as he describes his own isolating behaviors. We want connection. Through connection there is hope. "And when the light of hope shines on all the world, then our future will be connected with your future. That's what I want, above all."

When Harriet McBryde Johnson issued her challenge for people with disabilities to tell their stories, she wanted to offer a counterargument to Singer's assumption that people with disabilities have lives that are "worse off." "Are we 'worse off'?" she writes. "I don't think so. Not in any meaningful sense. There are too many variables. For those of us with congenital conditions, disability shapes all we are. Those disabled later in life adapt. We take constraints that no one would choose and build rich and satisfying lives within them. We enjoy pleasures other people enjoy and pleasures peculiarly our own. We have something the world needs."

I love this line: *We have something the world needs*. The first lesson a child with autism teaches his parents still grieving a diagnosis is to stop grieving and get on with life. There are passions to pursue, some universal, some peculiarly their own. Along the way, they teach us countless other lessons: Difference is not a tragedy. Success is measured in many ways. Happiness doesn't necessitate achievements as measured by the broader society.

But here is another conundrum: history doesn't determine what Ethan will make of his future. This is his story to write. Gunnar Dybwad, an early pioneer of deinstitutionalization, remembered an early slogan NARC (National Association for Retarded Children) often used in the 1960s on posters and leaflets: "We Speak for Them." "What faces parents today is that these children and young people are learning to speak for themselves," Dybwad writes. Parents must learn to listen. They will be challenged by "the very movement [they started] whose horizon is suddenly being widened by opinions which they didn't expect to hear from their offspring."

In 2002, when the state of Vermont abolished institutions and sheltered workshops about ten years before any other state, a collection of self-advocacy groups sprang up soon after. Most are member led, with some assistance for planning events and outings. "We help each other," one advocate says. 'We make things better for others in the community." Another puts it a different way. "I respect myself more because we give each other respect."

A University of Vermont researcher looked at the outcomes of belonging to a self-advocacy group and found that they have helped individuals achieve or make progress in many key goals like independent housing, jobs, sports, social life, and taking care of their health. Though the groups emphasize socializing—and many of their activities are strictly that—their founding mission was political activism and self-advocacy. They've visited the statehouse in Montpelier and organized rallies. On a local level, they've done what was never done nationally: put their faces forward, appeared on TV, made their case. So far, they've succeeded in putting a respectful language bill before their state legislature and getting it passed. They've also partnered with nondisability groups to build a stronger human rights movement. For Max Barrows, a self-advocate leader with autism at Green Mountain Self-Advocates, partnering with other twentysomethings at Vermont Workers' Center is exciting. He believes working with other social justice groups widens their world and raises awareness about other people's struggles: student debt crisis, income inequality, environment action. "We work together because we know that there is no climate justice without migrant justice, no workers' rights without disability rights."

As the population of Americans with IDD grows bigger every year, and the competition for funding grows tighter, I suspect political organizing will be a crucial piece of ensuring the fullest lives possible, and the strongest advocates will undoubtedly be the ones doing it for themselves. It won't be a political movement that looks exactly like any other, but it will have some similarities. Eddy Hougan has been working at Milestones, a community-based day program for adults in Hadley, Massachusetts, for five years. Before that, he was primarily a musician, artist, and social activist, but in 2014 his daughter Emma was born and diagnosed with Down syndrome. A few months later, he walked into the Inclusive Community Center, home now to Whole Children and Milestones. "The second I walked in here, I had a powerful feeling, like I was coming home," he tells me. Hougan was raised by politically active parents, with a father at the forefront of the gay rights movement starting at Stonewall and continuing through the AIDS crisis. Eddy witnessed that fight as a child and has come to see disability activism as a new civil rights movement. "One of the things I always loved about the gay movement was that they never wanted to fit in to culture, they wanted to be themselves, to celebrate their sexuality and everything that made them different. I was this little kid in gay pride marches shouting 'We're queer and we're here'" and I loved it because it's such a human message— we're all queer and we're all here. Why should other people change themselves to fit into a dominant culture's expectations?"

He started working in Milestones, teaching art and music classes he designed to celebrate the individuality of each participant. The longer he works at this the more connections he sees to his father's work back in the '80s. "This is a group that's only just discovering its own voice and sense of pride. But it's amazing to watch when it happens. Art and music are the best platforms to express themselves and release that sense of profound pride and tell the world—I am here, I matter, what I have to say is important. It wouldn't happen unless we were all together in this place, reinforcing each other, experimenting with different forms and ways to express ourselves. I watch these folks do something completely new—dance with their arms thrown up in the air, or sing into a microphone, and I feel like a kid again, watching my dad's friends come out of the closet and march down the street. It's breathtaking, and yeah, I have to say, it could never happen if I was working one-on-one with someone in the community, taking them to a grocery store. That's all about fitting into a status quo. That's not a movement." He gestures around him, at walls covered in self-portraits—drawings, paintings, photographs the participants have taken of each other. "This right here—this is a movement."

Ari Ne'eman echoes this belief that perhaps the most radically political act of all for people with autism and IDD is living an unapologetic life. For years he dreaded every April—Autism Awareness Month—and its outpouring of rhetoric "heralding autistic people as eternal children, diseased, broken, empty and imprisoned, putting our families through unimaginable suffering and single-handedly creating the greatest public health crisis of our time. More devastating than AIDS, more expensive than cancer, more common than diabetes: If your child stacked blocks or didn't make eye contact, it was the end of the end of the world." For Ne'eman, a new day is dawning and with it, he's got an alternate message to offer not just in April, but every month of year: "We aren't victims, we aren't monsters, and we aren't going anywhere. We are family members, friends . . . and fellow citizens. We can speak for ourselves and we have things to say. We are autistic. And we have a right to live in this world."

In the course of my interviews, I asked dozens of professionals what their advice was for parents hoping to ensure the best adulthood for their child. One vocational coordinator told me that parents should work more on the soft skills that will matter much more in a workplace environment than any academic skills: Following instructions. Taking criticism. Doing something over if you haven't done it right. An autism consultant told me, "Focus on the experiences where your child has had the most success." A longtime special-ed teacher: "Always stay open to the possibility that your child will surprise you."

Ethan recently wrote about his dreams for the future in a class for BHMA with a teacher who incorporates personal statements before every musical performance. It's a wonderful idea because it combines practice with public speaking along with a chance for parents to be surprised by the things their children say. Before his last performance, Ethan told the assembled crowd, "As a professional farmer, my dream is to someday own a farm of my own. I know it will be hard work, but this is my dream."

Mike and I looked at each other, eyebrows raised. We'd never heard this before.

What can we do, now that Ethan is an adult, to keep him moving forward toward his goals? I thought of the question as I watched him last December. Ethan loves Christmas—hands down, it's his favorite holiday—but every year he struggles to make a wishlist and, in the end, he usually settles on the same things he always asks for: restaurant gift cards, licorice, a six-pack of Mountain Dew. I realized in that moment what he really wants are the rituals, starting with the church pageant and dinner the night before, spent with the same family friends we've always shared Christmas Eve with. After dinner he wants to read "'Twas the Night Before Christmas" with a Santa hat on his head and, afterward, sit down by himself with several sheets of paper and write a note to Santa, which he'll leave with cookies he's squirreled away for this purpose along with some raggedy-looking carrots from the bottom of the crisper drawer, which he'll explain in his note are for the "rain deer."

He wants *Christmas* for Christmas, the same way he wants his life now to be his life forever. So how do we gently push him to want more? Or to believe he can do things he hasn't seen too many of his friends doing, either?

This is our challenge. We need to see possibilities he can't see for himself and believe in his capacity to rise to meet them. Families can't sit back and wait for the policy makers to take action. Our children need options before they reach middle age. Our thinking must align with other groups that have found solutions to similar challenges. The future we all want necessitates having faith in the possibility of communities we might not live near yet but that we can visit and see the surprises they offer: joy, connection, interdependence. This will depend on flexibility from every stakeholder. We must be ready and willing to do the work. We must do everything in our power to get our children as independent as they can possibly be, recognizing and accepting that there will be some measure of risk in allowing them to move out into the world and take their place there. We can't anticipate everything that might happen but we can teach them the same things we teach our neurotypical children: self-defense, advocacy, and resilience.

Above all we need to acknowledge that we are already creating that world. It's a far different place than it was thirty years ago before inclusive education laid a groundwork that can never be undone. People with IDD are not vilified or dehumanized the way they were in the first half of the twentieth century. But that doesn't mean we're out of the woods. They will still suffer from isolation and neglect unless we all take responsibility.

In Ethan's early years, I longed for a book that would tell me exactly what to expect. As every parent will learn sooner or later, the glorious challenge of disability is that every child with a disability is different, and each one has strengths you didn't foresee and deficits that linger in spite of years of determined effort to address them. No doctor, teacher, or therapist can predict the future for your child.

In his book *Uniquely Human,* Barry Prizant argues that the single most important thing parents can do for their autistic child while they're still young is get them out in the world as much as possible. Every parent of a child who has passed through a rocky infancy and a meltdown-filled toddlerhood knows how challenging this is. The impulse is always to run ahead of your preschooler, looking for landmines and rearranging the world to fit his expectations. Inevitably it doesn't work. Stores will be closed. The baby pigs you drove out to the farm to visit will not yet be born. (If it's possible, the mother pig will be even less sympathetic to your child's wails than you are. She has enough on her plate. She doesn't need a four-year-old screaming, *"Where are the baby pigs??"*) The world is rife with injustice that must feel heartrending to a four-year-old who desperately wants it to bend to his will.

"Let him get angry" was one of the best pieces of advice one of Ethan's preschool teachers once gave me. "And let him practice coming back from it. As often as possible. Every day if you have to. You'll see. Eventually he'll start to shorten his recovery time."

It was great advice for all our kids. Get mad and then come back to us. Prizant believes that parents who've done this have "exposed their child to challenges and offered opportunities to learn coping skills and stay well-regulated." I will also say this: in my experience, the children who found the fewest ways to engage with the world—with parents who steered them clear of restaurants, loud places, all situations that overwhelmed their sensory systems—now seem to be the young adults who wrestle the most with anxiety and depression. Even when this instinct toward protectiveness comes entirely from loving, good intentions (as it always does) it's an important cautionary note—sooner or later, your child will need to make their peace with the world's unpredictability in order to find their place in it.

At the end of his memoir, *Father's Day,* Buzz Bissinger asks himself the hardest question every parent of an aging child with IDD has faced: "Why had we never discussed, even in the broadest terms, [Zach's] long-term future, no matter how wrenching the subject might be? Maybe because I wasn't sure how much he would understand. Or maybe I couldn't bear to think about it. Because when I did, the same image always appeared: I am gone and his mother is gone and Zach is old now, in his sixties, stooped and scraggly, his brown eyes more dark and furrowed than ever, his voice raspier than ever when he talks to himself. . . ." He imagines his son living in a group home, sitting on a bed, with his hands clasped in front of him. "And then I see him talking aloud to himself some more, which no one tries to silence because no one else is there."

To any parent who has spent two decades living with a self-talker, it's a frightening image. What will happen to my son when no one is there to tell him to pipe down? We must look at the future. We must have these conversations.

At almost every residential site I visited, I experienced a moment of quiet revelation: the people living in a good situation away from their parents seem happier than the ones still at home. Even the ones less able to communicate how they are feeling seem older to me, and more sure of their place in the world.

Our children not only can do this; they will have to sooner or later.

. . . .

When Jason Kinglsey was diagnosed with Downs syndrome at birth in 1974, the doctor had blunt words for his mother, Emily: "His recommendation was that I not feed him, hold him or get attached to him—but to send him to an institution and tell our friends and family that he died in childbirth." Instead, Emily and her husband, Charles, became pioneers in the early intervention movement. "We surrounded him with motion and music, and we'd talk and talk to him," Emily recalls. Jason exceeded everyone's expectations. By age three he could identify letters; by four, he was reading simple words. A few years later, he was counting to ten in twelve languages.

Emily was a head writer on *Sesame Street*, which was the first children's television show to include characters with disabilities. Jason appeared on several episodes and, over the next ten years, on over fifty other TV and radio shows. He graduated from high school and then from Maplebrook, a postsecondary school for students with learning disabilities. In 1997, on the brink of moving into his own apartment for the first time, Jason told the *New York Times* about his plans: "I will do my own shopping, I will do my own cleaning. I will pay my bills. Intellectually in my brain, I am very excited. In my feelings, I'm still a little bit nervous. . . . Someday I will get married and start my own history of being my own family."

It didn't quite work out that way. Having outgrown his child-acting jobs, finding work got harder. For a while, he shelved videos in a library and came up with his own system to reorganize the collection. "It made sense to him, but nobody could find anything," his mother said. Living alone didn't pan out, either. He needed more structure. He was isolated; the apartment grew messy; he stopped shaving and bathing regularly.

"We were too optimistic," Emily decided. Now, she looks back at his childhood with clear eyes. When he was little, "it was so exciting. Everything they said he wouldn't do, he was doing." Soon enough, though, she saw his limitations. He could read at an early age, but he couldn't understand what he was reading. He'd make the soccer team but didn't know which way to run on the field.

Jason's isn't a cautionary story—it's a realistic, candid one. Emily is internationally famous for an essay called "Welcome to Holland," which most parents of a child with special needs have, sooner or later, read. The message is this: having a child with a disability is like packing your bags thinking you're going to Italy and winding up in Holland instead. Everything is different than you expected. It's not Italy, but if you open your eyes and look around, there are tulips and windmills, and you will grow to love Holland as well. But one essay can't be expected to reflect an entire lifetime.

The story I really love is one Emily shared in that *Times* article. Jason was living in a group home, with three other men with IDD. They were lobbying to get a sidewalk on the street they had to walk to catch a bus to their jobs. They'd gotten their neighbors' signatures and now they had to appear before a judge and make their case. Jason had a speech written out that he'd memorized, like the old days when he had to learn scripts. He was planning to explain to the judge that his job was important—he delivered mail in a law office—and he wasn't safe walking on the road.

The roommates won. They returned to their shared home and celebrated over cake. For me this is more reassuring than "Welcome to Holland." The article doesn't shy away from the details that comprise the life of an adult with developmental disability: the job he does, the daily struggle to get there, the apartment he shares. The closer picture isn't depressing. It's full of victories.

Jason, once the poster boy of overachievement for a child with IDD, has done something that's trickier and more elusive than counting to ten in multiple languages: he's become an adult with responsibilities and friendships, solving his own problems. His mother remains a guiding hand, but she's not controlling the outcome, because—as she undoubtedly learned years ago—she can't.

This is the kind of happy ending we need to see more often: one in which adults with IDD are charting their own path, reminding their families that they not only can, but should be celebrated when they do.

....

When Ethan was first diagnosed, floortime was one of the few mainstream therapies that parents were presented with. The idea is this: get down on the floor and do what they're doing. Join their endless wheel-spinning, their block-lining and make them give you a turn. Narrate what they're doing so they learn the words for what they care most about. If it sounds hard (and let's be honest, boring), it is.

"I'm terrible at floortime," I heard other mothers confess in a whisper. One mom told me she read magazines while she was doing it because her son never looked at her anyway so why not? I include myself in this camp. I was always awkward. Too shrill, too talky, too fake. Mike, who was more of a natural, was also more dubious. "Doesn't this all feel a little phony and unnatural?" he'd ask, putting in his hour of floortime after I'd put in four.

Yes. It did.

Still I forced us to soldier on as I forced us to do every therapy I'd bought a book about. They always opened with a host of appealing success stories. Though Dr. Stanley Greenspan wrote the essential bible on floortime, *Son-Rise* was an earlier book about a similar therapeutic approach created by Barry Neil Kaufman and Samahria Lyte Kaufman. Because their son Raun was in constant motion, easily distracted, and so hard to contain in one spot long enough to sustain joint attention on anything, the Kaufmans began their hours of therapy on the bathroom floor. You might forget some of the details, but you'll never forget the photos of Raun's mother displaying yogic flexibility as she played with her son, wedged into spaces between the toilet and the wall. You also don't forget the ending: the fully recovered child, writing thank-you notes to his parents and joining in their work to help other children for the last several decades.

These stories are only dangerous if you take them at face value and believe that money, time, and effort invested will guarantee a similar outcome. It won't. Required reading for every buyer of *Son-Rise* should be *Boy Alone* by Karl Taro Greenfield. The author is the brother of Noah Greenfield, made famous in the '70s when he was featured in their father's book, *A Child Called Noah,* about their family's tireless commitment to rescuing a child in the grip of autism. Karl writes with poignance about the adulthood of his "unrecovered" brother, "You can do everything in the world—invest all your money, move across the country to get the best therapists, do everything in your power and it still won't work out. That happens, too."

I know many more versions of the second story—extraordinarily committed families who still, fifteen years later, have a nonverbal child. Personally, I know only one version of the former, a single mom who moved to our town with her two young sons with autism. She was committed and smart but had limited resources. Her boys got school-based therapies and some outside therapies but mostly they did without the pricier ones the rest of us were pouring our money into. Her boys are now at MIT and Landmark College, respectively. Was she quietly doing something right that the rest of us missed or did she just get lucky with genetics that allowed the boys to find their own path? My instinct as a parent is that it's the latter.

This doesn't mean you don't try every therapy available; it means you measure your expectations for success against a realistic continuum. You are not a failure if your child doesn't speak before the age of five or eight or whatever benchmark you've written down so diligently. It means you'll have tried in every way possible to forge that mode of communication and now you'll move on to other methods.

Bissinger echoes this reminder to parents not to hinge future happiness on meeting certain goals or benchmarks. "There is no rose-colored ending to this. There is no pretty little package with a tidy bow. He will never drive a car. He will never marry. He will never have children. . . . He is not the child I wanted. But he's no longer a child anyway. He is a man, the most fearless I've ever known, friendly, funny, freaky, unfathomable, forgiving and fantastic, restoring the faith of a father in all that can be."

For those of us with older children who remember the hours of floortime and other labor-intensive interventions, maybe it's time to also remember the original impulse behind them: to get to know our child. To enter his world and see it like he does. To spin some car wheels, or fixate on a light switch and see how it feels. Chances are you won't get the same thrill your child does, but you'll see—maybe just for a split second—oh, yeah, this is kind of cool. How you flip a switch and boom, the whole room lights up.

Imagine living your whole life open to seeing the everyday magic of the world in this way. When Ethan was three, he taught me how to do this. It's not an easy lesson to hold on to, but there's a similar feeling when I watch him put his necklace wallet around his neck and head into town to buy himself another lunch of chow fun and a can of soda. *Isn't it amazing, that I can walk into town and do this?*

It is, I think. It really is.

Acknowledgments

The seeds of this book began fifteen years ago when Jo Sittenfeld, a graduate student at RISD in photography and documentary filmmaking, asked if she might include our family in a project chronicling the impact of autism on two different families. For two years, she visited our home regularly, traveled with us, and became a beloved member of the extended family. Ten years later, on the eve of Ethan's graduation from high school, she returned with the idea of reworking old footage and presenting a story we don't see often enough: how autism plays out over a lifetime. I loved the idea. Parents raising a child with autism obsess over therapies and choices with precious little scientific evidence for guidance on what will really make a difference in the final outcome for a child who faces so many challenges. For years, I wanted someone to come in, watch Ethan for a day, and tell me with some assurance: do this, it will make a difference; don't bother doing that, it won't matter in the long run. I loved Jo's idea not because I believed we were authorities on any of this, but because I had learned by then that the best information I got was often not from doctors but from other families, especially ones with children slightly older than Ethan. Maybe it'll help someone, I thought. When Jo's project morphed into an op-doc and a photo essay at the *New York Times*, accompanied by an essay I wrote that got widely circulated, many people suggested I write a book. I demurred for a long time, thinking our story was too common to warrant a book. Like every family raising an autistic child, it was very hard for a while and then gradually it became easier. We didn't have any secrets to success. Some days, it didn't feel like we'd succeeded at all. It was Jo's sister, Curtis Sittenfeld, writer extraordinaire and longtime friend, who convinced me otherwise on a hot summer day in Jo's backyard. "This could be a story for every parent of a younger child with autism and for everyone who knows a child with autism and wonders what will happen when they become an adult. You'll make it real and you'll make it hopeful. Telling your story will help people."

Her words back then and her belief in this project helped me enormously throughout, and I know this book would not exist without the mighty force of the Sittenfeld sisters.

Many thanks as well to:

Margaret Riley King (our sixth book together! How is it that you get better with every one?); Eric Simonoff of WME; from Penguin Random House, Megan Newman and Nina Shield for jumping in and enthusiastically embracing this book with such heart. And to the rest of the team at PRH: Hannah Steigmeyer, Casey Maloney, Farin Schlussel, and Lindsay Gordon. Many thanks for your help bringing this story out to the world.

Every service provider and professional who helped me understand the unique challenges of doing their work well. A few people were especially generous with their time, starting with Bill Zimmer who is such an articulate, thoughtful spokesperson for this population that he should be writing his own book. Also: Desiree Kameka, Dale Dileo, Amy Lutz, and Shawn Robinson were extraordinarily patient and thorough in explaining many of the basic issues around housing and employment. Tim O'Donohue for early help on research.

The mothers who helped me understand that being a proactive parent means building the world we want our children to live in and helped to create and sustain Whole Children/Milestones: Carrie McGee, Valle Dwight, Maggie Rice, Noreen Cmar-Mascis, Sue Higgins. Along those same lines, Jenny Koprowski deserves a special mention, too.

The educators who taught me that some of the best teaching happens with the students reaching for the lowest rungs of the academic ladder—the ones who might not go to college, but will lead fuller, richer lives thanks to their efforts: Grethe Camp, Denise O'Donovan, Crystal Cartwright, Faye Brady, Phyl Gerber, Lucy Robinson, Joan Epstein, Christa Smith, Sarah Wilson, Catherine Manicke, Paul Coffill, Michelle Kostek, Brian Melanson, Chris Harper. The teachers and school staff who widened Ethan's world and may appear in this book but aren't named directly: Erika Loper, David Ranen, John Bechtold, Mark Moriarty, Joelle Sanford, Jeff Stauder, Ahmed Gonzalez Berrios, Stephen Bechtold, Jackie Deiana, Brianna Rzeznik, Matt Meers, and Nancy Janoson.

The extended family who have watched this story unfold and helped us in so many incalculable ways, but mostly by making Ethan feel loved, celebrated, and appreciated for what he can do and who he is. Both sets of grandparents: Bill and Katie McGovern, Alain and Joanne Floquet. Also Monty McGovern and Kathy Graunke, Elizabeth McGovern and Simon Curtis, Manon Floquet and Rebecca Lee, and Susanna and Kevin Culver, and all the beloved cousins: Mattie, Grace, Richard, Brendan, and Blaine. All of you have been role models and heroes to Ethan.

Recently Ethan has made a new habit out of starting conversations with people he hasn't seen for a while not with his own news, but with convoluted, frequently exaggerated updates of his brother's accomplishments. It means Charlie and Henry have to clarify and explain. No, they aren't inventing robots or starring in any movies. They are patient and kind about this and I believe it is a measure of the superheroes his brothers are in his eyes—both of them, destined for greatness, capable of anything. I hope being his brother has given them as much as they've given him.

And last, but certainly not least: Mike's loving constancy and enduring patience doesn't get nearly enough page space in this book, but this story wouldn't exist without him. He has built our home and our family and filled both with laughter and love.

Notes

CHAPTER ONE

1 **a fighter pilot seeking a discharge:** Joseph Heller, *Catch-22* (New York: Simon and Schuster, 1961).

5 **"I've never met a child who has recovered from autism":** Cammie McGovern, "Autism's Parent Trap," *New York Times,* June 5, 2006.

6 **"Will we put in the work and open our eyes":** Dan Rather, Facebook post, September 4, 2016.

8 **entitled to receive vocational training, including community-based job internships:** "A Transition Guide to Post-Secondary Education and Employment for Students and Youths with Disabilities," US Dept. of Education, May, 2017.

9 **only 15 percent . . . will find paid employment:** Jean Winsor et al., "State Data: National Report on Employment Services and Outcomes though 2016," Institute for Community Inclusion, University of Massachusetts, Boston, p. 1.

9 **In Pennsylvania, over sixteen thousand . . . sit on waitlists:** Pennsylvania Wait List Campaign, https://pawaitinglistcampaign.org/.

9 **In Ohio, the waitlist is sixty-eight thousand names long:** Kaiser Family Foundation (KFF): Waiting List Enrollment for HCBS Waivers, 2018, https://www.kff.org/health-reform/state-indicator/waiting-lists-for-hcbs-waivers/.

14 **"Leon would talk to anybody":** "Levasseur's Will," *Bates College Alumni Magazine,* Summer 2013, p. 14.

18 **a whopping 56 percent, according to a 2014 survey:** Gary Siperstein, Robin Parker, Max Drascher, "National Snapshot of Adults with Intellectual Disabilities in the Labor Force," *Journal of Vocational Rehabilitation* 39, no. 3, 2013.

18 **only a quarter of adults with ASD . . . have community-based employment as a goal:** Anne Roux, Jessica Rast, Kristy Anderson, Paul Shattuck, *National Autism Indicators Report: Developmental Disability*

Services and Outcomes in Adulthood. Pennsylvania: Life Course Outcomes Program, A. J. Drexel Autism Institute, Drexel University, 2017, p. 13.

18 **By packing her lunches and limiting her expenses:** Rachel Simon, *Riding the Bus with My Sister: A True Life Journey.* (New York: Grand Central Publishing, 2002). p. 15.

18 **"No matter what people will say":** Wolf Wolfensberger, "A History of Human Services, Universal Lessons, and Future Implications," a lecture delivered at Millersville University, Lyte Auditorium, Millersville, Pennsylvania, on September, 1998. Posted online by Disability Minnesota, Council on Developmental Disabilities. https://mn.gov/mnddc/wolfensberger/.

20 **80 to 90 percent of adults with IDD who live with their parents into middle age:** Massachusetts Healthy People Autism Road Map Report, 2020: Understanding Needs and Measuring Outcomes, https://shriver.umassmed.edu /sites/shriver.umassmed.edu/files/CDDER/MA%20HP2020%20Autism %20Roadmap%20Report%20FINAL_tagged.pdf.

22 **seven million people with developmental disablity:** National Disability Navigator Resource Collaborative, https://nationaldisabilitynavigator.org/ndnrc -materials/fact-sheets/population-specific-fact-sheet-intellectual-disability

CHAPTER TWO

25 **"only one out of five students with special needs attended school":** Mental Retardation Past and Present, letter prepared by the President's Committee on Mental Retardation, Joseph Califano, chairman, January 1977, p. 48.

26 **"They can be taught to do some kinds of labor":** Ibid., p. 3.

27 **"Institutions are unnatural":** Ceremonies on laying the cornerstone of the New York State Institution for the Blind, Samuel Gridley Howe, Batavia, New York, September 6, 1866.

27 **"the morbid peculiarities of each":** *Mental Retardation Past and Present,* p. 5.

27 **"Even idiots have rights":** Ibid.

27 **"An idiot awakened to his condition is a miserable one":** Ibid., p. 9.

27 **"The tide is rising rapidly":** Charles Davenport, *Eugenics, the Science of Human Improvement by Better Breeding* (New York: Henry Holt, 1909), p. 31.

28 **"unspeakable debauchery and licentiousness":** W. E. Fernald, "The Burden of Feeblemindedness," *Journal of Psychoasthenics* XVIII, 1912, pp. 90–98.

28 **"We must protest and resist against this brutal pessimism":** Alfred Binet, *Les Idees Modernes sur les Infants* (Paris: Ernest Flammarion, editeur, 1909).

29 **"prevent the spread of and multiplication of worthless":** Adam Cohen, *Imbeciles: The Supreme Court, American Eugenics, and the Sterilization of Carrie Buck* (New York: Penguin Books, 2017), p. 25.

29 "wipe out defectives within fifteen or twenty years": *Imbeciles,* p. 25.

29 "If we prolong the lives of weaklings": *Imbeciles,* p. 56.

29 "Three generations of idiots are enough": *Buck v. Bell,* Oliver Wendall Holmes. 274 U.S. 200, 207, 1927.

29 "which families are reproducing these degenerates": *Imbeciles,* p. 136.

31 "[The hospital] has witnessed the heights of man's inhumanity": Peter Cranford, *But for the Grace of God: The Inside Story of the World's Largest Insane Asylum.* Old Capital Press (reprint edition, 2008), p. 9.

32 "a yearly increasing crop of half-wits": Michael Wehmeyer, *The Story of Intellectual Disability: The Evolution of Meaning, Understanding and Public Perspective* (Baltimore: Brooks Publishing, 2013), p. 170.

32 "Augusta women did much toward educating the members": Ibid.

33 "Disability is most often viewed through the lens": Katherine Castles, "Nice Average Americans, Post-War Parents Groups and the Defense of the American Family," anthologized in *Mental Retardation in America, a Historical Reader,* Steen Noll and James W. Trent, eds., New York University Press, 2004, p. 365.

34 "psychic trauma wrought upon the normal children": *Mental Retardation Past and Present,* p. 21.

35 1930 report from the National Children's Council: Ibid., p. 23.

36 "I have been a long time making up my mind": Pearl Buck, *The Child who Never Grew* (Rockville, MD: Woodbine House, 1950), p. 1.

36 "there is a whole personality not concerned with the mind": Ibid., p. 55.

37 "people behave as if it were": Ibid., p. 24.

37 "her life must count": Ibid., p. 6.

37 "all people are equal in their humanity": Ibid., p. 51.

37 "You're part of something larger": Pearl Buck, A *Community Success Story, the Founding of the Pearl Buck Center* (New York: John Day Co., 1972), p. 3.

38 "strapped in chairs like criminals": Eunice Kennedy Shriver, "Hope for the Retarded," *Saturday Evening Post,* Sept. 22, 1962.

38 "no better than a snake pit": The Minnesota Governor's Council on Developmental Disabilities, The ADA Legacy Project, Willowbrook Leads to New Protections of Rights, Moments in Disability History, 2013. https://mn.gov/mnddc/parallels/five/5b/bobby-kennedy-snakepits.html.

39 "what to do about the institution issue": *Valuing Lives: Wolf Wolfensberger and the Principle of Normalization;* interview with Wolf Wolfensberger, Jerry Smith, director and producer; Guy Caruso, producer; Amy Hewitt, executive producer, 2015. https://www.youtube.com/watch?v=QdQAFPAktR0.

39 "If you can view them as animals": *Valuing Lives: Wolf Wolfensberger and the Principle of Normalization;* interview with Wolf Wolfensberger, conducted at his home in Syracuse, Oct. 2009.

39 "normalization means living in their natural surroundings": Robert J. Flynn and Raymond A. Lemay, eds., "Formulating the Normalization

Principle," in *A Quarter-Century of Normalization and Social Role Valorization: Evolution and Impact* (Ottawa: University of Ottawa Press, 1999), p. 33.

40 **people deserve to have *a life*:** *The Principle of Normalization in Human Services,* Wolf Wolfensberger. (Toronto: National Institution on Mental Retardation, 1972).

40 **which he called the "Promised Land":** *Valuing Lives,* interview with Wolf Wolfensberger.

40 **"It swept through our field":** *Valuing Lives,* Steve Holmes, extended interview, 2015.

41 **"Is Basket Weaving Harmful?":** *Valuing Lives,* interview with Wolfensberger. Every poster child for a March of Dimes fundraiser: "An Interpreted Pictorial Presentaion on the History of Human Services," lecture delivered at Millersville University, Lyte Auditorium, Millersville, PA. September 1988.

42 **"You are going to get frustrated with me":** Ibid.

43 **"Our respectful treatment results in higher achievement":** Ibid.

43 **"an alcoholic retarded person":** *Valuing Lives,* interview with Wolf Wolfensberger.

43 **Nirje . . . stayed more positive about the developments:** Bengt Nirje, "The Basis and Logic of the Normalisation Principle," *Australia and New Zealand Journal of Developmental Disabilities* 11, p. 65–68.

43 **achieving true independence:** Bengt Nirje, in *Changing Patterns in Residential Services for the Mentally Retarded,* Washington DC, President's Committee on Mental Retardation, pp. 179–195.

44 **"there can be crippling indignity in safety,":** Robert Perske, "The Dignity of Risk and the Mentally Retarded," *Mental Retardation* 10, no. 1, February 1972.

44 **they had 'few or no friends':** Wolf Wolfensberger, "What is Still the Same, New Problems that Have Arisen, and Things that Have Gotten Worse," lecture delivered at Millersville University, Millersville, PA, September 1988.

44 **"People should consider living with a family member":** Ibid.

44 **"it's lies, lies, lies, and more lies":** *Valuing Lives,* interview with Wolfensberger.

45 **"their whole lives go down the drain as a result":** Wolf Wolfensberger, "What Is Still the Same," lecture delivered at Millersville University, September 1988.

45 **The majority of them had been "dumped":** Ibid.

45 **"These ideas lie on a continuum":** *Valuing Lives,* extended interview with Steve Eidelman, 2015.

46 **"We need people like Wolf":** *Valuing Lives,* interview with Chas Mosely, 2015.

46 **he'd become an ardent supporter of L'Arche:** John O'Brien, "Celebrating the Genius of Wolf Wolfensberger," *Georgia Lithonia Research & Practice for Persons with Severe Disabilities* 36, no. 1–2 (2011): 76–79.

46 **idleness was the gravest danger:** Wolfensberger, lecture delivered at Millersville University, September 1988.

CHAPTER THREE

50 **chilling candor from the administrators and staff:** "They Need Love, They Get Angry, They Bleed," a Channel 3 Public Affairs Presentation, originally aired in 1972.

52 **"he was afraid of his daughter getting raped":** *Purgatory, An Historical Analysis of the Belchertown State School.* Jeromie Whelan, producer, Whelan and Daniel Madson, directors, 2012.

52 **"Making them *part* of the community was not":** Bill Zimmer, interview with the author, 2019.

52 **"We believed the isolation would end":** Ibid.

53 **"We were never accepted there":** Ruth Sienkiewicz-Mercer and Steven B. Kaplan, *I Raise My Eyes to Say Yes* (New York: Houghton Mifflin Co., 1989), p. 204.

53 **"no family ever wanted to scale *back* on staff":** Bill Zimmer, interview with the author, 2019.

53 **"boredom and a tight budget":** *I Raise My Eyes,* p. 222.

CHAPTER FOUR

55 **Ninety percent of them will be unemployed or underemployed,** Bryna Siegel, *The Politics of Autism* (New York: Oxford University Press, 2018), p. xiii.

58 **"an accommodated curriculum is a waste of time":** Ibid., p 98.

61 **"truth in special education is a very vulnerable commodity":** Ibid., p.107.

63 **"the truth is so much dearer than any comforting falsehood":** *The Child Who Never Grew,* p. 78.

65 **"Make your child as independent as possible":** Jane Bernstein, "Love: The Challenges of Raising a Child with Disabilities," keynote speech presented at the Perkins School for the Blind, 2009.

CHAPTER FIVE

70 **some earned an average of fourteen cents an hour:** U.S. v. Rhode Island and City of Providence—1:13-cv-00442- (D.R.I. 2013).

70 **CNN investigated Goodwill:** "Agents raid Goodwill amidst growing investigation of AbilityOne," CNN News, September 4, 2014.

70 **working at a turkey processing plant in Atalissa, Iowa:** Dan Barry, "The Boys in the Bunkhouse: Toil, Abuse, and Endurance in the Heartland," *New York Times,* March, 2014.

70 **"a promising but overdue starting point":** Editorial Board, "Doubly Disabled in Life," the *New York Times,* April 11, 2014.

71 **"Sheltered workshops are fundamentally flawed"**: Dale Dileo, interview with the author, 2018.

71 ***getting ready* to have a life!"**: Ibid.

71 **"You could spend six years on shoe-tying"**: Dale Dileo, keynote address, APSE (Association of People Supporting Employment First) National Conference, 2018.

72 **"This person will spend a lifetime getting ready to have a life"**: Ibid.

72 **"given a chance to try"**: Ibid.

72 **get all people with disabilities earning minimum wage or higher:** APSE website, "Our Mission: Real Jobs for Real People," www.apse.org.

75 **"overcome the inertia of the status quo"**: Bill Zimmer, interview with the author, 2019.

76 **individuals around the country who are still employed in sheltered workshops:** David Sommerstein, "Advocates Fight to Keep Sheltered Workshops for People with Disabilities," *All Things Considered,* NPR, April 14, 2015.

76 **"People are going to die because of this"**: Ibid.

76 **"I was chilled by what I saw"**: Jane Bernstein, "Why Are People Trying to Take My Disabled Daughter's Job Away?" *Vice,* May 1, 2016.

77 **Massachusetts planned ahead for this process:** Margaret Van Gelder, Amanda D. Nichols, M.S.W., Larry Tummino (principal authors), *Blueprint for Success: Employing Individuals with Disabilities in MA,* prepared for the Dept. of Development Disabilities, November 2013.

77 **DDS reimburses provider agencies:** Provider Payment Rates: Purchase of Service, 101 CMR 401, https://www.mass.gov/lists/provider-payment-rates -purchase-of-service.

77 **employment has actually gone down slightly:** Jean Winsor, et al., *StateData: The National Report on Employment Services and Outcomes through 2016,* Institute for Community Inclusion, p 3.

77 **"why aren't we doing better, folks?"** Dale Dileo, keynote address, APSE Conference, 2018.

78 **"what they can't do, not what they can"**: Ibid.

78 **"We need to make them *see* this"**: Ibid.

78 **"is going to have trouble fitting in"**: Dileo, interview with author, 2018.

80 **"they'd wandered into a bingo parlor"**: Ron Suskind, *Life Animated: A Story of Sidekicks, Heroes, and Autism* (New York: Kingswell, 2014), p. 178.

80 **"I've been proven wrong so many times"**: Dileo, interview with author, 2018.

81 **nearly half will wander or bolt from safety:** "Autism Statistics and Facts," Autism Speaks, https://www.autismspeaks.org/autism-statistics.

82 **"as long as you make the choice we agree with"**: Bill Zimmer, interview with author, 2019.

82 **71 percent of people with IDD weren't interested in community employment:** National Core Indicators: 2017–18, Human Services Research

Institute (HSRI) and The National Association of State Directors of
Developmental Disabilities Services (NASDDDS), https://www
.nationalcoreindicators.org/charts/2017-18/?i=15&st=undefined.

83 **"It just doesn't work for them":** Lee Cieswekisz, interview with the author,
2018.

83 **"sitting with a job developer, right?":** Ibid.

84 **"already spending their days in congregate settings":** Ibid.

85 **the vast majority of former workshop employees didn't find jobs:**
Scott Spreat and James William Conroy, "Longitudinal Investigation of
Vocational Engagement," *Journal of Policy and Practice in Intellectual
Disabilities* 12, no. 4 (2015): 266–271.

85 **the first state in the country to close all sheltered workshops:** Halle
Stockton, "Vermont Closed Sheltered Workshops for People with Disabilities.
What Happened Next?" *Public Source,* September 2014.

85 **"we have grossly erred":** Scott Spreat, "Challenges of Employment First,"
Social Innovations Journal, March, 2017.

85 **they instituted a working age adult policy:** Gretchen Enquest et al.,
"Trends and Challenges in Publicly-Financed Care for Individuals with
Intellectual and Developmental Disabilities," Center for Health Care
Strategies, 2012, http://www.chcs.org/media/IDD_Service_Delivery_Systems
_082812.pdf.

86 **highest integrated employment rate in the country:** Chris Kardish,
"Hidden or Unemployed: America's Failure to Get Disabled People Jobs,"
Governing: The Future of States and Localities, June 2015.

CHAPTER SIX

88 **"we've got a much better program now":** Kyle Scheller, interview and site
visit, Riverside Industries, Easthampton, Massachusetts, 2018.

88 **"We can individualize a lot more than we used to":** Kyle Scheller,
interview with the author, 2018.

89 **"It was frustrating for all of us":** Ibid.

91 **"Boy, we sure made her day":** Ibid.

CHAPTER SEVEN

98 **sing opera in twelve languages:** Teri Sforza, Howard Lenhoff and Sylvia
Lenhoff, *The (Strangest) Song: One Father's Quest to Help His Daughter Find
Her Voice* (Amherst, NY: Prometheus Books, 2006).

98 **music impacted her own son:** Kay Bernon, interview with the author,
2019.

99 **It took about four years from their early brainstorming:** Sharon Libera,
interview with the author, 2019.

99 **Gloria and John were featured:** "A Very Special Brain: Morley Safer
Reports on People with Williams Syndrome," *60 Minutes,* January 2006.

99 **what stood out to researchers was their level of *responsiveness* to music:** *The (Strangest) Song,* pp. 179–181.

102 **has effectively erased disability from our cultural landscape:** Margaret Keller, "The Art of Seeing: How to Look at Disability, a TED Talk," December 2015.

102 **"captured the power of art":** Ibid.

104 **They won both their battles—for access and for arts funding:** National Disability Arts Collection and Archive, https://the-ndaca.org/the-story/.

104 **"We thought it might help to create theater pieces":** "Closing the Gap Between Disabilities and Drama, an Interview with Tim Wheeler," Mailout.co, https://mailout.co/articles/closing-the-gap-between-disabilities-and-drama-exclusive-interview-with-tim-wheeler-artistic-director-of-mind-the-gap/.

105 **Belchertown State School . . . supported a thriving theater program:** Robert Hornick, *The Girls and Boys of Belchertown: A Social History of the Belchertown State School for the Feeble-Minded* (Amherst: University of Massachusetts Press, 2012), pp. 37–38.

106 **There are now over forty disability arts festivals around the world:** Disability Arts International, a website coordinated by the British Council for the Arts, https://www.disabilityartsinternational.org/about-us/.

106 **people with disabilities were four times less likely to see a performance:** National Endowment for the Arts, Accessiblity Fact Sheet, January 2017, https://www.arts.gov/sites/default/files/accessibility-fact-sheet-jan2017.pdf.

107 **"I don't want to live in a world without art and neither do people with disabilities":** Bill Zimmer, interview with author, 2019.

107 **"It wasn't really a big debate":** Sharon Libera, interview with the author, 2019.

108 **"The biggest problem, in the state's eyes, was the dorm":** Michelle Theroux, interview with the author, 2019.

109 **"We've been allowed to exist in this gray area":** Andy Anderson, interview with the author, 2019.

110 **"they are undervalued or believed less worthy of citizenship":** "Holding Truths to be Self-Evident: Affirming the Value of People with Intellectual Disabilities, Letter to the President from the Committee for People with Intellectual Disabilities," Dallas "Rob" Sweezy, chairperson, 2007, https://acl.gov/sites/default/files/programs/2017-03/pr_2007_holding_truths_to_be_self_evident_5d36.pdf.

111 **They suggested establishing a "Disability History Week":** Ibid., p. 22.

111 **It would be an impressive résumé for any actor:** Tommy Jessop's website, www.tommyjessop.com.

111 **Potter . . . now works primarily as a professional advocate:** Cynthia Wang, "Glee's Lauren Potter: 'I am Still Bullied for Being Different,'" *People,* February 22, 2011, https://people.com/tv/glees-lauren-potter-i-am-still-bullied-for-being-different/.

CHAPTER EIGHT

115 **The success of Prospect Meadow has surprised even her:** Susan Stubbs, interview with the author, 2019.

115 **"Our folks need space like that":** Shawn Robinson, interview with the author, 2019.

117 **"by showing them where they fit into the scheme of things":** William J. McKee, *Gould Farm, A Life of Sharing* (Monterey, MA: Wm. J. Gould Associates, 1994), pp. 39–40.

118 **"This is the way I feel":** Frank Bayles, "Prospect Meadow Farm: Clients' Perspective on Beneficial Farming Activities," master's thesis, Smith School of Social Work, 2014.

118 **"Each day is a new opportunity":** Ibid., preface.

120 **"as if they were targeting us specifically":** Robinson, interview with the author, 2020.

121 **"fighting to sustain it":** Robinson, interview with the author, 2020.

122 **"Valued social roles for people need to be attained":** *Valuing Lives,* Wolfensberger interview.

123 **"deny people with disabilities the right to be themselves":** Bert Perrin, "The original 'Scandinavian' Normalization Principle and Its Continuing Relevance for the 1990s," *A Quarter-Century of Normalization and Social Role Valorization: Evolution and Impact,* RJ Flynn and RA Lemay, eds. University of Ottawa Press, 1999, pp. 188–189.

125 **"A community is only being created when its members":** Jean Vanier, *Community and Growth* (London: Darton, Longman and Todd Ltd, 1989), p. 109.

126 **"I can order what I want from the menu":** Buzz Bissinger, *Father's Day* (New York: Houghton Mifflin, 2012), p. 230.

126 **"They want to be whoever it is they've come to be":** Andrew Solomon, *Far from the Tree: Parents, Children and the Search for Identity* (New York: Scribner, 2012), p. 14.

CHAPTER NINE

128 **Morris has won a host of awards:** Blue Star Recyclers website, www .bluestarrecyclers.org.

128 **"they're *phenomenal* employees":** Bill Morris, interview with author, 2019.

133 **"He'd always been *almost* profitable":** Tom D'Eri, interview with the author, 2019.

134 **"you have a highly functional unit":** John D'Eri in interview with Tom D'Eri on podcast, *"The Autism Advantage: Lessons From Building a Successful Autism Enterprise,"* November 2018.

134 **"Those relationships can extend beyond the workplace":** Michael Alessandri, interview with Tom D'Eri on podcast, *"The Autism Advantage,"* November 2018.

134 **"The voice of the people being served must be heard":** Ibid.

135 **"We've also got all of them working more independently":** John D'Eri, interview with Tom D'Eri on podcast, *"The Autism Advantage,"* November 2018.

136 **"What is broken is the lens through which we view people with disabilities":** "Amy Wright is CNN 2017 Hero of the Year," CNN, March 18, 2018.

137 **in a multimillion-dollar business:** Jim Axelrod, "Father and Son Spread Happiness, One Pair of Crazy Socks at a Time," CBS Evening News, June 27, 2018.

137 **"too disconnected from the bigger picture of whatever the company is doing":** Michael Alessandri interview with Tom D'Eri on podcast, *"The Autism Advantage,"* November 2018.

138 **"I don't know—we're a team here":** Dee Dee Brodski, interview with the author, 2019.

CHAPTER TEN

139 **"start a school that focuses only on this":** Yudi Bennett, interview with the author, 2019.

142 **students also learn hard-to-teach soft skills:** "Project Search: Who We Are," video available on https://www.projectsearch.us/who-we-are/.

143 **"they really want to help":** Maria Ortiz, interview with the author, Ronald Reagan Hospital in Westwood, California, 2019.

143 **"This changes lives":** Bill Morris, interview with the author, 2019.

144 **"I think about that a lot":** Tom D'Eri, interview with the author, 2019.

144 **"It doesn't solve the massive problem we have around this country":** Yudi Bennett, interview with the author, 2019.

144 **"I felt like Chuck Yaeger, breaking the sound barrier":** Randy Lewis, *No Greatness Without Goodness: How a Father's Love Changed a Company and Sparked a Movement* (Carol Stream, IL: Tyndale House Publishers, 2016), p. 108.

145 **"The goal is teaching them the job and helping them succeed at it":** Randy Lewis, in interview with Tom D'Eri, *"The Autism Advantage," podcast,* December 2018.

145 **"We learned that performance comes in all different packages":** *No Greatness Without Goodness,* p. 154.

146 **"They just want to get back to work":** Jenny Koprowski, interview with the author, 2020.

CHAPTER ELEVEN

151 **"It doesn't just happen and the state can't buy it":** Bill Zimmer, interview with the author, 2019.

155 **Micaela Connery, who describes herself as a "radical inclusionist":** Micaela Connery, blog, The Kelsey, https://www.thekelsey.org/post/what-does -it-mean-to-be-an-inclusion-native-and-why-does-it-matter, 2018.

155 **"It's about how we can all learn from each other and be better together"**: Micaela Connery, interview with Kim Albrecht for LOMAH podcast, January 13, 2019.

156 **"residents who seemed quite happy in their daily life"**: Micaela Connery, "Disability Housing: Institutional Avoidance," Huffington Post, September 2015, https://www.huffpost.com/entry/disability-housing-instit _b_7849666.

156 **"that's where we need to put our focus"**: Ibid.

157 **"They would much rather have everyone live at home"**: Maggie Rice, interview with the author, 2020.

158 **"The gift of disability is that it cuts through the myths we weave around ourselves"**: Simon Duffy, "A Fair Society and the Limits of Personalization," https://www.centreforwelfarereform.org/uploads/attachment /261/a-fair-society-and-thelimits-of-personalisation.pdf.

159 **close to a million—live with parents or a caregiver over sixty years old:** "Majority of People with Intellectual and Developmental Disabilities Live with Their Families; Only 13.5% in Supervised Residential Settings," DD Blog, posted April 2018, based on data from: https://stateofthestates.org/.

CHAPTER TWELVE

161 **"then they ask me, 'What's a waiver?'"**: Desiree Kameka, interview with the author, 2019.

162 **the most important qualities of HCBS . . . were integration and supported access:** "Keeping the Promise: Self Advocates Defining the Meaning of Community Living," https://autisticadvocacy.org/wp-content /uploads/2012/02/KeepingthePromise-SelfAdvocatesDefiningtheMeaningof Community.pdf.

163 **"safety leaves the equation"**: Julia Bascom, "Space Lettuce," a speech delivered to ASAN's 10th Anniversary Gala, November 2016.

163 **"Residents fatally choked"**: Michael Berens and Patricia Callahan, "A Troubled Transition: In the Rush to Close Institutions, Illinois Glossed Over Serious Issues in Group Homes," *Chicago Tribune,* December 30, 2016, https:// www.chicagotribune.com/investigations/ct-group-home-investigations-cila-met -20161229-htmlstory.html.

163 **found that one in six of all the deaths:** Danny Hakim and Russ Buettner, "In State Care, 1,200 Deaths and Few Answers," *New York Times,* November 5, 2011.

164 **"If disabled people were simply warehoused"**: Alan Judd, "Mentally Disabled Suffer in Moves from Georgia Institutions," *Atlanta Journal-Constitution,* June 21, 2014.

164 **"Staff turnover—it's like a cancer,"** Michael Berens and Patricia Callahan, "A Troubled Transition: In the Rush to Close Institutions, Illinois Glossed Over Serious Issues in Group Homes," *Chicago Tribune,* December 30, 2016, https://

www.chicagotribune.com/investigations/ct-group-home-investigations-cila-met
-20161229-htmlstory.html.

164 **"we've been dealing with for more than thirty years"**: Rita Price,
"Direct Support Workers in Short Supply as Demand Surges," *Columbus
Dispatch,* June 18, 2018.

165 **7.8 million direct-care jobs that will need filling by 2026:** Long-Term
Services and Care: Direct Care Worker Demand Projections: 2015-2030, US
Dept. of Health and Human Services, March 2018, https://bhw.hrsa.gov/sites
/default/files/bhw/nchwa/projections/hrsa-ltts-direct-care-worker-report.pdf.

165 **"The status quo for staff these days is basically no training":** Ashley
Woodsman, interview with the author, 2019.

166 **fifteen hundred adults . . . under the age of sixty-five:** Chris Serres,
"Caregiver Shortage Forcing Young People with Disabilities into Nursing
Homes," *Minneapolis Star-Tribune,* May 9, 2018.

166 **a class-action lawsuit brought by three thousand residents:** Betsy
Blaney, "Texas Accused of Ignoring Mentally Disabled in Nursing Homes,"
Statesman, September 2018.

166 **"I feel like I'm missing out on life every day that I'm stuck here":**
"Caregiver Shortage Forcing Young People with Disabilities into Nursing
Homes," Chris Serres, *Minneapolis Star-Tribune,* May 9, 2018.

169 **"the less prepared they seemed to be for the reality of the challenge":**
Art Middleton, interview with the author, 2019.

CHAPTER THIRTEEN

173 **"Everyone keeps saying we're headed for a crisis":** Desiree Kameka,
interview with the author, 2019.

174 **Massachusetts, for example, is sticking by the stricter policy:** Mass
DDS Home and Community Based Services, Adult Waiver Guide, 2018, https://
static1.squarespace.com/static/518bb7cde4b0d1e7bd9c37b5/t/5877b7a5d1758e
26601bbcd1/1484240809653/DDS+Adult+Waiver+Guide+2016.pdf.

175 **"He'd go out to bars and spend all his SSI money":** Penny Hanson (not
her real name), interview with the author, 2020.

176 **Aidan can invite friends to live in the big house with him:** Valle
Dwight, interview with the author, 2020.

178 **"we hope will ultimately yield a higher quality of caregiver":** Martin
Moylan, "When a Caregiver Can Be a Roommate, It's a Win-Win," MPR news,
May 31, 2019.

179 **"they had their own apartment and lived independently":** Art
Middleton, interview with the author, 2019.

179 **"turns out to be the worst thing you can do to these folks":** *Valuing
Lives,* interview with Wolf Wolfensberger.

181 **"Allow them to make mistakes":** Glen Finland, *Next Stop: A Son with
Autism Grows Up* (New York: Amy Einhorn Books, 2012), p. 7.

182 **"Where does that pain go?":** *Next Stop,* p. 162.

183 **"I was just a parent":** Michael Bérubé, interview with the author, 2019.

184 **"they are a powerful social good":** Michael Bérubé, "Don't Let My Son Fall Off the Disability Cliff," *USA Today,* April 2, 2018.

184 **"They are not really integrated or community-oriented at all":** Cal Montgomery, "Developmental Disability Community Faces a Housing Crisis," *NOS Neurodiversity Culture and Representaion,* April 2018.

184 **"And neurotypicals are always in charge":** Ibid.

184 **"doesn't really exist anymore":** Desiree Kameka, interview with the author, 2019.

185 **"nostalgic for a more integrated sense of connectedness":** *Bowling Alone: The Collapse and Revival of American Community,* Robert Putnam (New York: Simon and Schuster, 2000), p. 381.

185 **the average adult still attended twelve meetings a year around civic engagement:** Bowling Alone, p. 19.

185 **there were four hundred such houses in cities around the US:** Bowling Alone, p. 393.

185 **"the internet-age equivalent of 4-H or settlement houses":** Bowling Alone, p. 401.

188 **"deeply brutalizing to the human spirit":** Sebastian Junger, *Tribe: On Homecoming and Belonging* (New York: Hatchette, 2016), p. 93.

188 **"our society does not allow for that":** Tribe, p.108.

189 **"The earliest and most basic definition of community":** Tribe, pp. 109–110.

193 **"Here, people are learning a life skill":** Vanessa Henry, interview with the author, 2019.

194 **"it's possible to celebrate their differences and *create new norms,*":** Maria Lyons, *Re-thinking Community Care: the Camphill Village Model,* Centre for Welfare Reform, 2015, https://www.centreforwelfarereform.org /uploads/attachment/473/rethinking-community-care.pdf.

195 **"85 percent of our students stay here after graduating":** Michael Storz, interview with the author, 2019.

196 **"Every parent comes here saying their child won't be able":** Catherine Sullivan-DeCarlo, interview with the author, 2019.

200 **"What they're looking for is integration, control, and choice":** Amy Lutz, "Who Decides Where Autistic Adults Live?" *The Atlantic,* May 2015.

200 **Florida currently has the fourth longest waitlist in the country:** Florida's DD Waitlist Campaign, University of South Florida, Tampa, http:// ddwaitlist.cbcs.usf.edu/numbers.html.

200 **number forty-nine in IDD funding:** Ibid.

200 **kept rent at an astounding $260 to $560 a month, per bedroom:** The Villages at Noah's Landing website, https://www.royalamerican.com /properties/villages-at-noahs-landing-lakeland-florida/floorplans.

200 **states join with Medicare to pay between $50,000 and $90,000 a year per resident in a group home:** National Council of State Legislators, "Public Support for People with Intellectual Disabilities," https://www.ncsl.org /research/labor-and-employment/public-support-for-people-with-intellectual -and-developmental-disabilities.aspx.

201 **"they wanted to keep in touch with this group":** Niki Johnson, interview with the author, 2019.

203 **"No one here is staying in their apartment all day":** Denise Resnick, First Place website, https://www.firstplaceaz.org/about/videos/.

204 **"Parents are the most invested in finding long-term, sustainable solutions":** Desiree Kameka, interview with the author, 2019.

204 **"transform the paradigm":** Dotty Foley, interview with Brian Ondrako, *Just Get Started* podcast, September 2019.

204 **"the only people that Dylan is connected with":** Ibid.

206 **"it's harder for them to say no":** Desiree Kameka, interview with the author, 2019.

207 **"It's happening faster and fewer people are talking about it":** Nancy Thaler, OACB Videos: Nancy Thaler on National Trends and CMS Rule Guidance, May 28, 2014, https://www.youtube.com/watch?v=-Q6SL9MoiPk.

207 **"She said no to everything":** Amy Lutz, interview with the author, 2019.

208 **"All I say is we're a legitimate way":** Sister Rosemary Connelly, as quoted by Michael Berens and Patricia Callahan, "A Troubled Transition," *Chicago Tribune,* December 30, 2016.

209 **30 percent are nonverbal:** Center for Disease Control, "Autism Facts," https://www.cdc.gov/ncbddd/autism/facts.html.

209 **A 2017 study found that about a quarter of autistic children:** Nicholette Zeliadt, "Large Study Finds Self-Injury Common Among Children with Autism," *Spectrum News,* January 2017, www.spectrumnews.org/news /large-study-shows-self-injury-common-among-children-autism/.

209 **"There's no single solution for a population that diverse":** Amy Lutz, interview with the author, 2019.

210 **Because there were no residential options left for him:** Lutz, "Who Decides?"

211 **"They have a much more flexible approach these days":** Desiree Kameka, interview with the author, 2019.

211 **"It was a wake-up call to all of us about an unaddressed need":** Michael Storz, interview with the author, 2019.

212 **"We are all part of many communities":** Lutz, "Who Decides?"

212 **"Before I die, my son will be in an intentional community":** Ibid.

CHAPTER FOURTEEN

213 **"overly optimistic about the potential for good in congregate settings":** Lutz, "Who Decides?"

213 **"Overprotection can keep people from becoming all they"**: Robert
   Perske, "The Dignity of Risk and the Mentally Retarded," *Mental Retardation*
   10, no. 1 (February 1972):24–27.

218 **"people with IDD are seven times more likely . . . to be the victim of
   sexual abuse"**: Department of Justice website, https://www.ncjrs.gov/ovc
   _archives/factsheets/disable.htm.

218 **"It could be as high as 75 percent"**: Joseph Shapiro, "Abused and Betrayed:
   The Sexual Assault Epidemic No One Talks About," *NPR: All Things
   Considered*, January 2018.

219 **only thirty-eight states require sex education**: Guttmacher Institute
   website, https://www.guttmacher.org/state-policy/explore/sex-and-hiv-education.

220 **Only one state in the country—Oregon**: FactOregon, "Empowering
   Families Experiencing Disability," https://factoregon.org/sex-ed-disability/.

220 **it most often happens in response to an emergency**: Andrew Maxwell
   Triska, *Sexuality and Intellectual Disabilities: A Guide for Professionals* (New
   York: Routledge, 2018), p. 2.

220 **By contrast, in 2017 the UK enacted a law**: UK Department of Education
   website, https://www.gov.uk/government/publications/relationships-education
   -relationships-and-sex-education-rse-and-health-education/relationships
   -education-primary.

221 **It's possible to buy books**: *Sexuality and Intellectual Disabilities*, p. 6.

221 **"the schools aren't going to suggest it themselves"**: Brian Melanson,
   interview with the author, 2020.

221 **"they were all hitting puberty"**: Maggie Rice, interview with the author,
   2020.

223 **Whole Selves is a comprehensive K-12 curriculum**: Whole Selves website,
   https://wholeselves.org/.

226 **"In the view of independence-minded clinicians, [sex ed] is useless"**:
   Sexuality and Intellectual Disabilities, p. 114.

226 **"they've never learned who is or is not appropriate to hug"**: Leslie
   Walker-Hirsch, *Facts of Life . . . and More: Sexuality and Intimacy for People
   with Intellectual Disabilities* (London: Brookes Publishing, 2007), p. 89.

CHAPTER FIFTEEN

231 **"that's what this legislation is all about"**: National Archives, transcript of
   speech made by George H. W. Bush upon signing the ADA, July 26, 1990,
   https://www.archives.gov/research/americans-with-disabilities/transcriptions
   /naid-6037493-statement-by-the-president-americans-with-disabilities-act
   -of-1990.html.

232 **"The disability rights movement was very good at getting laws
   passed"**: Mary Johnson, *Make Them Go Away: Clint Eastwood, Christopher
   Reeve and the Case Against Disability Rights* (Louisville: Advocado Press,
   2003), p. 38.

232 **"never really entered the national consciousness"**: Ibid., p. 235.

232 **"A law cannot guarantee what a culture will not give"**: Ibid., epigraph.

233 **"We couldn't galvanize our people into huge marches"**: Ari Ne'eman, speech delivered for the ASAN (Autism Self-Advocacy Network) Gala, 2016, https://autisticadvocacy.org/2016/12/2016-gala-speech-by-ari-neeman/#:~:text =Because%20what%20we%20try%20to,that%20you%20are%20welcome %20here.

233 **"The moment we stop lying to ourselves is the moment"**: Ibid.

234 **"Policy cannot make people with serious disabilities move as if they did not have them"**: Editorial Board, "Must Every Bus Kneel to the Disabled?" *New York Times,* November 18, 1979.

234 **"I am not one of them"**: Christopher Reeve, Senate testimony in support of the Kennedy-Feinstein Bill, March 5, 2002, https://www.help.senate.gov/imo /media/doc/reeve.pdf.

235 **"I think our movement has gotten too timid"**: John Kemp, keynote address, University of Washington, 2019, https://www.washington.edu/doit /videos/index.php?vid=95.

235 **"The sense of shame associated with having a disability"**: Sarah Triano, "The Definition of Disability Pride," *Encyclopedia of Disability,* (Sage Publications, 2013).

236 **"all they can do is suffer"**: Harriet McBryde Johnson, *Too Late to Die Young: Nearly True Tales from a Life* (New York: Henry Holt & Co., 2005), p. 253.

236 **"We need to bear witness to our pleasures"**: Johnson, *Too Late to Die Young*, p. 254.

237 **"I can sing along with whatever is around me"**: *In My Language,* Mel Baggs, YouTube video, https://www.youtube.com/watch?v=JnyIM1hI2jc.

237 **"I wonder if he is capable"**: Mel Baggs, "Cultural Commentary: Up in the Clouds and Down in the Valley: My Richness and Yours," *Disability Studies Quarterly* 3, no. 1 (2010).

240 **"Whatever shame her siblings felt about Rosemary"**: Timothy Shriver, *Fully Alive: Discovering What Matters Most* (New York: Sarah Crichton Books, 2014), p. 54.

240 **"knowing the joys of giving"**: Shriver, *Fully Alive*, p. 54.

240 **"would also give rise to a global movement"**: Shriver, *Fully Alive*, p 55.

241 **"It has the potential to transform society itself"**: Matthew Diller, as quoted by Mary Johnson, *Make Them Go Away*, p. 205.

242 **"Even at a museum"**: Naoki Higashida (author), KA Yoshida and David Mitchell (translators), *Fall Down 7 Times Get Up 8* (New York: Random House, 2017,) p. 157.

243 **"That's what I want, above all"**: Naokie Higashida (author), KA Yoshida and David Mitchell (translators), *The Reason I Jump* (New York: Random House, 2007), p.137.

243 **"We have something the world needs"**: Johnson, *Too Late to Die Young,* p. 256.

244 **"these children and young people are learning to speak for themselves"**: "Ed Skarlunis interviews Rosemary and Gunnar Dybwad," Parallels i2n Time: A History of Developmental Disabilities, produced by Council of Developmental Disabilities, Minneapolis, Minnesota, 1987, https:// mn.gov/mnddc/parallels2/one/dybwad-parents/rosemaryGunnar03.html.

246 **"If your child stacked blocks or didn't make eye contact"**: Ari Ne'emann, introduction, Julia Bascom, ed. *And Straight on Until Morning, Essays About Autism* (Washington, DC: The Autistic Press, 2013), p 2.

246 **"we have a right to live in this world"**: Ibid., p. 2.

CHAPTER SIXTEEN

249 **"stay well-regulated"**: Barry Prizant with Tom Fields-Meyer, *Uniquely Human: A Different Way of Seeing Autism* (New York: Simon and Schuster, 2015), p. 224.

250 **"I see him talking aloud to himself"**: Bissinger, *Father's Day,* p. 238.